"Patrick Morley pierces the facades men tend to live behind and presents biblical principles for evaluating—and changing—one's life. *The Seven Seasons of a Man's Life* is honest and practical, a great book for men who are searching—or who need to search—for answers."

Franklin Graham, Samaritan's Purse

"No one communicates with men at the level of Patrick Morley. *The Seven Seasons of a Man's Life* is another landmark work that will change thousands of lives, as did *The Man in the Mirror*."

Stephen Arterburn, author and cofounder of Minirth Meier New Life Clinics

"*Seven Seasons of a Man's Life* prods men of our culture to recapture the lost art of reflection. It challenges us to courageously embrace the questions that gnaw at our hearts in the midst of 'the race.' As you read, you'll begin to settle the most basic issues of this life while discovering, maybe for the first time, success of the soul."

Dennis Rainey, author of *The Tribute*, executive director of FamilyLife, and the host of "FamilyLife Today"

"There is a time in every man's life when he reaches a state of having what seems to be insurmountable family, spiritual, or work-related problems. Since Patrick Morley has also been there, he is able to provide guidelines based upon personal experiences and biblical principles, which will enable you not only to overcome these problems, but turn them into wonderful blessings."

Kenneth H. Cooper, M.D., M.P.H., author, lecturer, and founder of the Cooper Aerobics Center

"Pat Morley has done it again. *The Seven Seasons of a Man's Life* is must reading for any man who wants to find his way through the fog. This is not a book of overused clichés, but rather one filled with solid, biblically-based direction."

Dr. E. Glenn Wagner, vice president of Promise Keepers

"This book is immediately gripping, incredibly honest, penetrating, and brilliantly relevant to every man's inner struggles. All who sense an emptiness on life's road will find an understanding fellow traveler and friend in Pat Morley. Readers will be greatly inspired by what Pat has discovered."

Dr. Bill Bright, founder and president of Campus
Crusade for Christ International

"Patrick Morley challenges us to reflect honestly about ourselves—to see where we are in the context of life's seasons. I was tremendously moved by Pat's own openness and vulnerability. This should be required reading for every man!"

Gary Smalley, bestselling author and host
of the television show *Hidden Keys to
Growing Relationships*

"Patrick Morley has done it again, but this time, he takes us from in front of the mirror and puts us under an x-ray. *The Seven Seasons of a Man's Life* is a penetrating look into the hearts of men and a well-lit pathway to the heart of God—a proven plan for men who want their lives to add up and make sense."

Tim Kimmel, author of *Little House
on the Freeway*

"An incredible book! If you desire true success, you *must* read it."

Peter Lowe, president of Peter
Lowe International

"This is Patrick Morley at his best. Morley is gut-level honest as he deals with the real issues that men face. I saw myself in these pages. I think you will too."

Steve Farrar, author of *Point Man*

"Pat Morley has his fingers firmly on the pulse of today's man. He knows that every man's desire is that his life truly 'count for something'—and that it is impossible to have eternal impact apart from a relationship with the eternal God. *The Seven Seasons of a Man's Life* rings true. Read it—slowly and carefully—and prepare to encounter 'the God who *is*.'"

Ed Young, pastor and author of *Been There. Done
That. Now What?*, *Remembering the Home*, and
From Bad Beginnings to Happy Endings

"This book is vintage Pat Morley—practical, penetrating, persuasive, and powerful! It hits at the core of life—meaning! Thanks, Pat, for the jolt! I needed it! Every person I know needs it! This is bedrock stuff."

Dr. Ron Jenson, speaker, author, and chairman
of High/Ground and MaxLife

"Pat Morley amazes me. I stand awed by his ability to take ordinary events of life and put such spiritual relevancy to all of it. His new book, *The Seven Seasons of a Man's Life*, picks up where *Man in the Mirror* left off. If you liked *The Man in the Mirror*, you will love *Seven Seasons of a Man's Life*. If you want to discover if your life is really counting for God, Pat's new book is a must to read."

Pat Williams, general manager of Orlando
Magic basketball team

"Pat, in his book, *The Seven Seasons of a Man's Life*, has a very challenging and winsome way of making us confront some of the significant issues of the passages of life. I recommend this book to any man seeking to lead a fulfilling and purposeful life."

Ron Blue, author and managing partner of
Ronald Blue & Co.

"Pat Morley understands men! *The Seven Seasons of a Man's Life* accurately portrays the key issues a man must grapple with on his journey of manhood. I have worked with thousands of men who need a game plan when they make mid-course corrections in life. This book will keep transitions from turning into crises."

Rodney L. Cooper, Ph.D., national director of
Educational Ministries and Promise Keepers

"This is not just a good book, it's great. Patrick speaks to the issues, challenges your mind, and also penetrates your heart. This resource can bring a balance into any man's life. Well-written, easy to read, and insightful is an apt description."

H. Norman Wright, author and
marriage counselor

"If your philosophy of life is to go from one hospital (where you're born) to another (where you die) without making a terrible mess of things or thinking about it too deeply, this isn't your book. However, if you want to see God work in the time in-between, you now have a wonderful handbook. Read this book, and it will make you think. Utilize it, and it will change your life."

Steve Brown, professor of Preaching and
Practical Theology, Reformed Theological
Seminary, Orlando, president of Key Life
Network, Inc.

"Pat Morley is a man of uncommon insight, wisdom, and integrity. *The Seven Seasons of a Man's Life* is a reflection of his character. It is a superb book that is both challenging and wonderfully encouraging."

Howard Dayton, founder of Crown Ministries

"Men who realize that 'an unexamined life is not worth living' will profit greatly from Pat Morley's new book. His writing, as usual, shows much wisdom as well as the breezy, readable, and relevant style that has made Pat one of the foremost authors of our time."

William L. Armstrong, U.S. Senator, 1979–1990

The SEVEN SEASONS *of a* MAN'S LIFE

Examining the unique challenges men face.

PATRICK M. MORLEY

THOMAS NELSON PUBLISHERS
Nashville • Atlanta • London • Vancouver

Published in Nashville, Tennessee, by Thomas Nelson, Inc., Publishers, and distributed in Canada by Word Communications, Ltd., Richmond, British Columbia, and in the United Kingdom by Word (UK), Ltd., Milton Keynes, England.

Unless otherwise noted, Scripture quotations are taken from the HOLY BIBLE, NEW INTERNATIONAL VERSION®. Copyright © 1973, 1978, 1984 by International Bible Society. Used by permission of Zondervan Bible Publishing House. All rights reserved.

The "NIV" and "New International Version" trademarks are registered in the United States Patent and Trademark Office by International Bible Society. Use of either trademark requires the permission of International Bible Society.

Scripture quotations noted NKJV are from THE NEW KING JAMES VERSION. Copyright © 1979, 1980, 1982, Thomas Nelson, Inc., Publishers.

Scripture quotations noted TLB are from THE LIVING BIBLE (Wheaton, Illinois: Tyndale House Publishers, 1971) and are used by permission.

Scripture quotations noted KJV are from The Holy Bible, KING JAMES VERSION.

Library of Congress Cataloging-in-Publication Data

Morley, Patrick M.
 The seven seasons of a man's life / Patrick M. Morley.
  p. cm.
 Includes bibliographical references.
 ISBN 0-7852-7827-3 (hc : alk. paper)
 ISBN 0-7852-7583-5 (pb)
  1. Spiritual life. 2. Men—Religious life. I. Title.
BV4501.2.M58548 1995
248.8′42—dc20

95-14737
CIP

Printed in the United States of America
2 3 4 5 6 7 – 01 00 99 98 97 96 95

In memory of Tom Skinner

1942–1994

The significance of a life is not determined by its length. Yours, Tom, was a truly significant life. But you must go now. We have heard the hoofbeats pounding. It is the chariot of fire and the horsemen of Israel—they have come for you. You are being promoted to that heavenly choir of which you spoke so fondly. Sing a new song, Tom. Sing a song for us.

We will all miss you deeply, our dear brother. In your death as in your life, we pledge ourselves to continue breaking down the walls that divide us and to build relationships.

I was the better tennis player. Just for the record.

Contents

Acknowledgments

Rare is the wife who can in one breath inspire her husband to never give up, then with the next breath tell him to abandon a particularly stupid idea without disheartening him. That's my Patsy. She can inspire me to fly, but help me land safely when I run out of good sense. Thank you.

A particular word of thanks to my staff—Betty Feiler, B. J. Belton, Bill Miller, and David Delk—for enabling me to have the time to write while carrying on the work in a way that gave me peace of mind.

Thank you, Mike Hyatt and Robert Wolgemuth, for your enthusiastic support and for making this project possible. I am also indebted to the team at Thomas Nelson for conceiving the embryo that became *The Seven Seasons of a Man's Life*.

Introduction

When I die, if I live to be eighty, my tombstone will read *1948—2028*. From this small bit of information we can learn quite a lot.

- First, most of the rest of my life, and probably yours, too, will be lived in the twenty-first century. That means we ought to regear ourselves and get into some twenty-first-century thinking.
- Second, when we look at the length of the dash between the dates on a tombstone, we can see that it's short. That reminds us that life is short. Life's an inch.
- Third, the dates remind us that we live at a particular moment in history. Our cultural moment is unlike that of any previous generation. A continuing explosion of technologies, a global economy, immense prosperity, and a painful cultural war make the challenges of our time different from those that men have had to face before. And yet, paradoxically, human nature remains the same.
- Fourth, the first date on a tombstone reminds us that we were born. The Creator saw fit to give us the precious gift of life. It reminds us to appreciate our lives.
- Fifth, the second date reminds us that someday we are going to die. There is a certain inevitability to death. With each setting sun we march inexorably twenty-four hours closer to "that day." It reminds us to invest our time wisely.
- Sixth, the second tombstone date also prompts us to ponder what will happen after death. Where will we go? What determines where we will go? When we step across the threshold of eternity, will we be ready?
- Seventh, project your own death date. Do it right now. Now both of our tombstones tell us that we probably have quite a few miles left to travel. It makes us wonder, *Which roads will I take? Will they lead to victory or defeat? Will God watch over the changing seasons of my life?* and ten thousand more questions just like them.

And that is what this book is all about: the issues raised by the tombstone that will stand over your grave as a reminder of the life you lived.

As you begin reading, then, the question I would like you to reflect on is simply this: "What will you do with the dash?"

Every man goes through seven seasons in his life. These seasons don't come upon us in any easily ordered, predictable sequence (a disappointment for many of us linear-thinking, type A personalities).

Each of us will go through all of these seven seasons over the course of his life—many seasons more than once. Sometimes we may find ourselves in two or more seasons at the same time. For these reasons you don't need to read this book in any particular order. Go where your heart leads you.

The purpose of *The Seven Seasons of a Man's Life* is to help you sort out your life—to give you categories to help you think about yourself, where you are, and where you are going. It is a tool to help you stop, examine your life, be reconciled with God, and make needed changes. In a sense, it is an alternative to secular thinking about success and life.

I have written from the perspective of a Christian worldview. However, whether you are a Christian or not makes no difference. I have written so that the material will be profitable to you regardless of where you are on your spiritual pilgrimage.

The stories that follow are real (most names have been changed to protect the guilty!). They work hard, they struggle, they stumble, and sometimes they run scared. Sometimes they succeed; sometimes they fail. But at least they try. They have loved, and they have felt sorrow. And when they hurt, they cry out to God. They are men like us.

While writing this book I have constantly asked myself, "What can I offer you that has cost me a great price?" That is the way I wrote, and I hope you will find it helpful.

Questions and Decisions

At the end of each chapter (except chapters 1, 10, and 17) I will ask you to consider some specific questions and decisions based on what you've read. Please allow some time to reflect honestly on these issues.

Group Study

You may also want to use these questions as the basis for a book study and discussion group. (For additional ideas, please see the Discussion Leader's Guide at the end of the book.)

PART 1

•

THE SEASON OF

REFLECTION

The "Borneo" Christian:
A Case Study, Part 1

Here is my secret: I tell it to you with an openness of heart that I doubt I shall ever achieve again, so I pray that you are in a quiet room as you hear these words. <u>My secret is that I need God—that I am sick and can no longer make it alone.</u>

—Douglas Coupland, Life After God

1 This is my story.

I do not tell it to you because it is pretty—it is not. I do not tell it to you for fame or glory—it is far more likely to tarnish my reputation. Rather, I tell it to you for three reasons.

First, because it is true. Men today pretend too much. We put on airs. We wear game faces. I want us in this book to sink our teeth into something real. That requires some honesty, vulnerability, and transparency.

Second, because you are sure to see yourself mirrored in these pages. No matter how different our backgrounds, you and I share many more similarities than differences. Because all men have so much in common, I believe you will identify with my journey.

Third, because we are in this thing together—or at least we ought to be. We are fellow pilgrims, strangers in this world, just passing through. We can help each other along the way.

Life is a pilgrimage. Along the way we reach some milestones that make our spirits soar. We also fall back to places that make us wonder if maybe it isn't all a hoax, a cruel joke of nature.

I have gone through three major phases on my pilgrimage: Phase 1: The search for meaning and purpose; Phase 2: The commitment to the God I wanted; and Phase 3: The commitment to the God who is. In each of these major phases I have experienced seasons of reflection, building, crisis, renewal, rebuilding, suffering, and success.

As you read along, try to identify the major phase of life you are in right now. Maybe you will relate to one of the phases I have gone through, or maybe this chronicle will trigger some thoughts of your own. In any case, it will be profitable to grasp the larger perspective of where you are generally on your spiritual journey as together we go on to explore the seven seasons of a man's life.

Phase 1: The Search For Meaning and Purpose

It was a warm, muggy summer morning in central Florida. The white-frame elementary-school building sitting up on cement blocks doubled as our church on Sundays. In those days, in that neighborhood, it would never occur to folks to complain about the lack of air-conditioning.

Growing up, I had a drug problem—every Sunday my parents drug me to church. Actually, I enjoyed it, and found myself wide-eyed over all the rituals of religious life.

In my first major assignment as an altar boy, I stood before our small congregation to hand out the offering plates to the ushers, and then receive them after they were passed around. Instead of sitting back down while the plates were passed, I decided to stand at the front of the church facing the congregation.

All the women were fanning themselves with their bulletins, and I was sweating pretty good myself. What must have been a hundred gnats buzzed around my eyes, and I kept trying to blow them away. Under that hot robe I was suffocating, but I wasn't about to bungle my first major assignment. Many years later my dad told me that my face flushed, then turned pale, as I wobbled back and forth. He ached to tell me I could sit down, but because he knew how important it was to me to do this good deed for God, he didn't.

When I was eight or nine, I felt my first hunger to know God. During confirmation, I strained to hear the voice of God, but it was a rote exercise in memorization. As an altar boy, I pored over those catechisms and prayers searching for something to stir my soul, but I felt nothing. I went looking for God but could not find Him. A few years later we moved, my parents stopped attending church, and I lost interest in spiritual things. Girls and sports kindled awkward and exhilarating new feelings, respectively, that I had never known. By comparison, God seemed dull.

As a "first wave" boomer, I grew up in that post-World War II fantasy bubble we call the American Dream. It was an era when the entire population—every man, woman, and child—focused on things. Everyone. Virtually every conversation centered on the next thing, award, position, or achievement we were going to acquire. Anyone could be the next president if he tried hard enough. So it seemed natural to announce to my parents that my goal in life was to become a millionaire.

By my senior year in high school, the questions about life I had suppressed began to poke themselves into my conscious thoughts again with increasing regularity: "What's it all about? What is the purpose of life?" I assumed education would help answer those questions. So, I would go to chemistry class and learn about the chart of elements. I would go to English class and learn about the world of literature. I would go to history class and learn about the great events that shaped the world. I would go to geography class and learn about the stuff that makes up the earth's crust. I would go to mathematics class and learn about whatever it is they talk about in there. Unfortunately, at the school I attended we learned about all the *diversity* of the world, but nobody ever brought it all together into a *unity*. I had more questions than ever, and I assumed no one had any real answers.

During my high school years, I performed the duty of pallbearer twice. Randy and C. T. both died in grisly automobile accidents. We were a wild, reckless bunch. I began to be concerned over the question, "What happens when we die?" But I figured I was going to heaven because I was an American, and everyone knew God was on the side of America.

School bored me to tears. Discouraged, I threw myself into the party scene. I started cutting classes and hanging out at the local pool hall. By my senior year I only needed senior English to graduate, so I signed up for distributive education. I went to school in the morning and after lunch worked in the produce department of the local grocery store.

If I hated school, I loathed work. Everything seemed meaningless, a chasing after the wind. Religion had not helped me. Education had not answered my questions. I hadn't amounted to much as an athlete. Drinking, smoking, fighting, and chasing girls seemed shallow. Work provided no sense of direction. Depressed, I quit high school in the middle of my senior year.

My father was not about to let me hang around the house, so he made me join the army—a good thing, looking back (hindsight is 20/15—a little better than 20/20). I loved the discipline. I loved serving my country. But that, too, soon plateaued. With some buddies, I started making the sixty-mile drive from Ft. Bragg to Raleigh, North Carolina, several nights a week in search of the things young soldiers go looking for.

One morning I woke up in a ditch somewhere along that thin ribbon of asphalt between Raleigh and Ft. Bragg. As the hot sun scorched through the windshield of my car, my head pulsated and throbbed in pain. I had missed reveille, and I knew I would pay a price for that, but that's not what was bothering me. What really bothered me was the question: *What happened to you, Morley? You had potential. You were an honor student. You were supposed to be somebody. But here you are lying in a ditch somewhere in the middle of "who cares?" headed "who knows where?" You're just a nobody headed nowhere.* And it was true—and grim. I was lonely, empty, discouraged, confused, afraid of the future, and filled with guilt.

As I lay there across the bench seat of my Chevy, I made a decision to turn my life around, to find a meaningful life philosophy. But where should I turn? The only avenue that seemed open to me was education. So I took the GED exam, enrolled at North Carolina State, and attended classes at the extension building on the "beautiful" campus of Ft. Bragg.

One evening as I studied for an exam, I read some lines from Shakespeare, *Hamlet* to be specific:

> *This above all: to thine own self be true,*
> *And it must follow, as the night the day,*
> *Thou canst not then be false to any man.*

I thought, *Eureka! This is the most noble thought I have ever heard uttered in my entire life! I am going to adopt this as my life credo. I will try to do the right thing by every person I meet every day. That's how I will find the secrets of meaning and purpose.*

On that day I became a moralist. It's interesting. Once you sign up for any new group—Rotary, the Chamber, whatever—you begin to meet the other members of the group. So I began to meet the other moralists in the world. I quickly realized that all moralists have one thing in common. None of them has any money!

So I decided if I wanted to get rich, I needed to add a little more to my life philosophy. I chose to pursue a career in business, and became a materialist—a "moral" materialist.

After the army, I completed college by going year-round for two and a half years. I recall running into a girl I knew from high school and church in the university library one day. She had always treated me with kindness so I poured out my heart to her. I remember telling her how depressed I was because I would soon be twenty-one and wasn't a millionaire yet.

Graduation close at hand, I had to make a career choice. I wanted to make a lot of money. I had heard the best way to make a lot of money was to go into sales. So I asked myself, "What is the biggest thing I can sell?" reasoning that the bigger the sale, the bigger the commission. That led to a career in commercial real estate. Within a year I had started my own business with a friend from college.

Frankly, I thought I had broken the code. I signed up for the human potential movement: "If your mind can conceive it and believe it, you can achieve it." Just six short years after waking up in a ditch of despair, I was sitting on top of the world. Money poured in over the gunwales.

I shifted flawlessly into the accumulation stage. I married a perfect wife, bought a home using VA financing, leased a luxury car, started buying expensive Hickey-Freeman suits, began numerous real estate partnerships, wore the standard-issue Rolex watch, and generally thought I had gone to heaven.

My big thing was goal-setting. I read every book ever written on success, and I always had a motivational tape playing in my car. I was meeting every goal I set. (It never occurred to me that it might just be a good economy, not my genius.) Yet, my life seemed hollow, shallow. After meeting a goal, I would feel terrific. But two weeks later the novelty would wear off, and I would have to set a new goal that, of course, always had to be bigger, better, and brighter. It started to become boring. I found that met goals tended to become a string of hollow victories, increasingly frustrating as I accomplished more and more. Simply put, I found that success didn't satisfy.

The nagging questions that had so often haunted me started coming back as demons in the middle of the night: "Is this all there is? What's the meaning of it all? Are you sure you are on the right track?" I felt frustration so deep in my gut that I could not form words on the tip of my tongue to express the gnawing pain, the growing despair. It was so amorphous that it remained inarticulate, inexpressible.

Free-floating anger was always boiling just below the surface. You know what I mean. I would go ballistic if someone slighted me, cut me off in traffic, or kept me waiting on hold too long. God forbid someone should keep me waiting in a reception area.

The emptiness seemed like a hall of doors, with no end in sight. One day I pulled into our garage, calmly put down the garage door, and then began kicking a wall, hoping I would knock it down from the inside like an implosion. When we sold that house, I was embarrassed to think someone might ask how those footprints got on the garage wall.

One morning I ranted and raved around the house, taking my frustrations out on my wife, Patsy, saying things no man should ever say to a woman. I glanced over at her and saw large tears streaming down her cheeks from those beautiful fifty-cent-piece-sized eyes. She didn't say a thing—she just sat there taking the abuse. To be honest, that was not unusual at that point in our marriage. But there was something different that particular morning, and as I looked at her, I was transfixed—I couldn't look away. After she held my gaze for what seemed an eternity, she asked me, "Pat, is there anything about me you like?"

I felt like I had been hit with a cattle prod. I wandered off to my office, and I stared out my office window for the rest of the morning. *What happened to you, Morley? You wanted your life to count, to make a difference. You wanted to find meaning and purpose, to make an impact on the world. You wanted to make a contribution, to do something important, to be somebody, to lead a life of significance. Instead, you're still just a nobody headed nowhere.*

I realized the life philosophy I had adopted was not working. I realized I had to abandon it and start over. But where? I was driven to consider—honestly and deeply consider—those questions every man must face squarely at some point in his life. You know them.

- Who am I—*really?*
- Why do I exist?
- Why is life so hard?
- What happens when I die?

We began attending a local church over the next several months, something Patsy had wanted from the start. We met two young couples who took an interest in us. One of the wives asked me one evening, "Are you a Borneo Christian?"

"A what?" I answered.

"A Borneo Christian?"

"What in the world is a Borneo Christian?" I asked her back.

"No, I said are you a *born-again* Christian?" she pronounced more clearly.

"What's the difference?" I asked.

Through the example of true friendship demonstrated by the two young husbands who befriended us, through Patsy's prayers and the pastor's preaching, I began to understand the fringes of what it means to be a follower of Jesus Christ. Frankly, it sounded exactly like what I needed. It sounded inviting.

Yet, I had some preconceived ideas about religion that made some of what I heard pretty hard to swallow. My biggest barrier was that I thought I already was a Christian. After all, I was an American. I didn't have anything against God.

Since I already knew a *little* about Jesus, I thought I knew *enough*. C. S. Lewis once said that before you can make a man into a Christian, you must first make him into a pagan. Knowing a *little* only made me think I was already a Christian. After all, I had grown up in the church—and willingly. However, as Billy Sunday said, "Sitting in a church doesn't make you a Christian any more than sitting in a garage makes you a car." Sometimes it's better to know nothing than a little. A little knowledge about God can be dangerous to your eternal health. At least when you know nothing, you can't pretend you know more than you really do.

I had a lot of philosophical and religious baggage to sort through. I had always thought Christianity was a *task*, something I did for God. I began to learn that Christianity is a *relationship* with God, something He does for us. The issue is not, "What do I do with religion?" The issue is, "What do I do with Jesus?" The issue is not, 'What must I do to be good?' The issue is, "What must I do to be saved?"

I learned that I was separated from God because of my sins (I needed no convincing that I was a sinner—I've left out a lot). Further, no human effort on my part was sufficient to receive forgiveness for these sins and salvation. Instead, Jesus Christ came into the world to save sinners—like me. After living a sinless life, He voluntarily shed His blood and died on a cross as a substitute for me. He took the penalty for my sins. Remarkable.

I also learned that because He rose from the dead, I, too, could become like Him and live forever in heaven. To accomplish this, I needed to agree with God that I was a sinner, express genuine remorse and a desire to change directions (called *repentance*), and by *faith* receive Christ into my life as my Savior and Lord.

Faith means believing that Jesus is who He says He is (God), that He did what He said He did (died for our sins), and that He will do for us what He said He would do (forgive our sins and give us eternal life).

I was encouraged to express my desire for God's love, forgiveness, and salvation through prayer.

One day as Patsy and I pulled away from church in our big, long luxury car, I watched in the rearview mirror until we were out of sight from the church. Then I laid into Patsy for some stupid thing that had embarrassed me in church. I cannot for the life of me recall what it was, but something "significant" like bouncing a knee during the sermon.

She began to cry, then I began to cry. I had finally come to the end of my 'self.' As we drove along, I pulled out my white handkerchief and waved it to signal my surrender to Jesus Christ. I prayed, "Jesus, I cannot manage my life. I have made a mess of things. I need You in my life if You will have me. Thank You for dying on the cross for my sins and offering me eternal life. By faith I now ask You to come into my life, forgive my sins, and give me eternal life. Take my life and make it into something worthwhile. Amen."

By God's grace and mercy I had made the transition from "Borneo" Christian to "born-again" Christian. Enormous changes began to take place in some areas of my life. In other areas, though, progress was as slow as watching fingernails grow. Yet, it was clear that God had hold of my life. Nevertheless, I had big plans for my life—and now I had a Partner to make my dreams come true (or so I thought). Soon I found that I had entered into the second major phase of my spiritual pilgrimage.

Serving Two Masters:
A Case Study, Part 2

The trouble with many men is that they have got just enough religion to make them miserable.
—Billy Sunday [1]

2

In the last chapter I told you about my life before God (phase 1). Now I would like to tell you about my life with God, which has come in two major phases.

Phase 2: The Commitment to the God I Wanted

I became a follower of Jesus Christ because I was miserable. Success had brought not satisfaction but sorrow. At least when I was still chasing the dream, I could cling to the illusion that success would make me happy. On the other hand, I did enjoy using the nice things success brought.

To be a moralist and a follower of Christ is no contradiction. But to be a materialist and a follower of Christ just doesn't add up. In fact, the Bible says, "No one can serve two masters. . . . You cannot serve both God and Money" (Matt. 6:24). Looking back, I can see that in many ways I had simply added Jesus to my life as another interest in an already busy and otherwise overcrowded schedule. Call it the gospel of addition.

It was a partial surrender. I was like the man who cheated on his income taxes and felt guilty. Finally, he couldn't stand it any longer and wrote an anonymous letter to the IRS.

Gentlemen:

I cheated on my income taxes, feel horrible, and have had a difficult time sleeping. So enclosed please find my check for five hundred dollars.

P.S. If I still can't sleep I'll send the rest.

I had truly trusted in Christ, but I still wanted to run my own life. After all, I had big plans for my life—they would be good for God too! My credo was "plan, then pray." Since I knew what I wanted to happen, I would make my plan and then pray to God about it: "Dear Lord, I've got this great deal I'm trying to put together. If You will make my dream come true, then I'll split the profits with You, and we'll both be better off! Amen."

I tried to blend together what I saw as the best of both worlds: success in the material world and salvation in the spiritual kingdom. I tried to eat my cake and have it too. Success and salvation. In theology we have a technical term for this:

> **syncretism:** *n* The attempt or tendency to combine differing philosophical or religious beliefs.

My single greatest problem was the problem of self-deceit. After my conversion, God gave me an insatiable appetite to read the Bible, which I was doing every day. However, I found myself reading the Bible with a purpose: I was looking for evidence to support the decisions I had already made. (Doesn't sound very objective, does it?)

Here's what I would do. If I saw a verse of Scripture on the left-hand page that pointed in the direction I was going to go anyway, then I would underline that verse. Often I would memorize it. However, if on the right-hand page I saw a verse that veered off in a direction I didn't want to go, then I would pull out a large mental eraser and smudge that verse right out of my mind.

This is the essence of self-deceit: to decide what you want and then look for evidence to support the decision you have already made. We all do it, though, don't we? Demosthenes said it best: "Nothing is easier than self-deceit. For what each man wishes, that he also believes to be true."

So, in those days I followed the God I was underlining in my Bible, without following the rest of Him too. I had a plan for my life, and I just wasn't ready to give it up. So I remade God in the image I wanted. You could say I created a fifth gospel: Matthew, Mark, Luke, John, and Patrick. It was not much of a problem at the one-, two-, or even three-year mark in my spiritual pilgrimage because I didn't know much of anything. But by the time I hit the ten-year mark, I was starting to become pretty dangerous.

For example, I was regularly teaching "tell me what it means to you"

Bible studies. We sat around in a circle, and each told the others what a verse of the Bible meant to him. It never dawned on me that we should be asking each other, "What does it mean to God?"

After a decade of "plan, then pray," I began to sense a vague feeling of discontent lurking just below the surface of my conscious thoughts. I could not form the words to express it, but the feeling began to visit me more and more often. I began to see that my life was not as fruitful as it should be. I was like the man in Matthew 13:22: "The one who received the seed that fell among the thorns is the man who hears the word, but the worries of this life and the deceitfulness of wealth choke it, making it unfruitful." Something was still missing.

The awareness that something was wrong—desperately wrong—with the way I was following God gnawed on me. I decided to enter into a time of self-examination that I assumed would last a couple of weeks. Instead, I spent the next two and a half years studying my navel.

As I have already said, when I became a follower of Christ, I did not stop being a materialist. On the contrary, I became an addict. Materialism is an addiction just like alcohol, pornography, sex, or drugs. It has power to destroy completely and finally. An addiction is a desire so strong that it overly controls actions.

I was never a cross materialist. I was a refined materialist. I didn't flaunt it. I would buy things and experiences that didn't shout too loudly. But it inflated my ego to take "Fantasy Island" trips, even if no one knew.

For example, I have four leather briefcases. Two of them cost five hundred dollars each. How do you figure that? Whenever I would walk by a luggage store in the mall, I would be mesmerized by the aroma. You can almost see that delicious aroma wafting out of the store! I think they have fans blowing it into the concourse to lure in materialists like me.

For me, however, materialism was merely the symptom. The root problem was that I was not building the kingdom of God. I was building a kingdom of my own. The Living Bible puts it this way: "Happiness or sadness or wealth should not keep anyone from doing God's work" (1 Cor. 7:30).

My ambitions didn't focus on "Thy kingdom come. Thy will be done in earth, as it is in heaven" (Matt. 6:10 KJV). Oh, I did things for the kingdom—taught Bible studies, sponsored evangelistic events, read the Bible, prayed regularly, and attended church—but deep down in that secret place where motives lurk, my top priority was achieving my personal ambition, not loving God. God was a means to other ends. My devotion was to what I wanted for my life, not what God wanted for my life. All in all, I had become a thoroughly modern man. I was at the center of my life. God was more or less a cosmic genie to help fulfill my dreams.

Here is the problem: Whatever controls your life is your god. It may be things. It may be ambition. It may be an intense desire to insulate yourself from the problems of other people.

At the end of two and a half years of self-examination, I realized I had been living the life of a Cultural Christian, not a Biblical Christian. What I mean is that even though I believed in Jesus, there was nothing exceptional about my lifestyle that would recommend him to others. I was Jekyll on Sunday, but come Monday morning, I was Hyde. My life was shaped more by the forces of commerce than by Christ. I was reading my Bible for comfort, but *Forbes* for direction. And I hated it. I hated my life even more than before I became a follower of Christ because now I knew the difference between a statistical Christian and a true believer. Simply put, I was living a double life. Don't misunderstand. I was a "good" man. I was leading a moral life. But that only deceived me into thinking I was following the God of the Bible when in reality I was following the God of my imagination. That's why it took so long to sort things out. I was committed to the God I wanted.

Cultural Christianity means to seek the God (or gods) we want and not the God who is. I realized I could not eat my cake and have it, too, after all. I was ready to make some decisions. Key and foremost, I decided to change the purpose of my life. At a moment that became my turning point, I wrote in the front of my Bible, "I want to live the rest of my earthly life for the will of God." That's now my life-purpose statement.

My turning point was a change from *partial* to *full* surrender. It was a commitment to have *integrity,* which I define as a one-to-one correlation between my *Bible,* my *belief,* and my *behavior.* It was a commitment to change from "plan, then pray" to "pray, then plan." It was a commitment to stop following only the God I was underlining in my Bible and follow the rest of Him too. It was a commitment to not only add Jesus to my life but to subtract some things also. It was a commitment to stop seeking the God I wanted and start seeking the God who is. It was the commitment to stop being a Cultural Christian and start being a Biblical Christian.

As the martyred Jim Elliot wrote in his journal, "He is no fool who gives up what he cannot keep to gain what he cannot lose."

This led to the third major phase of my spiritual pilgrimage.

Phase 3: The Commitment to the God Who Is

When I wrote in my Bible, "I want to live the rest of my earthly life for the will of God," it was a lifelong commitment to know, love, serve, trust, and obey the God who is. That was February 1, 1986.

At the time, I thought I was signing up for some personal remodeling or redecorating, maybe even to add a new room on the back. I thought I was already quite a trophy for God.

Three months later Congress passed the Tax Reform Act of 1986. In case you don't remember, the Tax Reform Act stopped capital from flowing into real estate, eventually caused the collapse of the savings and loan industry, nearly toppled commercial banking, careened into the insurance industry like a runaway freight train, and caused multiplied thousands of businesses to go under.

My business was decimated. It looked like a nuclear winter. I had thought God was going to build on a new addition to my life. Instead, the bulldozers showed up and leveled me right down to the foundation. It was as though the Lord was saying, "Pat, I believe that you are sincere—that you really want to live the rest of your earthly life for My will. But you have given Me so little to work with that I need to start over with you. So I am going to have to go down to the foundation and rebuild you in a right way."

Thank God, I at least had the right foundation: "For no one can lay any foundation other than the one already laid, which is Jesus Christ" (1 Cor. 3:11). But I had built wrongly on this foundation with "wood, hay, stubble." God was giving another chance—a chance to build with "gold, silver, precious stones" (1 Cor. 3:12–15 KJV).

Over the next five years I experienced the most agonizing, torturous crisis of my life. My business problems loomed endlessly on the horizon like dark thunderheads. I woke up in crisis, worked through the day in crisis, came home in crisis, went to bed in crisis, tossed and turned in crisis, got up the next morning in crisis and started the process all over again.

One day I came home for lunch. I was alone in the house. I stood in the darkness of our kitchen, leaned against the sink, and stared into the sunny backyard. *Dear God,* I thought. *I am so weary. I just don't know how I can go on one more day.*

I had built a shakable kingdom. God decided to remove the shakable kingdom so that His unshakable kingdom would remain. He shook up my tidy little world. The reason *why* God does this to men, *what* He does, *how* He does it, and our appropriate response are uniquely recorded in Hebrews 12:25–29:

> SEE TO IT THAT YOU DO NOT REFUSE HIM WHO SPEAKS. IF THEY DID NOT ESCAPE WHEN THEY REFUSED HIM WHO WARNED THEM ON EARTH, HOW MUCH LESS WILL WE, IF WE TURN AWAY FROM HIM WHO WARNS US FROM HEAVEN? AT THAT TIME HIS VOICE SHOOK THE EARTH, BUT NOW HE HAS PROMISED, "ONCE MORE I WILL SHAKE NOT ONLY THE EARTH BUT ALSO THE HEAVENS." THE WORDS "ONCE MORE" INDICATE THE REMOVING OF WHAT CAN BE SHAKEN— THAT IS, CREATED THINGS—SO THAT WHAT CANNOT BE SHAKEN MAY REMAIN. THEREFORE, SINCE WE ARE RECEIVING A KINGDOM THAT CANNOT BE SHAKEN, LET US BE THANKFUL, AND SO WORSHIP GOD ACCEPTABLY WITH REVERENCE AND AWE, FOR OUR "GOD IS A CONSUMING FIRE."

Why does God shake things up? God shakes us up when we "refuse Him who speaks"—when we go our own independent way. We cannot escape His loving discipline. What does He do to us? When we build our own kingdom rather than God's kingdom, He will remove what is shakable. Why? So that "what cannot be shaken may remain." In other words, He graciously sends the refining fires of adversity to purify us from our shakable kingdoms.

It's fascinating to me. When I was "blowin' and goin'," I could often tell men were looking at me and thinking, *Wow! He must really be under God's blessing!* I was thinking, *If they only knew. I hate my life. I am addicted to materialism. I don't know how to escape. I'm not under God's blessing. I'm under His curse.*

Then when I was crumbling right before everyone's eyes, I could tell men avoided me like a leper, thinking, *Wow! Whatever he did, it must have really been bad. He must really be under God's curse!* I wanted to shake them and say, "You don't understand! I'm not under God's curse. That was before, when things appeared to be so good. No, I'm under God's blessing!" God was faithfully, graciously removing what was shakable so what is unshakable would remain.

How did he know it was a blessing? you may wonder. Notice the last sentence in the Scripture passage above. It says, "Therefore, since we are receiving a kingdom that cannot be shaken, let us be *thankful*" (emphasis added). Now, I ask you, what are we to be thankful for—a blessing or a curse? Only a fool would thank God for a curse. We thank God when He gives us a blessing. In other words, the removal of the shakable kingdom is a blessing. Surgery hurts, but it brings healing.

So, at the thirteen-year mark on this spiritual pilgrimage, I began thanking God for loving me enough to chasten me. I further repented of my deeply ingrained Cultural Christianity. I began seeking the God who is with a passion. I found a new level of trusting Christ with the everyday details of my life.

Along the way I decided to become a recovering materialist. (I've thought about starting a new group called Materialists Anonymous. You may want to write me for a membership application!) The Living Bible says, "Those in frequent contact with the exciting things the world offers should make good use of their opportunities without stopping to enjoy them; for the world in its present form will soon be gone" (1 Cor. 7:31). As a friend said, "The world is not the *prize*—it's the *price.*" I still have nice things. But now I use them differently.

How is this working itself out in practical ways? I had never used a budget for personal finances. Patsy and I decided we should live on a budget, so we made one up. Not long after, I was invited to speak at an evangelistic dinner meeting in a beach resort community. The hosts invited me to bring Patsy and our two beach-aged children to stay in a luxury condominium right on the water. They also offered us a discounted rate if we wanted to stay over for extra days.

Though we didn't plan to stay over, when I saw the *Lifestyles of the Rich and Famous* view from this exquisitely appointed condo, I urged Patsy that we should extend our stay. After discussion and prayer, however, we decided that we couldn't afford it—it wasn't in our budget. We had more than enough money on hand to do it, but it wasn't in the budget. It's difficult to express, but that experience of turning down a great opportunity so that we could glorify God by living on a budget meant more to me than a million dollars. It was a sacrifice of praise.

I have by no means arrived. Every day brings new challenges, new temptations, and new opportunities to trust God or depend on self. I still have a lot to sort through, but I am committed to live the rest of my earthly life for the will of God.

QUESTIONS AND DECISIONS

Note: Whatever kind of man you and I are today, we will pretty much be the same one year, five years, or twenty years from now unless we decide to make changes. For the remainder of the book, at the end of most chapters, I will ask you to consider some specific questions and decisions based upon what you've read. Please go to a quiet place. Allow yourself some time to reflect honestly on these issues. Then, put yourself in the presence of God through prayer, and make some life-changing choices.

You may also want to use these questions as the basis for a book study and discussion group. (For additional ideas, please see the Discussion Leader's Guide at the end of the book.) Here are the questions and decisions for the first two chapters.

1. Which of these three major phases of spiritual pilgrimage are you in right now? Explain your answer.

   Phase 1: The Search for Meaning and Purpose
       Seeker: Have not found God yet through His Son Jesus Christ
       Description: A time of *experimentation*
   Phase 2: The Commitment to the God I Wanted
       Cultural Christian: Still wavering between two opinions
       Description: A time of *vacillation*
   Phase 3: The Commitment to the God Who Is
       Biblical Christian: Fully surrendered to the pleasure of God's will
       Description: A time of *submission*

2. Which situations mentioned in these first two chapters have you also wrestled with? How have you handled them? Have you handled them?

3. What are the situations not mentioned with which you are struggling right now? What would you like to do about them?

4. What do you hope to gain from reading this book?

Wounded Warriors:
Men under Pressure

Michael's job required him to leave town on Sunday afternoon, and he would be gone until Friday afternoon. One day he came home and greeted his two daughters, four and two years old. They turned from the TV, said hello, then turned back around.

3 Sources estimate the net worth of Bill Gates, the under-forty chairman of Microsoft, at around $6,000,000,000 (in case all the zeros make your eyes cross, that's six billion dollars). Despite the fact that his company is, by a wide margin, the largest software producer for personal comput-ers in the world, Gates said he continually worries about competition.

"In this business, by the time you realize you're in trouble, it's too late to save yourself," he said. "*Unless you're running all the time, you're gone.*"[1]

I once heard a parable expressing the same thought:

> Every morning in Africa when the sun comes up, a gazelle awakens and knows that it must run faster than the fastest lion, or it will perish. Every morning in Africa when the sun comes up, a lion awakens and knows that it must run faster than the slowest gazelle, or it will go hungry. It doesn't make any difference if you are a gazelle or a lion. Every morning in Africa when the sun comes up, you had better be running.

It's the law of the jungle, and the world you and I occupy *is* a jungle. As the dawn of the twenty-first century approaches, most men I know feel like they "had better be running."

Common Threads among Men

I have worked with men for more than twenty years. Rarely a day goes by in which I don't spend some time listening to and praying over a painful story. The problems invariably revolve around marriage, family, career, health, and/or money. Since *The Man in the Mirror* was released in 1989, I have heard from hundreds of men struggling to make ends meet, to put it all together, to keep it all from coming unraveled.

In my work I regularly share with men how they can know Christ personally, teach men in a weekly Bible study, counsel men, and travel to preach, to speak, and to teach men and leaders. I say all this only to convey that I think I have a pretty good handle on men's issues.

All that said, if I were limited to making only one observation about men today, it would be that everywhere I go I find that men are tired. And I don't mean just physically tired, although that too. But I find that men are mentally, emotionally, psychologically, and spiritually tired. Exhausted by life. Worn to a thread. Beat up. Bone tired.

Not only are men tired, but they often have a lingering feeling something isn't quite right about their lives. A vague, indistinct, pervasive feeling of angst often chews away at their guts. They cannot form the words to express this amorphous feeling, so it remains unarticulated.

Many times things are not turning out the way they planned. Richard was brushing his teeth one morning while his wife of fifteen years lay in bed. She said, "Richard, I don't love you anymore. I filed for a divorce yesterday." Another man, Bill, had to ask his parents for financial support to feed and house his family during a protracted time of unemployment. Another man, Sam, was laid off during a corporate downsizing. Seven months later he hasn't even had a nibble on his resume.

Why is this happening? Where do we turn? What do we do? The meteoric pace of on-line modern life ironically leaves most men feeling isolated and lonely. Too often, when a man finally does reach out and trust someone he ends up feeling betrayed. As a result, it frequently doesn't seem like anyone really cares. (That's not true, of course. God cares—but we'll get to that later.)

For many men, managing their lives has become like trying to tie two pieces of string together that are not quite long enough. They are long enough to touch, long enough to manipulate, and long enough to create hope that they can be tied together, but they simply are not long enough to tie the knot. Close, but not close enough. No cigar.

The problem is that we have created a culture that requires more energy than men have to give. Sometimes we call this the rat race.

All in all, men are under a lot of pressure.

Performance Pressure

Chuck has conservatively managed his financial affairs. He gives 10 percent of his income to his church and other charitable causes, and he typically saves more than 10 percent of his income. He has no debts other than his share of the mortgage on an office building he owns with a few other men. He houses his insurance business and four employees in the building so, in a sense, he pays rent to himself.

Yet, Chuck feels the pressure. He is the only one in his office who sells; everyone else supports him administratively. So he must generate enough cash flow every week, week in and week out, to support not only the office expenses and his family, but four other paychecks as well.

As a result, Chuck constantly feels the cold chill of failure. He feels like he must constantly be on the run. Even though he is financially conservative, even though he doesn't live high, even though he has no debts, Chuck feels the pressure to perform that comes from meeting an overhead.

What is your monthly "nut," or overhead? How much do you have to earn to keep the wolves at bay? What kind of pressure does it put you under? Is it worth it?

Technological Pressure

Remember that old promise that computers would lighten our workloads? Have you noticed how nobody says that anymore?

Computers did not reduce workloads; they increased capabilities. Actually, computers could have reduced workloads if we had only used them to streamline the tasks we already performed. Instead, we discovered (and keep discovering) myriad new capabilities and applications.

Every eighteen months the capacity of the computer doubles while its price gets slashed in half. All the available information since the beginning of time will double over the next three years.[2]

In 1969, the United States Department of Defense designed an experimental network of four computers to enable scientists to communicate among themselves. By 1972, fifty universities and military research sites had access. During the 1980s, other public and private computer networks sprang up. Today these networks have been combined into a single information superhighway called the Internet, which combines more than twenty million users from academic, military, government, and commercial networks from the United States and more than forty other countries. You can find out everything you need to know about anything with a few strategic key strokes on your computer.

We have discovered endless ways computers can give us information that before we could only dream about—and when it's good, it's *very* good! On the other hand, computers have buried us under an avalanche of reports that no one could possibly ever read.

To make the world a better place for *mankind*, we build new technologies that ironically often sacrifice the lives of too many *individual* men on the altar of progress. It's a technological war out there.

The rapidity of change today makes corporations vulnerable. Because corporations can be knocked out by competitors, employees no longer have long-term job security. Not only do employees worry about competitors, but they also must fear the risk of being replaced by machines. All in all, it's a volatile business climate.

Here is the question: Does a better machine necessarily mean a better life? Ask the slaves of 1793, the year the cotton gin was invented. The cotton gin created enormously increased processing capabilities, but there was not enough labor. So inventive white entrepreneurs created a market in human flesh to man the plantations with enough labor to supply the insatiable appetite of the hungry cotton gin.

In the same way, much of today's technology has unwittingly made us into slaves. And for what? A bigger house? A better car? An easier life? A better lifestyle? Is all the stress, anxiety, and pressure worth it? The Bible says, "'Everything is permissible'—but not everything is constructive" (1 Cor. 10:23). Perhaps we need to manage our technology better. Maybe some of us can learn to get by with low tech. Building a better machine doesn't always mean a better life. It may only add more pressure.

Has the technology in your life lowered or raised your workload? Have you become a slave to your laborsaving devices? These are appropriate questions for a season of reflection.

Corporate Downsizing Pressure

Bill just turned fifty-eight. His company tried to let him go two years ago, but he protested—threatened to sue for age discrimination. The managers backed off, and the following year Bill was the top national salesman for the company. But the former incident left him feeling that his company had no loyalty to him, so he started looking around.

He took another position, but that didn't work out. For the last several months he has been unable to find suitable work. He has from time to time kept himself busy by painting, substitute teaching, and doing factory assembly work.

"I'm scared," he told a group of us one morning. "Sometimes I feel so lonely. Technology is passing me by. I find myself afraid of younger people who are more technologically current and have more energy to keep up. I just don't know what to do."

According to a study by James Medoff of Harvard University, American men aged thirty-five to fifty-four in this decade are 25 percent more likely to suffer permanent layoff or job loss than in the 1980s. A corporate environment of downsizing (what spin doctors want to call rightsizing), has put tens of thousands of men on the street looking for work. Many must face the reality that the new job will pay them less money for longer hours. Others, their skills no longer state of the art, their age considered over-the-hill, find themselves virtually unemployable. All in all, it puts a great strain on a breadwinner.

Long-term employees run scared because they realize corporate loyalty is a thing of the past in these turbulent, unpredictable times when competition and regulatory changes eat major companies for breakfast. Tensions and stress rise as supervisors demand more productivity from fewer employees. Employees know if they complain, they could easily be out the door, and they work longer hours for fear they could be next. Internal competition for existing jobs in a downsizing environment creates an almost predatory atmosphere among coworkers.

Communications Pressure

According to the Electronic Messaging Association, 23 percent of Fortune 2000 companies had E-mail (electronic mail) in 1991, but by 1993 the number had more than doubled to 65 percent.[3] Through E-mail I can finish writing this chapter on my computer in Orlando, push a key, and deliver a copy to my publisher in Nashville and my editor in Colorado Springs seconds later. Truly amazing.

Through technology we have defeated time and distance. I am completely in favor of overnight express mail, faxes, cellular phones, E-mail, Internet, and whatever comes next. These technologies have made life so much easier and convenient. At the same time, the increased expectations of an on-line lifestyle make life a lot more hectic.

Recently, I was negotiating for a new nonrecourse loan on one of our real estate projects. I received a fax asking for a huge change in the terms of the deal, and the lender wanted me to fax my answer within the hour. Give me a break!

Some days I feel bombarded with urgent requests for urgent answers to urgent problems that have urgent consequences. Some days I get the impression that the world will cease to spin on its axis unless I, Patrick Morley, personally take swift action. Sometimes, however, when I stop to analyze the significance of these seemingly weighty matters, I realize there is a lot of chaff, a little wheat, and a great deal of chasing after the wind.

Improvements in telecommunications have resulted in our putting more pressure on each other, not less. The possibility of a speedy reply has only increased people's expectations. A few short years ago you could take a couple of weeks to think over a major decision. Today people expect you to think, ruminate, consider, decide, and fax them your "wise" answer in five minutes! When we move so fast we lose the value of letting a decision "sit" for a season. Wisdom gets watered down. Creativity gets cut short. Blood pressure gets a spike. Get a life!

Each of us operates best at a particular pace. When we let our communication devices determine our pace, we invariably run too fast. After all, going faster captures the whole purpose of these devices! We need to set our thermostat and control our own pace, rather than react like a thermometer that merely adjusts to the demands of whoever clamors the loudest and most persistently. We have the *technological* capacity to make ourselves available at a level that we may not have the *physical* capacity to service. Yes, instant access is a good thing, but only when used with wisdom.

Men need times of peace. Men need times of reflection. Without reflection and wisdom we can quickly find ourselves chasing our technological tails. I don't have a car phone. I'm not against them, but my car is one of the few places where I can find some peace from all the devices hurling "important" questions at me. Without some time to think things over we will bounce from one urgent task to another, and in the process miss out on what's really important. We must take time out to keep things in perspective. We must control our technologies rather than let them control us.

We live in an information-driven society. Although it appears we have mastered the acquisition of vast sums of information, I cannot help but wonder if all this information has mastered us.

Have the improved communication tools you use really simplified your life? Or have they only added to the pressure you are under? If you could, would you go at a slower pace? What's holding you back from doing so?

Travel Pressure

Michael's job required him to leave town on Sunday afternoon, and he would be gone until Friday afternoon. One day he came home and greeted his two daughters, four and two years old. They turned from the TV, said, "Hello," then turned back around.

At that moment Michael, thirty-one years old, decided enough was enough. He had been on the road for 156 consecutive weeks.

With trepidation he met with his boss who turned out to be quite sympathetic. His boss said, "Michael, some things are more important than a job."

His company arranged a one-year severance package, so Michael had plenty of time to look around—and get reacquainted with his two daughters and wife.

"As I would look around the restaurants in all those hotels," Michael now recalls, "I could spot the men like me instantly. We all had that lonely look. The road is a dangerous place. It's full of temptations. It's a vulnerable place. Many of these men end up in a bar trying to drown their sorrows."

Bruce was channel surfing in his motel room. For some still unknown reason, when he crunched on channel one, a soft-porn pay-per-view movie flashed onto the screen. He felt as though some force lunged at him, enticing him to watch. Bruce couldn't believe what was happening. He knew he had to flee this toxic testosterone temptation. He smashed the off button and hurled the clicker across the room.

Recently, a Dallas-based hotel conducted a "Search for the Most Stressed Business Traveler." The prize was an all-expense-paid trip to the Virgin Islands (a discouraging sign of the times)!

The road adds to life's pressures, both *relationally* and *morally*. If you travel, do you find your family relationships under pressure? Do you find yourself under the pressure of moral temptation? What should you do?

Business-Deal Pressure

Business negotiation usually boils down to arguing about who gets to keep the money.

I'm sure you, like me, constantly come in contact with people who want to put you under a lot of pressure. Whether wittingly or unwittingly, who knows? Why do they do it?

Some people are entrepreneurs who thrive on stress and tension. They love the scent of a deal. They see business as a game of winners and losers. As a result, they create a world of pressure for those against whom they negotiate. They create chaos and havoc for us because it serves their hard-boiled self-interests. They are in the game for ego satisfaction and the money.

Others are the employees of companies that push them to perform. They may fear for their jobs and want to find job security. Or they may think beating you down will increase their prestige. Or they may see defeating you as the means to winning a promotion.

Whatever their reasons, the world is full of sinners who want to win at our expense. They can create a ton of turmoil and pressure.

"We're Killing Each Other"

My fourteen-year-old son, John, had an echocardiogram made to verify that some chest pains were not related to his heart. The doctor promised to phone my understandably concerned wife that same evening with the results.

He didn't call, and I didn't appreciate what he put my wife through. Finally, he called at 9:30 A.M. the next day. With earnest sincerity he said, "I'm terribly sorry I didn't call last night like I promised. I didn't get home until 11:00 p.m., and I didn't want to disturb you that late at night."

His answer satisfied me. I felt good about it, and felt it justified his not calling. Then I realized that, meanwhile, by getting home at 11:00 P.M., he is destroying his family. Do I care? Yes, in a vague, general way. But to be completely honest, only if I get good service or am satisfied that he killed himself trying. (I'm not suggesting that is the proper attitude.)

Our tendency is to like people who give us what we want, agree with us, and do what we ask. And if they don't, we are often not very forgiving. We might even call them selfish or strong-willed. When others have called me selfish or strong-willed, I notice it's usually because I won't cave in and give them what they want. What does that make *them*?

We put stressful expectations upon each other to perform. If we are completely honest, we are not happy with people unless we keep them running, especially when we feel we are putting forth more effort than they are.

What kind of pressure do you put on the people around you? Do you think it's healthy for them?

Ten Seconds of Respect

In June 1994, my best friend for eighteen years, Tom Skinner, died suddenly of acute leukemia. Not a day goes by that I don't think of him.

After his death, those friends who knew we were close would express some form of condolence. What is particularly interesting to me is that the average length of those condolences was about ten seconds. Then the subject would change, and in most cases, that's the last time his name was ever mentioned.

Tom was a man who always had people trying to get a piece of his time. I'm talking about *hundreds* of people. Let's be honest. Most people who ask you for time don't really care that much about you personally. I'm not blaming them. I'm simply pointing out that for most people in your life, you are good for about ten seconds of respect, and then life must go on. Only a handful of people will even attend your funeral, much less shed a tear.

Why? Because we're on the run. When someone wants to set you to running, ask yourself, "Is this person *really* going to miss me when I'm gone?"

Build in "Hang Time"

Speaking of Tom Skinner, together we helped leaders in Jackson, Mississippi, begin a citywide mission of racial and denominational reconciliation and evangelism appropriately called Mission Mississippi.

Over a two-and-a-half-week period, Tom and I spoke roughly fifty times to people in high schools, civic clubs, churches, and a crusade. The organizers faxed a demanding schedule to Tom. When he got off the plane, Tom, who was black, said, "After looking over this schedule, I realized there really are differences between white people and black people. Obviously, white people don't have to go to the bathroom!"

Frankly, as a type A personality, I have the natural tendency to plan to arrive at the last possible moment and leave at the earliest possible moment—maybe even sneak out early. One thing Tom taught me is the importance of building "hang time" into our calendars, time to "hang" with people. He said some of the most helpful conversations take place during hang time.

I've adopted this philosophy, and I can attest to its power. Some of the best business contacts you will ever make will come by simply "being there." The best moments I have with my kids happen because "I'm there." My relationship with my wife turned around when I started building in hang time around the dinner table after the kids split.

Your real friends are the ones who will spend hang time with you. Friends who will be with you when there is no agenda. Do you spend hang time with the people you really care about?

I used to have incredibly painful migraine headaches. My doctor gave me a prescription for a painkiller that I ate like chocolate chips. One day I was surprised to see on the label that the medication was a barbiturate. Months later the medicine burned a hole in my stomach, and I was hospitalized.

The first night, as I lay in bed with tubes sticking out of my nose, I awakened to see one of my best friends, Bill, sitting at my bedside. Bill is as busy as any four people I know, but there he was. I tried to talk, but he told me to rest. I kept talking anyway. Finally, he said that if I didn't stop talking, he was going to leave. I kept talking, so he left.

Until the day I die, I will never forget the message he sent by sitting quietly next to my bed when I was asleep. He is a true friend. He gave me some hang time.

Don't fill up every waking minute with activities. Be sure to build in some hang time to be with the people you care about the most, and those who need you the most. You don't have to be on the run. Running is a choice. And it creates a lot of pressure.

How to Say No

I wrote a friend and asked him to do a favor for me. It wasn't a big thing, just a tiny, little, teeny-weenie, itsy-bitsy thing. He wrote back, "I appreciate the invitation to help you out, but I must regretfully decline. With my present commitments *I have to be realistic about what else I take on.*"

"Hey!" I wanted to shout. "I didn't ask you to be realistic! I asked you to help!"

Isn't this how we usually treat each other? We want what we want when we want it, so we put a lot of pressure on each other.

What is it, anyway, about our culture? Culturally, men are not allowed to say no unless we can also say the magic words, "I'm too busy." Until a man can sigh deeply, let his shoulders sag, and show the creases in his brow from the pressure he is already under, he isn't supposed to say no. It just isn't the culturally acceptable thing to do. So we run wide open.

Whenever we are asked to serve on a committee, attend a meeting, or do a deed, most of us feel an obligation to say yes unless we can gaze at our calendar with the afflicted look of a martyr and note, with some satisfaction, that every waking moment is already spoken for.

A better way is the approach my friend used on me, a method I have adopted with tremendous results. I have prayerfully decided my priorities in advance. I have made some decisions about how I am going to spend my time before anyone has asked.

When someone asks me to do something, I no longer feel obligated to say yes merely because I have unscheduled time. Instead, like my friend said to me, I reserve the right to answer, "I'm sorry. I can't do it. I have to be realistic."

How do you respond when someone asks you to do something? Do you tend to feel guilty saying no if you have any unscheduled time on your calendar?

Instead of feeling guilty about not meeting everyone else's needs, be realistic. If you don't, you will end up as a wounded warrior, helping people who care the least, shortchanging those who need you the most, but still under a lot of pressure.

QUESTIONS AND DECISIONS

1. Carefully consider the following questions:

   • Are you tired?
   • Do you have a lingering feeling something isn't quite right about your life?
   • Is your life turning out the way you planned?
   • Do you feel you have some people in your life who really care?

   What do your answers tell you about the way you are spending your life?

2. Do you feel that every morning when the sun comes up, you had better be running? Why is that not healthy?

3. What is your monthly "nut" or overhead? What kind of pressure does it put you under? Is it worth it? What changes should you make?

4. If you travel, do you find your family relationships under pressure? Do you find yourself under the pressure of moral temptation? What should you do?

5. Has the technology in your life lowered or raised your work load? Have you become a slave to your laborsaving devices? What should you do?

6. Have the improved communication tools you use really simplified your life? Or have they only added to the pressure you are under? If you could, would you go at a slower pace? What should you do?

7. What kind of pressure do you put on the people around you? Do you think it's healthy for them? What changes should you make?

8. What kinds of pressure are others putting on you? Do you tend to feel guilty saying no if you have any unscheduled time on your calendar? How can you handle this area better?

The Search for Meaning and Purpose

Man's search for meaning is the primary motivation in his life.

—Victor Frankl

4 The "Felt" Need

"What motivates me," said Dick, a self-proclaimed agnostic, "is the desire to make a contribution. I have always wanted to do something significant with my life. That's why I became an airline pilot. A man needs to have a sense of direction, a sense of excitement. That's why I hated it so much when I was forced to retire at age sixty.

"After retiring, I threw myself into volunteer work on airplane safety. I have received a number of awards for my work. The other day I noticed a cake of dust growing on those plaques. That's what it's all been worth—dust.

"At least I have my integrity. A man said to someone about me, 'He's never lied to me.' That makes me feel good. To me, the real question is, 'Can you really look at yourself in the mirror and say you're happy?'"

Are you happy, Dick? *Really* happy? I hope so. Yet, my friend, these "felt" needs—to be significant, to make a contribution, to have a sense of direction, to possess a sense of excitement, to be recognized, to have integrity, to be able to look in the mirror and say, "I'm happy"—are surface needs. When satisfied, these felt needs still don't answer the deeper questions of life: "Who am I? What am I here for? What is my purpose? Where am I going when I die?

"There Is Something Missing"

What happens when you have achieved significance in the eyes of the world? Is that enough to satisfy a man? Ask Mickey Mantle. Few names in baseball conjure up as many warm feelings of nostalgia. The greatest batter of his era. In *Sports Illustrated* and a televised interview, Mickey Mantle described his long battle with alcohol, the agony of a son who died, and the grief of having a son on drugs.

The interviewer asked, "So how are things going for you today, Mickey?"

"Better," he replied. "I haven't had a drink in eight months. I'm starting to get my life back together, but I just feel like there is something missing."

The "Real" Need

"There is something missing." These words must ring in the ears of millions of men—men who did it "my way" for ten, fifteen, twenty, or more years. But it still has not come together. The meaning and satisfaction they expected have eluded them.

Jim said, "Even though I was saved at eighteen years of age, I was not taught and discipled, nor did I get into the Bible myself. Instead, I got into the world system and lived by reacting to the five human senses for forty years. I concentrated on work, family, and fun. I didn't wake up until they told me at the age of fifty-eight that I had inoperable terminal cancer. Prostate cancer had metastasized to my bones in more than fifty-eight places. I hope the men hearing this story won't wait as long as I did to wake up to the real meaning of life."

Men today are filled with angst, fears, worries, and doubts. They are under a great deal of stress. It often takes two incomes just to keep up. The half-life of a college education is about four years. Every other marriage ends in divorce.

The world's answers have not worked. Men find themselves feeling empty inside, like there is something missing. They are lonely and wonder, *What is the meaning of it all?* Men feel guilty about their pasts and afraid of their futures. Men today want something satisfying. Even in the church, *especially* in the church, men are hungry for God. A pervasive feeling is that "there must be more—there's gotta be." Men are coming to the end of themselves. They are reaching out for answers.

Are men so frustrated because life has no meaning? No, it is exactly because God has set eternity in men's hearts that they have a built-in sense that life does have meaning, and their frustration is that they have not yet found it.

Men Need God

In his book *Life After God*, Douglas Coupland, who wrote *Generation X*, captures this troubled, frustrating, sometimes terrifying feeling many men have about life when he writes for millions of American men:

> I think I am a broken person. I seriously question the road my life has taken and I endlessly rehash the compromises I have made in my life. I have an insecure and vaguely crappy job with an amoral corporation so that I don't have to worry about money. I put up with halfway relationships so as not to have to worry about loneliness. I have lost the ability to recapture the purer feelings of my younger years in exchange for a streamlined narrow-mindedness that I assumed would propel me to "the top." What a joke.

At the end of his book, Coupland confesses:

> Now—here is my secret: I tell it to you with an openness of heart that I doubt I shall ever achieve again, so I pray that you are in a quiet room as you hear these words. My secret is that I need God—that I am sick and can no longer make it alone. I need God to help me give, because I no longer seem to be capable of giving; to help me be kind, as I no longer seem capable of kindness; to help me love, as I seem beyond being able to love.[1]

Coupland has found the center of the problem, and it applies to men, whether they are spiritually lost or already know Christ but have wandered from the path. This is the core issue: Men need God. We are sick and cannot make it alone. Simply stated, apart from God, life has no meaning.

Coupland writes to his peers in *Generation X*, "You are the first generation raised without religion." I've got news for Douglas Coupland. You don't have to be part of Generation X to miss out on religion. In reality, in every generation there are men who are raised without *true* religion, both inside and outside the church.

"The Trouble with Many Men . . ."

The vast majority of us have been exposed to religion—to the gospel—but we have other interests and affections. We are busy people. Our responsibilities weigh heavily on our shoulders. We carry around the weight of the world. So religion becomes for us merely another competing attraction on the midway of this carnival called life. The preacher becomes a barker for *self-denial,* competing against a throng of silk-stocking pitchmen hawking sensuous pleasures up and down the midway of *self-fulfillment.*

So we tend to have a form of religion, but we miss out on the true meaning of that religion because we are so busy, so tired, so distracted. We don't have enough religion to make us happy when we look in the mirror, but we do have enough to remind us how unhappy we have become.

The Desire for God

Dave said, "I had a beautiful marriage of twenty-two years and three wonderful children, but something was still missing. It was like a picture without a frame."

Augustine said, "There is a God-shaped vacuum in every man that only Christ can fill." Every man, sooner or later, has a deep yearning within his soul to know God. I don't just mean to know *about* God, but to really *know* God. It is an intense, consuming desire to meet his maker. Augustine put it this way: "Thou hast made us for Thyself, and the heart of man is restless until it finds its rest in Thee."

Billy Graham said, "The human heart is the same the world over. Only Christ can meet the deepest needs of our world and hearts. Christ alone can bring lasting peace—peace with God, peace among men and nations, and peace within our hearts. He transcends the political and social boundaries of our world."

Knowing God and Knowing Self

At some point every man must face his doubts and answer life's seminal questions: "Who am I? Why do I exist? Why is life so hard? And what happens when I die?" These are questions that can be answered only when he knows himself and knows God.

How do we get past the hollow victory of satisfying our *felt* needs to the triumph of meeting our *real* needs? The answer is twofold: *I need to know who I am so that I can know God, and I need to know who God is so that I can know myself.*

Great thinkers have expressed this thought in different ways through the ages. Descartes wrote, "I hold that all those to whom God has given the use of reason are bound to employ it in the effort to know him and to know themselves." Augustine said, "I desire to know God and the soul," and he prayed, "Let me know myself, let me know thee." John Calvin, in the first sentence of his masterful tome, *Institutes of the Christian Religion*, said, "Nearly all wisdom we possess, that is to say, true and sound wisdom, consists of two parts: the knowledge of God and of ourselves."[2]

The secrets of meaning and purpose are revealed as we know God and know ourselves. In other words, the more deeply we sink into the knowledge of God and the knowledge of self, the more clearly we see the meaning of life and the purpose for which we were created.

What are the tools for knowing ourselves and knowing God? We answer life's most important questions through the tools of *self-examination* and *studying the character of God*.

The Call to Self-Examination

Clement of Alexandria was of the opinion that "if one knows himself, he will know God."[3] The simple decision of becoming open to knowing ourselves is a giant leap forward to meaning and purpose. As Plato said, "The life which is unexamined is not worth living."

The idea of self-examination may cause a concern that we are somehow not trusting the Lord, that we are acting self-centeredly. We may be tempted to ask, "Shouldn't we just leave well enough alone?" Actually, the Bible commends self-examination: "Examine yourselves to see whether you are in the faith; test yourselves" (2 Cor. 13:5); and "Let us examine our ways and test them, and let us return to the Lord" (Lam. 3:40). Self-examination is a biblical concept.

What should we know about ourselves? The call to self-examination is not the contemporary call to discover who is at fault for the way we turned out so we will have someone to blame. Rather, it is a call to understand our human nature so we can take responsibility for our lives.

Two questions in self-examination will drive us to God: "Why am I so blessed?" and "Why am I so unhappy?" Let's take them in order.

"Why am I so blessed?"

Reflect upon God's gifts and benefits to you. Consider your wife (if you are married), your children (except teenagers—smile), your health, your lifestyle, your occupation or job. Where did they come from? How is it that you breathe, think, talk, and walk? These gifts are hardly from yourself. Each benefit leads upstream toward God.

"Why am I so unhappy?"

Reflect upon your miseries and problems. Some troubles come *unintentionally* through ignorance, vanity, poverty, infirmity, or circumstances. A health problem could result from not exercising, poor diet, high cholesterol, or a genetic defect. A finance problem could result from being a spendthrift or losing a job. A relationship problem could develop because you didn't invest time in your wife or kids. These are unintentional troubles. You didn't plan to hurt yourself or others, but you did.

Other woes come *intentionally* through malice, depravity, corruption, and willful sin. You may lead a double life. Perhaps you have a secret thought life. Maybe the problem is dishonesty or sexual immorality.

It is not necessarily bad to be miserable. As someone has said, "We must be stung by our own unhappiness before we attain a knowledge of God."

Reflecting on our blessings and our unhappiness will inexorably give us a hunger to know ourselves and a thirst to know God.

Five Suggestions To Help in Self-Examination

1. The Bible

The single best searchlight of self-examination is the Bible. When we read self-revealing portions of the Bible (such as Psalms, Proverbs, Ecclesiastes, and James, among others) the Holy Spirit of God quickens truth to our minds. Try reading the Bible after you pray, and ask God to reveal to you a knowledge of self.

2. Christian Literature

Francis Bacon said, "Reading maketh a full man." In the last twenty years we have witnessed an explosion of good Christian literature (as well as some not so good). Many of these books by reputable authors can take you deeper into self-understanding. Ask your pastor or an employee of a Christian bookstore for suggestions.

3. Men's Bible Study

After you have read yourself full you will probably find that you still lack some self-understanding. Try out a men's Bible study that includes discussion time. It's profitable to hear a sermon, but for self-examination you need some "air time" to flesh out ideas for yourself.

4. Accountability Group

Positively the best tool of self-examination is a small group relationship with two or three other men who also seek to know God and know themselves. In an accountability group you give each other permission to ask the hard questions about how you are doing in key areas of your life: your relationship with your spouse and kids, your finances, your relationship with God, and any areas of personal struggle. Although it represents a vulnerable commitment, men who practice accountability swear by it. (For details about how to start an accountable relationship see *The Man in the Mirror*, chapters 10 and 23.)

5. Your Wife

Nobody knows you better than your wife. In fact, that's the very reason many men won't discuss their private thoughts with their mates. However, if you explain to your wife that you want to get a better handle on who you are and ask for her support, you will most likely find her a gifted and sensitive helpmate. If she's open to the idea, set aside some time—say thirty minutes to one hour—two or three times a week. You will find this type of self-examination naturally includes your roles as a husband and father. Take a walk, have a cup of coffee together, or go out for a bite to eat. (What should you talk about? If you don't know, try the discussion questions from the two-page devotionals in my book *Two Part Harmony*, or find some other materials designed to help couples have a deeper relationship.)

If we cannot know God unless we know ourselves, it is equally true that we cannot know ourselves unless we know God.

The Call to Study the Character of God

I have a deep concern for men today. We live in such a narcissistic culture that I am afraid we want God to know us more than we want to know Him. Have you *really* wanted to know God, or have you just wanted Him to know you? Be honest with yourself. Open your heart to what follows, especially if you gave the latter answer.

What is the principal task in doing business with someone new? Isn't it to get a feel for him—his credibility, his ability, his character, his personality, his likes, his dislikes, and his "ticks"? Doing business with God is no different. We need to ask, "What is He like? How do we get to know Him?"

Too often we settle for secondhand information about God. It is impossible to know anyone unless we personally spend time with him. Especially

God. How can we get to know God? We know God by studying His character. We do not press God into the mold of our expectations, but come humbly searching for the unchanging God. How does God reveal Himself?

Three Ways God Reveals Himself

1. Works

God reveals Himself through His *works* in creation and redemption. The way Calvin put it says a lot: "The painter reveals something of himself through his painting." The Bible says, "Since the creation of the world His invisible attributes are clearly seen, being understood by the things that are made" (Rom. 1:20 NKJV). Also, the power of a changed life (a redeemed life), which is a work of God, provides compelling evidence of God.

2. "Whisper"

God reveals Himself through a "whisper" to our *instinct*, what Martin Luther called the *divinitatis sensum*—the "sense of the divine." Billy Graham was sitting in the office of the president of Harvard University one snowy day. He asked, "What is the greatest problem your students face?"

The president stared out the window at the falling snow for a moment, then replied, "Emptiness."

When men feel empty, it is because they instinctively know there is more. The Bible puts it this way: "He has put eternity in their hearts" (Eccl. 3:11 NKJV). Cicero said, "There is no nation so barbarous, no people so savage, that they have not a deep-seated conviction that there is a God." The idols we make should offer ample proof.

3. Word

God reveals Himself through His *Word*. One day a man was reading his Bible on a bumpy plane ride. The woman next to him grabbed the armrests, and with every bump her knuckles turned a shade whiter. Finally, the plane took a really terrific jolt, and the woman screamed at the man, "You're religious! Do something!"

So he took up an offering.

This funny story illustrates a profound truth: People know the Bible contains answers. Through the Bible, God reveals a knowledge of Himself, as this passage illustrates: "Jesus did many other signs in the presence of His disciples, which are not written in this book; but these are written that you may believe that Jesus is the Christ, the Son of God, and that believing you may have life in His name" (John 20:30–31 NKJV).

Through these three means—His works, His "whisper," and His Word—God reveals a knowledge of Himself. What should we be looking for? We should look for the attributes of God.

The Attributes of God

God has attributes that are both *transcendent* (God out there) and *immanent* (God with us).

What are His transcendent qualities? He is the self-existent Creator God; He is "the King eternal, immortal, invisible" (1 Tim. 1:17 KJV). He is infinite, omnipotent, omniscient, and omnipresent. He is holy and just. By reflecting upon the supreme character of God, we come to appreciate, respect, and revere Him.

What are His immanent attributes? God possesses the attributes of love, grace, and mercy. His Holy Spirit lives within us to guide, comfort, counsel, convict, and encourage us. By considering His tender, long-suffering care for us, we are driven to our knees in love, affection, and gratitude. We wonder, "What is man that you are mindful of him?" (Ps. 8:4).

Three of God's attributes in particular merit special attention.

1. God is our Creator.

This attribute addresses the issues of our dignity and identity. It answers the question, "Who am I?"

In the movie *Days of Thunder*, Tom Cruise plays Cole Trickle, a maverick stock car driver who takes too many chances. While he is recovering from a serious race injury, Claire, his doctor-turned-girlfriend, wants to know what drives him to keep racing and why he is willing to risk being hurt again.

Cole replies, "I am more afraid of being nothing than I am of being hurt."

The fear of being nothing. Many are the men driven by the desire to not be nothing.

God created the cosmos, and He created you and me. Who are you? You are God's crowning achievement. You are His most excellent creation. You are the full expression of God's creative genius. God was at His best when He made you. Because of this identity as a creation of God, you have intrinsic value and human dignity.

You are everything God intended you to be, even if you are missing a limb or an eye. He created you for His own glory. If you are ordinary, it is because God wants you that way. A sign chiseled above the entrance to the New York Daily News building says, "God must have loved the common people most because He made so many of them."

When Martin Luther tacked his *Ninty-five Theses* on the Wittenberg door, one of them read, "God does not love us because we are valuable. We are valuable because God loves us."

As Francis Schaeffer said, "Man is not nothing."

2. God is our Redeemer.

This attribute answers the question, "What happens when I die?" It has always been God's plan to redeem (to save from sin and its consequences) a people to live with Him in heaven forever. Read carefully how that plan works as the apostle Paul writes to followers of Jesus Christ:

> God has told us his secret reason for sending Christ, a plan he decided on in mercy long ago; and this was his purpose: that when the time is ripe he will gather us all together from wherever we are—in heaven or on earth—to be with him in Christ, forever. Moreover, because of what Christ has done we have become gifts to God that he delights in, for as part of God's sovereign plan we were chosen from the beginning to be his, and all things happen just as he decided long ago. (Eph. 1:9–11 TLB)

All who belong to Christ will become part of God's plan to be with Him in Christ forever.

3. God is our Lord.

This attribute answers the questions, "Why do I exist? What is the purpose of my life?" Not only did God create the world and people, and not only does He redeem people who yield their lives to Christ, He also sovereignly rules over the affairs of men—both good and evil. Jesus said, "He makes His sun rise on the evil and on the good, and sends rain on the just and on the unjust" (Matt. 5:45 NKJV). Every poetic move Michael Jordan ever made flowed from the natural abilities he received as a gift from

God, whether he acknowledges it or not. Even the man who curses God only draws his next breath by God's kindness. He is the Supreme Ruler.

As our Lord, God calls us to become obedient disciples of his Son, Jesus Christ, and to live as faithful stewards, humble servants, and bold witnesses. Our destiny is to "produce fruit" in keeping with our identity: "Different kinds of fruit trees can quickly be *identified* by examining their fruit" (Matt. 7:17 TLB, emphasis added).

Ultimately, however, each of us wants to experience God personally. As the psalmist wrote,

> AS THE DEER PANTS FOR STREAMS OF WATER,
> SO MY SOUL PANTS FOR YOU, O GOD.
> MY SOUL THIRSTS FOR GOD, FOR THE LIVING GOD.
> WHEN CAN I GO AND MEET WITH GOD? (Ps. 42:1–2)

This will be our subject in the next chapter.

QUESTIONS AND DECISIONS

1. When was the last time you thought, *There is something missing?* What did you do about it?

2. How have you answered each of the following questions about life?

   - Who am I?
   - What am I here for?
   - What is my purpose?
   - Where am I going when I die?

3. "This is the core issue: Men need God. We are sick and cannot make it alone. Simply stated, apart from God, life has no meaning." Do you ☐ agree/ ☐ disagree? Explain your answer.

4. Billy Sunday said, "The trouble with many men is that they have got just enough religion to make them miserable." Has this been true in your life? How?

5. "I need to know who I am so that I can know God, and I need to know who God is so that I can know myself." Do you ☐ agree/ ☐ disagree? Explain your answer.

6. What are the five tools of self-examination mentioned in this chapter? Which of these are you already using to your satisfaction? What changes should you make?

7. Have you studied the character of God? What are the benefits of studying His character and attributes? What do you still need to know about God?

8. Three attributes of God were briefly mentioned:

   - Creator
   - Redeemer
   - Lord

   Have you settled in your mind that God is your Creator? Your Redeemer? Your Lord? Which one do you struggle to accept?

How Can We
Know God Personally?

—*Matthew 16:26*

5 Jesus made the claim: "I am the way, the truth, and the life. No one comes to the Father except through Me" (John 14:6 NKJV). Jesus proclaimed, "I and My Father are one" (John 10:30 NKJV). He also said, "He who has seen Me has seen the Father" (John 14:9 NKJV). And He declared, "If you had known Me, you would have known My Father also" (John 8:19 NKJV).

These are remarkable statements. What should we make of them? Anyone who would make such claims is a *liar,* a *lunatic,* or *Lord.* If these claims are false, Jesus had to be either a malevolent liar or a deluded lunatic. But if these claims are true, we have only one option left: He is Lord.

C. S. Lewis said,

> A man who was merely a man and said the things Jesus said would not be a great moral teacher. He would either be a lunatic—on a level with the man who says he is a poached egg—or else he would be the devil of hell. You must make your choice. Either this man was, and is, the son of God; or else a madman or something worse. You can shut him up for a fool; you can spit at him and kill him as a demon; or you can fall at his feet and call him Lord and God. But let us not come with any patronizing nonsense about his being a great moral teacher. He has not left that open to us. He did not intend to.[1]

How can we know God personally? This chapter is written especially for men who yearn to know God personally, although every man will profit from a careful reading.

You cannot be a Christian on your own terms. That is Cultural Christianity. You must be a Christian on God's terms. That is Biblical Christianity. The former is counterfeit; the latter is authentic. So let's explore the terms of knowing God personally.

The way we know and experience God personally is through His Son, Jesus Christ. Where are you on your spiritual pilgrimage? Are you tired? If so, Jesus says to you, "Come to me, all you who are weary and burdened, and I will give you rest" (Matt. 11:28). Do you have a lingering feeling that something isn't quite right about your life? If so, Jesus says to you, "I have come that they may have life, and that they may have it more abundantly" (John 10:10 NKJV). Do you feel nobody really cares about you? That's not true—Jesus cares. Matthew noted, "When [Jesus] saw the crowds, he had compassion on them, because they were harassed and helpless, like sheep without a shepherd" (Matt. 9:36).

The Great Desire of God

Do you know what the great, great desire of God is? His great desire is to be reconciled with you personally and individually. The Bible says,

> The Lord is . . . not willing that any should perish but that all should come to repentance. (2 Peter 3:9 NKJV)
>
> I take no pleasure in the death of the wicked, but rather that they turn from their ways and live. (Ezek. 33:11)

[God] desires all men to be saved and to come to the knowledge of the truth. (1 Tim. 2:4 NKJV)

For God so loved the world that He gave His only begotten Son, that whoever believes in Him should not perish but have everlasting life. (John 3:16 NKJV)

Why then are we alienated from God? We are alienated from God because we are sinners: "For all have sinned and fall short of the glory of God" (Rom. 3:23 NKJV). Sin is estrangement from God through rebellion against Him or indifference toward Him.

We have a dilemma. On the one hand, God desires to be reconciled with us. On the other hand, we are separated from Him by our sins. What is the solution to this dilemma?

Jesus Christ is the solution. God reconciles us to Himself through Jesus Christ: "This is a faithful saying and worthy of all acceptance, that Christ Jesus came into the world to save sinners" (1 Tim. 1:15 NKJV).

How did He do that? Again, the Bible gives us the answer: "For scarcely for a righteous man will one die; yet perhaps for a good man someone would even dare to die. But God demonstrates His own love toward us, in that while we were still sinners, Christ died for us" (Rom. 5:7–8 NKJV).

He had no army or organization. He came from an unknown family. He never wrote a book. He never traveled more than one hundred miles from His hometown. He was poor. His only possession was a robe. Yet of Him, Napoleon said,

> I die before my time and my body shall be given back to the earth and devoured by worms. What an abysmal gulf between my deep miseries and the eternal kingdom of Christ. I marvel that whereas the ambitious dreams of myself and of Alexander and of Caesar should have vanished into thin air, a Judean peasant—Jesus—should be able to stretch his hands across the centuries and control the destinies of men and nations.

Here is the heart of the matter: "Christ died for our sins according to the Scriptures, . . . He was buried, . . . He rose again the third day according to the Scriptures, and . . . He was seen by Cephas [Peter], then by the twelve. After that He was seen by over five hundred of the brethren at once" (1 Cor. 15:3–6 NKJV).

How to Be Reconciled to God

How can you be reconciled to God personally? Personal reconciliation to God through Jesus Christ occurs by taking these two steps:

Step 1: Acknowledge and confess that you are a sinner separated from fellowship with God and His purpose for your life.

Sin separates us from God.
"For the wages of sin is death. . ." (Rom. 6:23 NKJV).

We must acknowledge we are sinners.

"If we say that we have no sin, we deceive ourselves, and the truth is not in us. . . . If we say that we have not sinned, we make Him a liar, and His word is not in us" (1 John 1:8, 10 NKJV).

We must confess our sins.

"If we confess our sins, He is faithful and just to forgive us our sins and to cleanse us from all unrighteousness" (1 John 1:9 NKJV).

Step 2: Turn to God and by faith receive Jesus Christ as your Savior and Lord.

Christ is the way to reconciliation with God.

"Jesus said to him, 'I am the way, the truth, and the life. No one comes to the Father except through Me'" (John 14:6 NKJV).

We must receive Christ.

"But as many as received Him, to them He gave the right to become children of God, to those who believe in His name" (John 1:12 NKJV).

We receive Christ by faith.

"For by grace you have been saved through faith, and that not of yourselves; it is the gift of God, not of works, lest anyone should boast" (Eph. 2:8–9 NKJV).

We receive Christ by faith by inviting Him in.

Jesus said, "Behold, I stand at the door and knock. If anyone hears My voice and opens the door, I will come in to him and dine with him, and he with Me" (Rev. 3:20 NKJV).

The issue is not what you do with religion, but what you do with Jesus Christ. The issue is not about how to be good, but about how to be saved. The issue is not about being committed to a set of Christian values, but about being committed to the person of Jesus Christ.

The core message of Christianity is that Jesus Christ entered into the stream of human history to redeem lost sinners. Our faith is to be not in an idea but in a historical person. As J. Gresham Machen said, "Jesus is not merely an *example* for faith; He is the *object* of our faith."[2]

Does this make sense? If you have never received Christ, or if you are unsure of your salvation, you can settle the issue right now. Would you like to receive Jesus Christ right now? God looks at the attitude and motives of your heart. If you sincerely desire to confess your sins, change the direction of your life by turning to God from self (repentance), and place your faith in Jesus Christ for salvation, then you can do so right now by expressing your desire to Him. Prayer is an excellent way to express yourself to God. Here is a suggested prayer:

Lord Jesus, I need You in my life. I desire to be reconciled to You and to experience Your love and forgiveness. I acknowledge that I have sinned against You, and as a result, my life has not turned out the way I had planned. Thank You for dying on the cross for my sins. I open the door of my life and receive You by faith as my Savior and Lord. Thank You for forgiving my sins and for giving me eternal life. I now ask You to take control of my life and make me into the kind of person You want me to be. I pray You will let me experience the true meaning and purpose of life. Amen.

Does this prayer express the desire of your heart? If it does, pray this prayer right now, and Jesus Christ will come into your heart and life as He promised. The result? Your sins will be forgiven, you will begin to experience God's love, you will receive eternal life, you will begin the great adventure of living the Christ-controlled life, and you will find true meaning and purpose. Do this now.

Recommitment

What if you have previously received Christ, but you have not been walking with Him? Once you have Christ in your life He will never leave you. However, by controlling your own life, fellowship with Him can be broken. It is possible, indeed, common, for men to receive Christ but live by their own ideas.

If you have not been walking with Christ, if you have hit the wall, if you are burned out, if you are ready to acknowledge and repent of controlling your life, if you are tired of "kicking against the goads," if you are weary of being a Cultural Christian, you will have the opportunity to recommit and rededicate your life in a deep and meaningful way in the parts of this book entitled "The Season of Crisis" and "The Season of Renewal." Feel free to skip over "The Season of Building" if you want. You can come back to it later.

Next Steps

If you have just given your life to Jesus Christ in repentance and faith I would like to be the first one to congratulate you. Welcome to the family!

Speaking for multiplied millions of other men who have made this same decision, I know that in the days, weeks, months, and years ahead, you, like me, will look back upon this decision as the single most important choice a man can ever make. You are now eternally and irrevocably connected with God.

Let me suggest five steps for you to consider taking:

1. Tell someone today.

Share your experience with someone close. Don't put this off. Sharing will further help you conceptualize your commitment. The Scriptures say, "If you confess with your mouth the Lord Jesus and believe in your heart that God has raised Him from the dead, you will be saved. For with the heart one believes unto righteousness, and with the mouth confession is made unto salvation" (Rom. 10:9–10 NKJV).

2. Read the Bible daily.

Purchase a Bible or dust off the one you have. Be sure you have a translation you can understand. Your pastor or an employee of a Christian bookstore can help you select a good version. Read the Bible on a daily basis. Pick a consistent time and place if you can. I can honestly report to you that I have never known a man whose life has changed in any significant way after receiving Christ apart from the regular study of God's Word.

The Bible is the principal means God uses to speak to us. So if we want to know God, we must read His Word. Begin by reading the four Gospels, Matthew, Mark, Luke, and John. Read a chapter or two each day. Discuss what you read with someone if you can.

Then move on to Romans, Ephesians, Galatians, and James. The book of Proverbs is filled with practical wisdom. The book of Psalms provides tremendous comfort when you are under pressure. Paul declared, "For whatever things were written before were written for our learning, that we through the patience and comfort of the Scriptures might have hope" (Rom. 15:4 NKJV).

3. Pray daily.

Set aside some time each day to pray, preferably immediately before or after you read the Bible. It doesn't need to be long. You can pray the Lord's Prayer (Matt. 6:9–13). You can pray for loved ones, confess sins, ask for blessings, and seek courage to reconcile broken relationships. Peter urged, "Cast all your anxiety on him because he cares for you" (1 Peter 5:7). (Chapter 20 goes into greater detail about reading the Bible and praying.)

4. Attend church consistently.

It is impossible to be a Christian on your own—a "Lone Ranger" Christian. The Bible encourages believers not to forsake assembling together. Many temptations tug at us, and we need the fellowship and accountability of like-minded people to keep us thinking clearly. We attend church to worship God. The church gives us a special place to humble ourselves in reverence to the God who saves us from our sins. A good church will preach from the Bible and be evangelistic (the church will encourage people to give their lives to Christ). Ask around, and don't be shy about visiting a number of churches.

5. Attend a men's Bible study.

A Bible study with other men is a golden key to unlocking the mysteries of Christian life. If you have met before in a group with other men, you already know how much men share in a common struggle. If not, you will be amazed at how common the struggles, challenges, and opportunities you face are among other men too. (More will be said about this in chapter 22.)

QUESTIONS AND DECISIONS

1. How would you answer these questions?

   • Are you tired?
   • Do you have a lingering feeling that something isn't quite right about your life?
   • Do you feel nobody really cares about you?

2. Where are you on your spiritual pilgrimage?

3. Reread the claims of Jesus in the first paragraph of this chapter. "Anyone who would make such claims is a *liar,* a *lunatic,* or *Lord."* Do you agree with this assessment? Why or why not? If Jesus' claims are true, how should you live differently in response?

4. Has there ever been a time in your life when you received Jesus Christ as your Savior and Lord?

5. If you answered no to the last question, did you pray to receive Christ at the end of this chapter? If not, would you like to? If you sense a desire to be reconciled to God through Jesus Christ, why not express that desire to Him right now through prayer? You can pray the prayer on page 48, or use your own words.

6. Which of the following five suggested steps are ones you would benefit by taking? Why?

   • Tell someone today.
   • Read the Bible daily.
   • Pray daily.
   • Attend church consistently.
   • Attend a men's Bible study.

PART 2

•

THE SEASON OF

BUILDING

Building a Career

At a corporate retreat for a major real estate company, the senior executive was leading a discussion about how to develop a new vision for the firm. The business environment had changed, and the company floundered because of a lack of direction.

He said, "What we need is a vision that will inflame the imaginations of our employees, a vision that will make them excited to get out of bed in the morning! We need a business plan people are willing to give their lives to! A plan that can give them the satisfaction they are looking for! Blah, blah, blah, etc., etc. . . ."

Sitting quietly at the table, a young executive's thoughts began to drift into a daydream. He considered how one-dimensional his life had become. He had worked seven days a week to make his dream come true. Now he was filled with regret for the ten years he had made this company his idol and had poured all of his time and creativity into building a temporal kingdom for himself. He wondered how he could build some balance into his life. He wondered how his daughter ever got to be three and a half years old without spending more than a few minutes with her daddy.

As he considered what his boss was trying to accomplish related to what his own life had become, he wrote on his pad, "You can't get there from here."

Myth #1

<u>Without reflection any of us can be lured into an unbalanced life.</u> This chapter explores the first of three myths men often buy into as they are building a life.

Myth #1

"To succeed means to have a dynamic career."

You could tell it from the moment you met him. Don was exceptional. He was going to do something special with his life. He had fire in his belly.

During the first ten years of his career, he rose predictably to become the manager of his company. To accomplish such a feat, he worked twelve-hour days, six days a week.

He forgot one thing. The fire that fuels can also consume.

Truth #1

There are many ways to succeed besides having a dynamic career. You are only as successful as the way you balance your priorities as worker, husband, father, friend, provider, and follower of Christ.

Actually, career success is how the people who care about you least evaluate your worth as a person. In a word, you are expendable.

"Charm School"

General H. Norman Schwarzkopf became a national hero and instant celebrity in 1991 by decimating the Iraqi military forces and driving them out of Kuwait during the Persian Gulf War.

When Schwarzkopf was first promoted to the rank of brigadier general, he was instructed to report to the Pentagon along with thirty-five other general-officer designees for a ten-day orientation affectionately known as "charm school." A general officer is one who has risen to a whole new sphere of responsibility, and the Pentagon designed "charm school" to give the new generals a broader view and better manners.

On the first day of class, Schwarzkopf and the others tingled with excitement as the army chief of staff, General Bernard Rogers, strode to the podium to address the newly appointed batch of "Protecters of the Free World." The square-jawed, ramrod-straight man was the same man who had approved their promotions. Now he would surely congratulate them, tell them what a credit they were to the army, describe the outstanding careers they could look forward to, and ask their advice on sensitive problems only they could help him solve.

As General Rogers stood at the lectern, he stared at the men before him for a long moment. Then he said, "If all of you had taken the same airplane to Washington, and that airplane had crashed and you had all been killed, we could go right back into the ranks of colonels and find thirty-six more just as good as you."[1]

No one is indispensable. We may be irreplaceable in some sense—each of us is a unique creation by God, no two people are exactly alike—yet there are many more who could be found to do our tasks just as good as we do, maybe even better.

Although we are dispensable in our work, it is a wise man who remembers the two or three places where he truly is indispensable.

The Need for Fulfilling Work

Men have a God-given need to perform fulfilling work. As early as the second chapter of the Bible, we read, "The Lord God took the man and put him in the Garden of Eden to work it and take care of it" (Gen. 2:15).

Work was not the result of Adam's Fall. It was instituted as a holy vocation beforehand. In other words, work was given as a *blessing* to man. Work was something to occupy his days. Work was a way for man to glorify God. It still is. The difference now is that through the Fall, work has been made difficult.

> THEN TO ADAM [GOD] SAID, "BECAUSE YOU HAVE HEEDED THE
> VOICE OF YOUR WIFE, AND HAVE EATEN FROM THE TREE OF WHICH I
> COMMANDED YOU, SAYING, 'YOU SHALL NOT EAT OF IT':
> "CURSED IS THE GROUND FOR YOUR SAKE;
> IN TOIL YOU SHALL EAT OF IT
> ALL THE DAYS OF YOUR LIFE.
> BOTH THORNS AND THISTLES IT SHALL BRING FORTH FOR YOU,
> AND YOU SHALL EAT THE HERB OF THE FIELD.
> IN THE SWEAT OF YOUR FACE YOU SHALL EAT BREAD
> TILL YOU RETURN TO THE GROUND,
> FOR OUT OF IT YOU WERE TAKEN;
> FOR DUST YOU ARE,
> AND TO DUST YOU SHALL RETURN." (Gen. 3:17–19 NKJV)

What is man if not a worker? We are made for the task. Notwithstanding the Fall, in the breast of every man burns a deep, God-given desire and need to accomplish and be fulfilled. From the earliest days of our manhood, we look for a cause, a mountain to climb, a mission in life, something worth making a sacrifice to accomplish, a world to change and conquer.

We are made to contribute, to be spent in a worthy cause. Nevertheless, fulfillment through work can be elusive.

Fulfillment Is Elusive

- He became the chief executive officer of a great empire.
- By his trading skills, he was acclaimed as the world's foremost merchant.
- As the leading shipping magnate, he had a fleet of merchant ships that sailed throughout the world collecting treasures.
- By his wealth he easily topped the Forbes 400 list.
- He was a master builder who constructed mammoth projects.
- His architectural designs became the world's most important buildings.
- He built vineyards, gardens, parks, and reservoirs.
- Tired of commerce, he turned to science, relentlessly pursuing the classification of nature.
- He was the chairman of the Joint Chiefs of Staff, building a vast army to defend and conquer.
- He was unanimously elected president of his country.
- He became the poet laureate for his nation.
- He had a distinguished career as a writer.
- He was a singularly gifted musician.

Wise and wealthy, president, poet, patron of the arts, teacher, musician, writer, scientist, botanist, master builder, architect, merchant, shipping magnate. No man ever had a more dynamic career than Solomon.

Though Solomon enjoyed the most successful, varied career in history, it is worth noting the reflections he penned about his work:

MY HEART TOOK DELIGHT IN ALL MY WORK,
AND THIS WAS THE REWARD FOR ALL MY LABOR.
YET WHEN I SURVEYED ALL THAT MY HANDS HAD DONE
AND WHAT I HAD TOILED TO ACHIEVE, EVERYTHING WAS
MEANINGLESS, A CHASING AFTER THE WIND;
NOTHING WAS GAINED UNDER THE SUN. (Eccl. 2:10–11).

What was Solomon saying? Simply that no amount of career accomplishment could satisfy him. Here is the problem: *Our work will not be fulfilling if it is our principal means of being fulfilled.* That dog won't hunt! It won't carry the whole burden of making us feel fulfilled. Part, yes, but not all.

Identity

Jim left his position as an executive with an OTC-traded company over a matter of principle. For twenty-two months he could not find employment. For the first several months he was strong. But doubts about his value as a human being crept in. He realized that he had allowed his identity to be wrapped up in his title, the status, the income, and the privileges of his position in commerce rather than his position in Christ.

In addition to the problem of elusive fulfillment, a second great problem is that we tend to get our identity too wrapped up in our careers. We expect our careers to produce more than God intended in terms of worth, value, significance, meaning, and purpose. Nevertheless, let's not throw the baby out with the bathwater and think none of our identity will come from our work.

We men have two disturbing tendencies. First, we tend to think *how we are is how our day went at work.* If our day was extremely interesting, we arrive home in an elated state. If our day was a bummer, we show up depressed. How should our mood be determined? By circumstances, or by walking in the Spirit?

Second, we tend to think *what we do is who we are.* The first question you ask someone when you want to know him is, "What do you do?" What would you think if someone answered, "Well, I sleep a lot"? Or how about, "Well, when I'm at home, I'm a real couch potato"? That, of course, isn't what you wanted to know. You wanted to know his vocation. We tend to wrap identity up in vocation. What would you think if instead of asking you what you do, someone asked you, "Who are the people that give you your identity and why?"

There is a thread of truth that identity is marked by occupation, but here's the problem: If what you do is who you are, then who are you when you don't do what you do anymore? Suppose you are a lawyer, a business owner, or an elected official. Who are you when you are retired, not re-elected, or fired; when business is bad; or when you become unemployed?

Accepting Your Lot in Life

Solomon applied his wisdom—the greatest human wisdom ever known—to the problems of fulfillment and identity. Here is his considered conclusion:

THEN I REALIZED THAT IT IS GOOD AND PROPER FOR A MAN TO EAT
AND DRINK, AND TO FIND SATISFACTION IN HIS TOILSOME LABOR
UNDER THE SUN DURING THE FEW DAYS OF LIFE GOD HAS GIVEN
HIM—FOR THIS IS HIS LOT. MOREOVER, WHEN GOD GIVES ANY MAN
WEALTH AND POSSESSIONS, AND ENABLES HIM TO ENJOY THEM, TO
ACCEPT HIS LOT AND BE HAPPY IN HIS WORK—THIS IS A GIFT OF
GOD. (Eccl. 5:18–19)

Chuck Swindoll once said, "Life is like a coin. You can spend it any
way you want, but you can only spend it once." Let's sink down into our
careers and enjoy them. But let's not lose perspective. Career is only one
dimension of a successful life.

Hard Work Vs. Workaholism

Jim worked seventy hours a week as a sales manager. He was committed
to it—and proud of it. He believed it was the American thing to do. He
believed he was being patriotic. He believed people respected him more
for it. He thought people not as committed were slackers. His devotion had
its effect. He was enormously successful at the professional level. He made
gobs of money, and he earned many prestigious awards.

Yet, Jim never had much time for his three sons. He never could
break free for parent-teacher conferences. He couldn't tell you the name
or location of any of the professional caregivers for his boys, like doctors,
dentists, barbers, and so on. Sunday mornings belonged to him—he usually
played golf with buddies from work. He believed spiritual and moral instruction for his boys was paramount, but he delegated that responsibility to his
wife.

If you asked Jim what drove him to work so hard, he would be hard-
pressed to give you an answer. Let's face it. Workaholism is not rational.
Here is a key idea: People don't always act *rationally*, but they do always act
with *purpose*. In other words, there are reasons *why* we do *what* we do.

Men may work too hard because of fear, because of their values, because
they selfishly enjoy work, or because they hope to escape conflict in the
home. They may still be seeking to win the approval of their own fathers.
Whatever the reason, it is not rational.

The Bible commends hard work. Our culture and society esteem hard
work. Hard work, industry, initiative, excellence, and diligence represent
the values that made America great. On the other hand, the family also

made America great. But today the economy takes first place at the expense of the family. The family is hurting. When we get our work and family priorities out of balance, we tend to shortchange family.

Let's face it. You and I could work twenty-four hours a day. But for what? The Bible says, "Don't weary yourself trying to get rich. Why waste your time? For riches can disappear as though they had the wings of a bird!" (Prov. 23:4–5 TLB). And also:

THE SLEEP OF A LABORING MAN IS SWEET,
WHETHER HE EATS LITTLE OR MUCH;
BUT THE ABUNDANCE OF THE RICH WILL NOT PERMIT HIM TO SLEEP.
(Eccl. 5:12 NKJV)

If you can't sleep, you may be trying to do too much.

As I have said before, no amount of success at the job will compensate for failure at home. To succeed in work but fail at home is to fail completely.

QUESTIONS AND DECISIONS

1. "Men have a God-given need to perform fulfilling work" (see Gen. 2:15). Do you ☐ agree/ ☐ disagree? Explain your answer.

2. Is work to be our principal means of gaining fulfillment? How about you personally? Has your career been your principal means of gaining fulfillment? How are you off track? What should you do?

3. In what ways do you tend to get your identity too wrapped up in your career? Comment personally on these two tendencies:

   • How I am is how my day went at work.
   • What I do is who I am.

   How are you off track? What should you do?

4. How are you building your career? Is it a means to other ends? Or is it the ultimate end?

5. Do you need to accept your lot in life?

6. To what extent are your work and family priorities out of balance? Are you trying to do too much? Comment on these Bible verses: "Don't weary yourself trying to get rich. Why waste your time? For riches can disappear as though they had the wings of a bird!" (Pro. 23:4–5 TLB). If applicable, can you pinpoint the reason you try to do too much?

7. What are the characteristics of a workaholic? Are you a workaholic? (Answer carefully.) What changes do you need to make?

8. Do you have "fire in your belly"? Does it fuel you or consume you?

Building Our Families and Wives

Myth #2: "I'm doing this for my family."

7 My son, John, was playing in a basketball game in a nearby city at 4:00 P.M. on a weekday. Since I can arrange my own schedule, I decided to drive to the game with Patsy, my wife.

I knocked off work at about 3:00 P.M., jumped into some jeans, and we headed off for the game. On the way we passed the father of one of the other boys, who I assumed was also on his way to the game. We rolled down the window and exchanged a forty-mile-per-hour greeting.

Turns out he was not going to the game after all, but he asked us to wish his son good luck. A couple of miles later we came to a traffic light. We turned toward our son's game, but the other father turned the other way. He headed off in a different direction. I wondered why.

When we arrived at the game, I was surprised to see only one other father. He had apparently come directly from the office because he still had on his tie. We sat down next to him, and I said something benign like, "Isn't it great to be able to watch our sons play basketball?"

"It sure is," he said, then added, *"I really wanted to come but I know I shouldn't be here"* (emphasis added).

Bombs began bursting in my mind, and before I could catch myself, I blurted out, "Oh, yeah? According to whose value system?"

Actually, instead of taking my remark as an insult, this off-the-cuff comment led to a lengthy and healthy discussion about values and priorities. The man explained that he felt a sense of guilt and failure—that he was somehow letting his fellow workers down.

We agreed that this false sense of guilt drives many men to neglect their families. We also agreed that many men were addicted to their work—they would rather work than watch the game.

We also realized that the deceptive desire for an ever-increasing prosperity drives many men to create so many debts and duties that they operate too close to the edge. Their worlds are wired so tight that two hours off might topple their kingdom. *Come on! Get a life!*

Solomon wrote,

BETTER ONE HANDFUL WITH TRANQUILLITY
THAN TWO HANDFULS WITH TOIL
AND CHASING AFTER THE WIND. (Eccl. 4:6)

I know work can be intoxicating. I know there are deadlines. I know the pleasure of feeling needed at the office. But as I sat in the bleachers at the basketball game that day, I could not help wondering, *How many men are not here today because they have both hands full?*

Obviously, many men have jobs that won't allow them to take time off for a late afternoon game, but where were the men who *could* take off? A missed game is gone forever. We don't get a second chance.

What Is Failure? –

This incident really set me to thinking. What is *failure?* I looked it up in my *Webster's New Riverside University Dictionary,* 2nd edition, which says, "1. The condition or fact of not achieving the desired end. 2. One that so fails." Well, that certainly clears it up! Actually, this definition is not all that satisfying.

Failure is not just a matter of bombing out, of not achieving the desired end result. The problem with many men's careers is not so much that they are failing. The greatest problem is that many men are achieving the desired end result, but it's the wrong result! They are succeeding at work but failing in life. Many men are failing but think they are succeeding. They have bought the lie.

We can think of failure in two ways. First, it's not achieving the desired result. Second, it's actually achieving the desired result only to find out it didn't really matter. As someone said, "I climbed the ladder to the top, only to find out it was leaning against the wrong wall." Simply put: *Failure means to succeed in a way that doesn't really matter.*

Myth #2

In the last chapter we saw the first of three myths men buy into in the process of building a life—"To succeed means to have a dynamic career." In this chapter let's explore the second myth.

Myth #2: "I'm doing this for my family."

In the movie *The Paper*, the publisher, Bernie, is sitting in a bar. He says to the bartender, "Ninty-nine percent of your time goes to your house, your family, and your job, and there is not enough time to do all of them."

"Yeah," chimes in the bartender, "so we dump on our families."

When all the responsibilities we accumulate to build a better life for our families pile up and we have to cut someone or something, we ironically often give short shrift to the family for whom we took on those responsibilities in the first place.

Truth #2

Our families could care less about all the dreams and the stuff. What our families want is *us*. We have a God-given responsibility to nurture our families. We are told, "Husbands, love your wives, just as Christ also loved the church and gave Himself for her" (Eph. 5:25 NKJV); and "Fathers, do not exasperate your children; instead, bring them up in the training and instruction of the Lord" (Eph. 6:4).

The problem is that we tend to steal time from those who need us the most to give to those who need us the least.

Did you know that 40 percent of Christian marriages end in divorce? I get sweaty palms every time I hear about yet another friend whose marriage is in trouble. In my opinion, the failure of marriages is the number-one issue in Christendom today, followed closely by the number-two issue, the breakdown of the family.

Making marriage work constitutes the single greatest issue facing men today. Many of us see marriage as a process of give-and-take. Our wives give and we take. Many men are not fulfilling their wedding vows. If we will pay the price to make our marriages work, then our families will work too. But a failed marriage is a death sentence for the family.

Relationships create responsibilities. When we say, "I do," or bring a child into this world, we create responsibilities to love, nurture, and care for family members. Slowly, over time, through neglect, many of us crush out the feelings of love, warmth, and joy in our families. Many men are not giving wives and children enough time.

The Price of Failure

I said that, statistically, 40 percent of Christian marriages end in divorce. But what does that look like in real life? It looks like failure.

In many marriages the wife doesn't put forth enough effort. Yet, all in all, we men tend to contribute more to failed marriages than our wives do. Too often a Christian man doesn't work at his marriage. He doesn't invest in his wife. He creates feelings of isolation and loneliness in the woman for whom he was once willing to die. Her heart cries out to God for mercy, but her husband will not cooperate. Silently, alone, she swallows the bitterness of her tears.

Let's imagine for a moment that we are talking about what could happen to *your* marriage. The further you sink into the sins of neglect, the further she sinks into despair. She may or may not have an affair—those things are rarely planned in advance. Finally, she screws up her courage. On a fateful, tearful day of unsure emotions, she decides the marriage is dead and asks you for a divorce. Numbed to the bone, you drive away from the house blinded by your tears, terrified by your fears.

You stay in a cheesy motel the first few days, thinking it's all a mistake— a nightmare. While you're sitting alone before dawn one morning, reality strikes you like a thunderbolt. A sickening, clammy feeling creeps under your skin. That morning you search the classified ads until you find a cheap, dimly lit, furnished one-bedroom apartment that doesn't require a lease.

Her lawyer calls. The bile of betrayal rises in your throat. Seething anger rages in your chest. *How could she do this?* you wonder. A friend suggests you need a lawyer and gives you the name of a real barracuda. You meet this fish-man who testifies that he eats women like your wife for lunch. He wants five hundred dollars up front.

After a bitter eight-month custody battle, your wife gets the house and the kids, and you get the mortgage payment and child support, neither one of which you can afford. The judge allows you to see your kids every other weekend. *The judge is deciding how much I can see my kids? You've got to be out of your mind! What gives him the right?*

After a few months the children complain that they don't want to come to your place as much anymore because there is nothing to do. Besides, they have their regular friends back in the neighborhood.

A year later she remarries. "He" showers your ex-wife with dates, flowers, and too much touching. He "buys" your kids with gifts. Slowly, subtly, you watch their capacity for fatherly affection shift from you toward him. You can't stand sharing this love. It is driving you crazy. You realize that your fate—the consequence of not working at your marriage—is to watch another man raise your children. It is almost too much.

The Bible says, "If anyone does not provide for his relatives, and especially for his immediate family, he has denied the faith and is worse than an unbeliever" (1 Tim. 5:8). There are many ways we provide for our families: money, protection, education, spiritual training, value system, emotional support, food, shelter, and love—to name a few. What, though, are their greatest needs? How can we best provide for them?

If four out of ten Christian marriages get ugly enough to end in divorce, then many more couples must also be in trouble that don't get that far. How about you?

As much as any other thing you do in the whole wide world, you should make certain your marriage stands on firm ground. The areas we are about to discuss can add pizzazz to your marriage—no matter how good or bad you think it is.

Emotional Bank Account

Every human being has what has been variously called an *Emotional Tank*, a *Love Bank*, or an *Emotional Bank Account*. Personally, I like Stephen Covey's term: Emotional Bank Account.

Into this Emotional Bank Account we make deposits and withdrawals like a savings account. Every time Patsy and I come in contact with each other, we are making deposits and withdrawals. If I don't greet her cheerfully, I make a withdrawal. If she tells me she forgot to pick up my shirts *again*, she makes a withdrawal. If I help her make the bed, I make a deposit. If she surprises me (which she often does) with a candy bar in my sock drawer, she makes a deposit.

Doing what we say, spending time with each other, engaging in meaningful conversation, helping each other out, walking closely with the Lord, becoming each other's soul mate, keeping ourselves fit, being a fun and faithful sex partner—these represent some examples of areas where we can make deposits or withdrawals.

Couples who don't get along, don't feel much love, or are considering separation or divorce do so because the Emotional Bank Account of one or both partners is running low or empty. Couples divorce when they emotionally bankrupt their mates. Doesn't it make sense to make sure we have built up reserves of love and trust? In the same way a businessman always late paying his bills is foolish, so also is the husband who doesn't make deposits into his wife's Emotional Bank Account when due.

Every one of us is going to make withdrawals. The issue is how to make deposits faster than withdrawals. Everything you do with or to your wife is either a deposit or a withdrawal. Let's make a commitment to remember this concept, and to build up reserves of love and trust in the accounts of our wives.

Right now, today, what is the balance in your Emotional Bank Account? What would you estimate the balance of your wife's Emotional Bank Account?

Time and Conversation

Two great problems lurk in the bushes of every marriage. First, we don't carve out enough *time* to be together. Second, when we are together, our *conversation* is not meaningful. Tragically, when we are together we often don't connect. "In the same room" doesn't necessarily mean "together."

The most precious commodity we have is time. The greatest gift we can give another is a piece of our time. The most insensitive offense against us is having someone waste our time. Each second that ticks off the clock records our choices of how we spend this gift. One of the main ways our wives measure the *quality* of our relationships with them is by the *quantity* of time we spend with them.

What our wives possibly want and need more than any other single thing today is some meaningful conversation, as the following excerpt from a letter received by pastor and author Weldon Hardenbrook illustrates:

Letter from a Lonely Lady

The kids are in bed. There's nothing on TV tonight. I ask my husband if he minds if I turn the tube off. He grunts.

As I walk to the set my mind is racing. Maybe, just maybe, tonight we'll talk. I mean, we'll have a conversation that consists of more than my usual question with his mumbled one-word answer or, more accurately, no answer at all.

Silence—I live in a world with continuous noise but, between him and myself, silence. Please—oh God, let him open up. I initiate (once again; for the thousandth time). My heart pounds—oh how can I word it this time? What can I say that will open the door to just talk? I don't have to have a deep meaningful conversation. Just something!

As I open my mouth—he gets up and goes to the bedroom. The door closes behind him. The light showing under the door gives way to darkness. So does my hope.

I sit alone on the couch. My heart begins to ache. I'm tired of being alone. Hey, I'm married. I have been for years. Why do I sit alone?[1]

The wife with a "time and talk" deficit will inevitably feel like her Emotional Bank Account is empty. The principal value of time and talk is that they fill our mates up with emotional love.

One friend and his wife have what they call the Six O'Clock Rule. If he isn't home by six, he has to take her out to dinner. Another friend walks with his wife in the morning. Another man and his wife do daily devotions together.

When the party is finally over, the crepe paper is drooping, and the horns and hats are strewn about the floor, there will be only two rocking chairs sitting side by side. You are the only two who are really in this thing together. What are some ways you could insure that you will spend more time together?

Intimacy

The wives of two of Jim's close friends died only weeks apart. He called both men to comfort them. Both were depressed. Both said essentially the same thing, "There is so much I want to say, but it's too late."

A few days later Jim called his wife, Helen, from work and said, "How are you?"

"Fine," she replied.

"Well, uh, I was calling, uh, to tell you . . . Well, uh, I was calling to tell you . . . Helen, I love you!" He was fifty-eight years old.

"Thank you. I love you too."

The husband is the thermostat in his marriage; his wife is the thermometer. He controls whether the climate is hot or cold; she adjusts to the temperature he sets. He can make it saucy and romantic, or he can make it cold and boring.

Every wife's dream is that the romantic affections of her knight in shining armor will not stiffen up like creaking, rusty armor left out in the rain. What does a man need to know to satisfy his woman?

The overarching goal of marriage is, biblically speaking, oneness: "And they will become *one flesh*" (Gen. 2:24, emphasis added). *Oneness* is a synonym for *intimacy*. Intimacy means, "I know who you are at the deepest level, and I accept you."

We become one flesh by loving our wives three ways: *morally, emotionally,* and *physically.*

AGAPE: Moral Love

Moral love is *agape* love. (*Agape* is the first of three Greek words used for love.) *Agape* love means "an assent of the will to love as a matter of principle, duty, and propriety."[2] It is also the kind of love God commands husbands to have for their wives. *Agape* love is the right thing to do. It demonstrates responsibility and commitment. To not love in this sense is morally wrong. We have a duty to love our wives morally.

It will come as no surprise that our wives want more than *duty;* they also want some *romance!* Romantic love is both *emotional* and *physical.*

PHILEO: Emotional Love

Emotional love is *phileo* love. *Phileo* love means "to be a friend, to be fond of, to have affection for. It denotes personal attachment as a matter of sentiment or feeling."[3] *Phileo* love is to love as sentiment or feeling. *Phileo* love is to love in an affectionate sense. It means to love our wives because we like being around them. We *phileo* love because we want to. It demonstrates that we really care. If *agape* means to love with the *head,* then *phileo* means to love with the *heart.*[4] We have a duty to love our wives emotionally.

Emotional love includes nonsexual touching—hugs, kisses, pats, squeezes, and hand-holding. Emotional love means small, routine kindnesses like holding the door or washing dishes.

According to the U.S. Census Bureau, 19.6 percent of married women worked in 1950. By 1990, 74 percent of all women between the ages of twenty-five and fifty-four were in the workforce, and 58 percent of them were married.[5] In other words, the norm in the 1950s was for wives not to work, while the norm today is that our wives are just as likely to work as not. If your wife works, she is just as tired at the end of the day as you are. Be sure to share the load of home-life responsibilities.

EROS: *Physical Love*

Physical love is *eros* love. *Eros* love means sexual love. We *eros* love because it is God's gift, even command, to married couples (1 Cor. 7:3–5). It is the consummate expression of intimacy, the icing on the cake. *Eros* love means to love in a sexual sense. We have a duty to love our wives physically.

Men, we need to be loved *physically* so that we can love *emotionally*. Our wives, on the other hand, need to be loved *emotionally* so that they can love *physically*. As the spiritual leaders of our homes, we must take the leadership to love our wives in the ways they need to be loved.

We achieve oneness by loving each other morally, emotionally, and physically. How do we get there? Intimacy and oneness are not so much built by the big things we do (like trips, clothing, and diamond rings) as by the little things we do consistently, day in and day out. What are the little things that build intimacy? Try these out: buy her flowers, look directly into her eyes when you speak, smile when your glances meet, wink occasionally, say "I love you" every day, hold hands, catch the door for her, help make the bed, clear the dinner table. Get the picture? We build intimacy by doing many little things in a single direction.

The greatest decision a man can make to build a strong marriage and family is to make his wife his top priority, after God, but before all others. Remember: your wife is the only one who is truly in this thing with you to the end. All others will phase out of your life, just as they phased in.

In the next chapter we will look at some practical, constructive ways we can provide for our children.

QUESTIONS AND DECISIONS

1. Myth #2: "I'm doing this for my family." To what extent have you kidded, tricked, and fooled yourself into thinking your family wants you to work so hard that you miss out on important chapters of family life?

2. "Failure means to succeed in a way that doesn't really matter." Do you ☐ agree/ ☐ disagree? How does this apply in your own life?

3. Solomon wrote, "Better one handful with tranquillity/ than two handfuls with toil/ and chasing after the wind" (Eccl. 4:6). In what ways are you neglecting your wife and kids because you have both hands full?

4. If four out of ten Christian marriages get ugly enough to end in divorce, then many more couples must also be in trouble that don't get that far. What's the state of your marriage?

5. Right now, today, what is the balance in your Emotional Bank Account? What would you estimate is the balance of your wife's Emotional Bank Account?

6. Are you spending enough time with your wife? Why or why not? Are you having enough meaningful conversations with your wife? Why or why not? What changes should you make?

7. Is your wife your top priority, after God, but before all others? If not, do you agree that she should be? What do you need to do?

8. Make plans to build more intimacy into your marriage by implementing the changes suggested by questions 5, 6, and 7. First, make the commitment to think in terms of your wife's *Emotional Bank Account*, and make regular deposits. Second, spend more *time* with your wife. Third, have more meaningful *conversations* with your wife. Fourth, make your wife your *top priority*, after God, but before all others.

9. Make deposits of intimacy into your wife's Emotional Bank Account over the next several days by making some of the following suggested deposits:

- Buy her flowers.
- Look directly into her eyes when you speak.
- Smile when your glances meet.
- Wink occasionally.
- Say "I love you" every day.
- Hold hands.
- Catch the door for her.
- Help make the bed.
- Clear the dinner table.

Building Our Kids

8 One day an acquaintance cornered me and said with an angry edge to his voice, "I tried to call you the other night, but you have an unlisted phone number."

"Yes," I said.

"Well, I had important ministry business that I wanted to discuss with you. I can't believe you have an unlisted phone number! How can you be a Christian and have an unlisted phone number?"

"It's real easy, actually. All you do is call the phone company, tell them what you want, and they take care of everything!" I said.

Perhaps I was a bit too sarcastic because at that point he really let me have it. "I can't believe someone would make himself inaccessible on purpose. *Jesus* wouldn't have an unlisted number! Yak, yak, yak . . . Yip, yip, yip . . . Etc., etc." he droned on.

Finally, I said, "Look, I'm willing to die for you until 6:00 P.M. But after six o'clock I only die for my family."

The only way to know for sure that we will have time for our families is to put it on the schedule like any other appointment. If not, we will find ourselves running right out of their lives.

I would rather be a nobody in the world but be somebody to my kids.

Let's continue our discussion about how to provide for our families by turning to our kids. Our children have some significant needs that we can provide: time, structure, prayer, faith, and worldview.

Time

Many dads today suffer from the Weekend Dad Syndrome. They slave away at their work so hard Monday through Friday that they rarely see their kids except on weekends. They become two-day-a-week dads. Is two-sevenths of a dad a real dad? You be the judge.

The principal ways we provide for our families require *money* and *time*. We err when we give them enough money but not enough time. Money represents everything that is *not* you, but your time *is* you.

Time is everything to a relationship, whether with your wife or your kids. You are everything to your kids. Here is a principle worth remembering: *Give time to whom time is due.* Don't give your time to those who don't really need you at the expense of those who really do.

Successful fathering with our time requires *flexibility, creativity,* and a *willingness to subordinate our own selfish interests* to the interests of our kids. Let's look at these ideas.

Flexibility

The best way to give your children time is the way in which they want to receive it. If they like eating out, eat out. If they like movies, go to movies. If they participate in sports, go to their games. Be a chameleon. Change as their circumstances and interests change.

Patsy and I discovered that once our children became interested in activities like cheerleading and basketball, we basically had to follow them around if we wanted to spend time with them. On the other hand, it has been pure joy to watch them develop and grow as individuals, and we were always there to help them fit together the pieces they didn't understand.

Creativity

When our kids were very young, we did everything together. When they hit twelve years old or so, they wanted to be with their friends most of the time instead of always with the family. To stay close to them, I scheduled a date night once a week that we alternated between the two kids.

When they became teenagers, we stopped this tradition—they got real interested in the opposite sex, parties, dating, sporting events, cheerleading, etc. To keep up some form of tradition, we began going out as a family every Sunday night to different "cheap eats" restaurants.

Figuring out how to interact with teenagers can be especially hard. As one friend said, "Raising teenagers has brought out the worst in me." With a friend's help, I entered my name and my fourteen-year-old son's name into a lottery for an annual gator-hunting permit. I asked another friend if my son and I could crew for him when he races his car in an amateur event at Sebring next year. I took my son out of school for one day, and we went to Cape Canaveral to watch a space shuttle launching. Before my daughter went off to college, I used to "date" her periodically—either dinner or dinner and a movie. Spending time with our kids can tax our creative juices, but the greater tax is to not be with them. If you can't think of how to spend time creatively, ask your wife or your friends, or buy a book on fathering.

A Willingness to Subordinate Selfish Interests

My son, John, lives, eats, and breathes basketball. I read an article about a father who pledged to never say no when his son asked him to play ball because his own dad never had time for him. I decided to make the same pledge. I have not kept it. At first I felt guilty all the time. Then it occurred to me that I was saying yes 80 to 90 percent of the time. I realized I was being legalistic and needed to cut myself some slack. Now I enjoy saying yes a lot more because I don't feel the drudgery of duty calling. On the other hand, if a dad isn't saying yes very often, he may want to set a higher goal for himself.

If you have kids at home, you can't be a big man around town and a good father at the same time. Once, as a young businessman, I recall reading with awe and wonder the accomplishments and organizational involvements of a leading businessman. Only later did I discover that he had sacrificed his family on the altar of ego satisfaction. You can't have it all. We all work with the same 168 hours each week. Are you giving time to whom time is due?

Structure

At the office King David was the greatest leader, administrator, and executive of his day. At home he was a dud.

History records that his son, Amnon, raped his daughter, Tamar. Another son, Absalom, then killed Amnon in revenge. Later Absalom conspired against his father and was assassinated. After that, his son, Adonijah, also conspired to ascend David's throne. Finally, after being proclaimed king, Solomon had Adonijah killed.

One raped daughter, one son a rapist, two murdered sons, one son a murderer, and two conspiracies to take over the family empire. Where did David go wrong? The Scriptures give us the answer. When Adonijah conspired to be king, the Bible says, *"His father had never interfered with him by asking, 'Why do you behave as you do?'"* (1 Kings 1:6, emphasis added). David simply abdicated his responsibility to provide *structure*.

Parenting is the task of giving children structure, boundaries, and limits. It is the business of guiding, directing, and encouraging. It is the work of supervising and controlling. It is the responsibility to instill values, morals, and ethics. In short, it is positive interfering.

When his son was eighteen, Craig found a *Playboy* magazine under his son's bed. As soon as his son came home, he confronted him.

"Get it out of here," Craig said.

"But all my friends have it," answered his son.

"Then read it over there, but not in my house."

Craig's son just turned thirty-eight and now he has an eighteen-year-old son of his own. Recently, Craig's son found a "guess what?" in his son's room.

"How did you handle it, son?" asked Craig.

"Well, Dad, I told him to get rid of it—that I wouldn't allow that trash in my house!"

Too often we neither guide nor question our children's behavior. We are tired, we've been through this before, we get frustrated repeating ourselves, the message doesn't seem to be getting through, and so on. Even when our children rail against the discipline we provide, however, in their heart of hearts it is exactly what they want. Children want structure. And as the story above illustrates, the bonus check arrives in the next generation.

It will be a hollow victory if we succeed at work but fail at home. We need to evaluate the amount of structure and accountability we provide our kids. Do you put the question to your children, "Why do you behave as you do?" Interfere with their lives—that's what they want.[1]

In a national survey of high-school juniors and seniors commissioned by Sylvan Learning Centers and the National Association of Secondary School Principals, teenagers say parents don't give them enough structure. A lot of students wish their parents would say no. Teenagers want their parents to get involved (to interfere, if you please) in their schools, to take interest in homework, and to clamp down on how they spend their free time.[2] Remarkable? Not really. Our children long for structure, interest, and guidance. Our children crave our interference!

Prayer

In the Bible, Job prayed for his children. As far as we know, he is the only one who prayed for them.

You and your wife may be the only two people in the whole world willing to pray for your children on a regular basis. Prayer is the currency of our personal relationship with Christ. This capital does no good if we leave it on account. We must make a withdrawal and spend some of it on our kids.

Pray with a pencil. Write down specific prayer requests for your children. Writing down prayers creates visibility as a reminder to pray. Write down long-term prayers and tape them up in a high-visibility location such as your mirror. Write short-term prayers on Post-its and stick them where you will see them often, perhaps in the front of your Bible.

In *The Man in the Mirror* and *Two Part Harmony*, I included my daily prayer list for my children. I think it's important enough to include again. Since then I've added some additional items. Here is the revised list. If you don't already have a list, you may find that by adding and subtracting a few subjects you can tailor a list of your own:

- that there will never be a time they don't walk with You
- a saving faith (thanksgiving if already Christian)
- a growing faith
- an independent faith (as they grow up)
- persevering faith
- to be strong and healthy in mind, body, and spirit
- a sense of destiny (purpose)
- a desire for integrity
- a call to excellence
- to understand their spiritual gifts
- to understand the ministry God has for them and their spiritual gifts
- values and beliefs, a Christian worldview
- to tithe 10 percent and save 10 percent of all earnings
- to set and work toward realistic goals as revealed by the Lord
- that I will set aside times to spend with them
- to acquire wisdom
- protection from drugs, alcohol, tobacco, premarital sex, violence, rape, and AIDS

- the mate God has for them (alive somewhere, needing prayer)
- to do daily devotions
- forgiveness and to be filled with the Holy Spirit
- glorify the Lord in everything
- any personal requests or matters in discussion with their mother

Faith

Seven men at a weekly Bible study accepted the challenge to determine for sure where each of their children stood with the Lord. They agreed that for those kids who were unsure of their salvation, they would share *The Four Spiritual Laws* booklet (a publication of Campus Crusade for Christ, available in Christian bookstores) with them.

The following week when they met again, one man reported that he had, indeed, shared the gospel with his son and that he had received Jesus Christ as his Lord and Savior. With some degree of embarrassment the other six reported that they had chickened out—they just couldn't screw up the courage to find out where their kids stood with Christ.

If we, blood of the same blood, don't take responsibility (as God's agents) for the spiritual state of our children's souls why should we think someone else would care more? If we don't take the time, who will? Take responsibility for the spiritual nurture of your kids. We cannot make them have faith, but we can create the most likely environment possible for them to also have saving faith in Christ's redemptive work.

Worldview

One of the greatest investments we can make in our children is to give them the gift of Christian worldview thinking.

When I was growing up, parents didn't question what worldview teachers were pumping and pouring into our innocent eyes and ears. That's because when I was growing up, it was assumed the values taught at our schools were "Christian" values because they were "American" values. They were considered interchangeable.

Dr. Ron Nash defines a worldview as "a collection of answers to the most important questions in life."[3] By definition, a worldview is a religious choice because the most important questions in life consider, among other things, the meaning of life, the existence and nature of God, and so forth.

All secular worldviews believe the world is a closed system. God may or may not exist outside this closed box, but it doesn't matter because we—human beings—are in charge. We chart our own destinies.

On the other hand, the Christian worldview says that God not only exists outside the box, but He created the box (system) and He acts inside the box through prayer, providence, and miracles. God is in charge.

So why is it important to know this difference? The way in which we build our lives is determined by our basic assumptions about how God, man, and the world work. What we think determines who we are. More than anything else, what goes into the minds of our kids while they are young will determine their character and conduct when they grow up—whether they are *self-centered* or *God-centered*, and whether they locate their authority in themselves or in God's Word. The difference can be devastating.

Looking back, we can now see that an entire generation was lulled into believing that a bulldogged, self-reliant cowboy spirit pursuing the American Dream was synonymous with being Christian. We didn't stop to ask if those ideals fit into the biblical ideal of a humble, self-sacrificing servant spirit. There may not have been as much relationship between cowboy-American values and servant-Christian values as we once thought.

Today we have an advantage over yesteryear. Today there is no possibility of confusing the values being taught (or not taught) at our schools with the values of the Christian faith and worldview. The humanistic secular worldview is at war with the Christian worldview, and the classroom is the front line where this war rages on.

There is something you need to know about public education in America today. In a study conducted for the National Institute of Education, Paul Vitze found that public-school textbooks commonly exclude the values of those who believe in the traditional family, those who believe in free enterprise, those whose politics are conservative, and those who are committed to their religious tradition. Beyond that, most sex education is really only contraceptive education.[4]

We have saved the whales, the rain forests, the minks, the manatees, the sea turtles, the eagles, and the snail darters. It's time we save our kids. As a friend says, "America's at war, and the church doesn't know it."

Today more than ever before, fathers need to be proactive in teaching their children a Christian worldview. What they think will determine who they are. If not us, then who? We do not live in an age when any government-sponsored program can be considered safe for our children without careful review.

If a man wants an effective ministry, discipling (training) his family is the most powerful thing he can do.

These ideas can help each of us build our kids up "in the training and instruction of the Lord" (Eph. 6:4)—a noble goal.

Seven Developmental Tasks

When we dropped our daughter off at college for her freshman year, the director of counseling for the school told us they were going to concentrate on seven developmental tasks with our precious child.

1. *Sense of competence:* Faith in self intellectually and socially. "I can do this." A need to believe in themselves.
2. *Manage their emotions:* What information are these emotions giving me? Learn appropriate responses.
3. *Develop autonomy:* To move from dependence to independence to interdependence. (In relation to parents, not God.)
4. *Establish identity:* They will "try on" different identities. Help them sort out who they really are.
5. *Interpersonal relationships:* Begin looking deeper at people. May develop committed relationships. Develop lasting friendships. Learn true caring.
6. *Sense of purpose:* "How can I put what I am learning to use?"
7. *Sense of integrity:* Family values is the foundation under it all.

If these are the tasks identified as most important for a college student, how much more important is it for us to build these qualities into our children before they walk out our doors? If our kids are not well down these trails before they leave home, they will not master the tasks at college. These are the tasks for a father to work on.

The Gift of a Child

Someone handed me this on a tattered piece of paper. From where it comes I do not know, but it expresses a beautiful thought for the season of building up our kids:

"I'll lend you, for a little while, a child of mine," He said,
"For you to love while he lives, and mourn when he is dead.
"It may be six or seven years, or twenty-two, or -three,
"But will you, 'til I call him back, take care of him for me?
"He'll bring his charms to gladden you, and shall his stay be brief,
"You'll have his lovely memories as solace for your grief.
"I cannot promise he will stay, as all from earth return,
"But there are lessons taught down there I want this child to learn.
"I've looked the wide world over in my search for teachers true,
"And from the throngs that crowd life's lanes, I have selected you.
"Now will you give him all your love—not think the labor vain,
"Nor hate me when I come to call to take him back again?
"I fancied that I heard them say, 'Dear Lord, thy will be done.
'For all the joy this child shall bring, the risk of grief we'll run.
'We'll shower him with tenderness and love him while we may,
'And for the happiness we've known, forever grateful stay.
'And should the angels call for him much sooner than we planned,
'We'll brave the bitter grief that comes, and try to understand.'"

God has selected you "from the throngs" to be the father of your children. Demonstrate your love by giving them time, prayer, structure, and the foundation of faith, and by building into them a Christian worldview.

QUESTIONS AND DECISIONS

1. "The principal ways we provide for our families require *money* and *time*. We err when we give them enough money but not enough time." Do you ☐ agree/ ☐ disagree? Explain your answer. Do you need to make any changes?

2. Do you suffer from the Weekend Dad Syndrome? Is two-sevenths of a dad a real dad? What should you do?

3. King David reaped a terrible result by not providing enough structure, boundaries, and limits for his children. Do you think you are doing a good job in this area? Why or why not? What changes do you need to make?

4. Do you pray for your children on a regular basis? If not, will you? If so, how can you adapt the list provided in this chapter to your use or incorporate some other ideas to pray for your kids?

5. Do you agree or disagree that it is important in this day and age to carefully monitor what our kids are learning in school? Why?

6. Do you agree or disagree that there is a battle for the minds of our children taking place in our country? Why?

7. What practical steps can you take to give your children a Christian worldview? What do you think would be the advantages of such a worldview?

8. Do you know the spiritual condition of each of your children? Plan to share the gospel with those children of whose spiritual condition you are unsure (who are old enough to understand). You can use chapter 5 of this book, obtain a gospel tract from your church, or purchase one from a Christian bookstore. Will you do this?

Money and Lifestyle

Myth #3: "Money will solve my problems."

In 1923, an important meeting was held at the Edgewater Beach Hotel in Chicago. In attendance were eight of the world's most powerful financiers:

1. the president of the largest independent steel company
2. the president of the largest gas company
3. the greatest wheat speculator
4. the president of the New York Stock Exchange
5. a member of the president's cabinet
6. the greatest "bear" on Wall Street
7. the head of the world's greatest monopoly
8. the president of the Bank of International Settlements

By all accounts these men had ascended to the upper reaches of success. They had discovered the secrets of making money. As they left the hotel, life took them in different directions. What happened to them? Twenty-five years later. . .

1. The president of the largest independent steel company, Charles Schwab, died bankrupt, having lived on borrowed money for the last five years before his death.
2. The president of the largest gas company, Howard Hopson, became insane.
3. The greatest wheat speculator, Arthur Cotton, died abroad, insolvent.

4. The president of the New York Stock Exchange, Richard Whitney, went to Sing Sing Penitentiary.
5. The member of the president's cabinet, Albert Fall, was pardoned from prison so that he could die at home.
6. The greatest "bear" on Wall Street, Jesse Livermore, died a suicide.
7. The head of the world's greatest monopoly, Ivar Krueger, died a suicide.
8. The president of the Bank of International Settlements, Leon Fraser, died a suicide.

David was right when he said, "The sorrows of those will increase who run after other gods" (Ps. 16:4). Money makes a wonderful servant but a ruthless master.

Myth #3

A friend told me, "I have enough money to live on for the rest of my life—as long as I die by the day after tomorrow!"

Some people say money isn't important. The three groups of people who say money isn't important are (1) those who already have theirs, (2) those who want to spiritualize about money, and (3) those who can't make any, and want everyone else to be just as miserable as they are. They are all wrong.

I'll never forget the image of going as a boy with my father to deliver a grocery sack of oranges we had picked to a down-and-out family in our church. It wasn't much, but it was all we could give. They were really hurting.

Money is important, and when you run out, it becomes extremely important.

The first two myths we examined were, "#1: To succeed means to have a dynamic career" and "#2: I'm doing this for my family." Let's look at the third myth that drives us when we're not alert.

Myth #3: "Money will solve my problems."

Money represents a central motif for every man. When our income level drops below a certain level, the fight to survive consumes our daily lives. We live from paycheck to paycheck, under siege from creditors, dodging impending doom from day to day. Poverty is no spiritual badge of courage.

On the other hand, once we rise to the level of income that meets all of our reasonable needs, more money only creates more headaches.

Solomon wrote well when he penned,

WHOEVER LOVES MONEY NEVER HAS MONEY ENOUGH;
WHOEVER LOVES WEALTH IS NEVER SATISFIED WITH HIS INCOME.
THIS TOO IS MEANINGLESS. AS GOODS INCREASE,
SO DO THOSE WHO CONSUME THEM.
AND WHAT BENEFIT ARE THEY TO THE OWNER
EXCEPT TO FEAST HIS EYES ON THEM?
THE SLEEP OF A LABORER IS SWEET,
WHETHER HE EATS LITTLE OR MUCH,
BUT THE ABUNDANCE OF A RICH MAN
PERMITS HIM NO SLEEP. (Eccl. 5:10–12)

As Solomon said, and the eight financiers above succinctly illustrate, "rich" has its own slough of problems. Poor people often say, "If I could just get hold of some money, then everything would be all right." Anyone who has ever had money, even lots of money, knows that isn't even close to true.

On the television program *20/20* a megamultimillionaire was asked, "Has money made you happy?"

"No," he replied. "Anyone who thinks money will make you happy doesn't have money."

I often think that the poor have an advantage over the rich. At least they can still cling to the illusion that money will make them happy.

Truth #3

Once we get above a certain level, money creates more problems than it solves. In reality, the more money you have, the more hassles you have. Managing money distracts from other interesting uses of time. Men who have money usually end up with a garage full of rusty toys. For many men, their lives revolve around their possessions. The car needs waxing, the lawn needs mowing, the boat needs to be hauled in for repair, the front tire on the camper went flat, someone broke into the mini-warehouse where you store all that stuff you never use—just in case you ever find the time.

Those who own beach property or a mountain home have to worry about pipes bursting, tenants stealing, toilets leaking, and property taxes accruing.

Divide the annual cost of ownership by the number of nights occupied, and the nightly occupancy cost exceeds the most expensive resorts in Hawaii, Hong Kong, or anywhere else in the world! Do you want a condo at the beach? Go rent one from a friend! Let him worry about all that sand accumulating between the couch pillows! Let him hassle with the leaky faucets! Let him have the headaches while you have the fun! It's better to know someone who owns a condo than to actually own one yourself.

Another problem with money is its power to lure us away from weightier matters. Money is temporal, and souls are eternal. Preoccupation with one often leads to neglect of the other. In real life, both must receive attention. Yet the Bible cautions, "No one can serve two masters. Either he will hate the one and love the other, or he will be devoted to the one and despise the other. You cannot serve both God and Money" (Matt. 6:24).

The Bible also says, "What good is it for a man to gain the whole world, yet forfeit his soul?" (Mark 8:36). Poverty and prosperity are both great tests, but biblically speaking, prosperity is the greater test. Poverty risks the body, but prosperity risks the soul. All the *benefits* of money are *temporal*, while all the *risks* of money are *eternal*.

The Purpose of Money

We decided to purchase a car for our daughter on her sixteenth birthday. We certainly didn't feel obligated to do so, but we felt she had been a responsible, hardworking student, and we trusted her. In the four-month-long process of researching cars, our daughter decided a five-year-old Honda was the car she most wanted. I liked her choice, because the price looked right.

However, after I studied her *Consumer Reports* research, I became concerned about the safety of her choice compared to the new cars arriving in the showrooms at that time. In that model year most new cars came equipped with a driver's side air safety bag and anti-lock brakes, either standard or available as an option.

After much soul-searching, my wife and I decided we simply could not let our daughter drive around in a car without an air safety bag and antilock brakes if we were financially able to afford it. Frankly, I wish it could have happened five years later—then all the five-year-old cars would have these safety features. But it didn't happen that way, and we had to make a priority choice.

Since at the time God had blessed us with enough money to purchase the new car, we had to ask ourselves, "What is the purpose of money if not to spend like this?" We wouldn't have to skimp on our stewardship responsibilities, so we decided to trust that God had enabled us to purchase the safer car.

If we had not had the money, we would have trusted just as much that it was God's will to purchase the five-year-old car. Or if we had no money, no car at all. On the other hand, since we had the funds, I would never have been able to forgive myself if something tragic happened to my daughter that could have been prevented by my willingness to invest the money in her safety instead of something else.

What is the purpose of money? Money is a resource to acquire what we need and/or want. The choices we make with money indicate the priorities we have chosen. Understanding that everyone has their own opinion about how to prioritize spending, I would like to offer what I believe are the top ten uses of money.

The Top Ten Uses of Money

What are the best ways to spend and invest our money? As will become obvious, not everyone has enough income to satisfy all of the following uses of money. However, these are, in my opinion, the ten *best* ways we can use our money. Until we take care of these areas, I don't think we should be considering that new boat, a bigger house, or a better apartment. Also, if a man is fortunate enough to satisfy these ten uses, what is the eleventh idea? You decide, but I think it's best to use any extra funds to build the kingdom.

1. Give 10 percent or more to the work of the church.
2. Purchase catastrophic health insurance (to prevent wiping out savings after a life of toil).
3. Pay off all consumer debts.
4. Purchase a home (or retire the mortgage as soon as possible).
5. Save and invest 10 percent of income for retirement (this can and should include life insurance).
6. Save for emergencies (e.g., a washing machine or major car repairs).
7. Provide college educations for your children.
8. Purchase the safest possible transportation for your family (after careful examination of consumer reports about cars within budget range).

9. Acquire and maintain marketable job skills (seminars, courses, etc.).

-10. Purchase a few occasional nice things that will bring pleasure (e.g., a work of art, an antique, a nice piece of furniture, a fishing boat, or new golf clubs).

Everyone's Struggle

My dictionary defines *materialism* as "the belief that *physical well-being* and *material possessions* constitute the highest value and the greatest good in life." While few will agree that materialism is true, many live as though it is.

Materialism is not just the problem of the rich. My friend and financial author Ron Blue tells the story of a trip he took to Africa to meet with a missionary. As Ron drove up to the missionary's mud hut, the missionary's two-year-old daughter was playing on a trash heap—her only toy a used size D battery.

As they talked, Ron asked, "What is the greatest barrier to the spread of the gospel in this part of the world?"

Without batting an eye, the missionary answered, "Materialism."

Incredible! thought Ron. "How could that be?" he said. "The people here live in abject poverty. Your daughter's only toy is a used battery."

"Well, it's really quite simple," he said. "If a man has a manure hut, he wants a mud hut. If a man has a mud hut, he wants a stone hut. If his hut has a thatched roof, he wants a tin roof. If he has one cow, he wants two cows. If he has one wife, he wants two wives, and so on."

Everyone struggles with materialism.

A question we all wonder about is, "How much is enough?" The usual answer is, of course, a little bit more. It can be profitable for a man who wants to live a successful life to carefully think through his current lifestyle level and decide if that's where he should be. Let's look at the four different lifestyle choices a man can make.

Deciding on a Lifestyle

The lifestyle we pick today will determine the level of pressure under which we will live later, when college tuition, retirement, and the vicissitudes of life come knocking on the door. When we spend all or more than we make (more by accumulating debts), we threaten the stability of our marriages, our ability to finance college educations, and the quality of our retirements.

We choose from among four possible lifestyles. No man will totally fit into one category, but read these reflectively, then decide which one best describes you.

1. Living "Above" Your Means

The man who spends more than he earns by accumulating debt is a spendthrift always teetering on the brink of financial disaster. From the outside he may look rich, at least richer than his neighbors.

What drives this man? Motivated by self-indulgence and insecurity, he tries to outdo his neighbors with better cars, bigger vacations, fancier clothes, and more accessories and gadgets around the house. Yet every bit of it is financed up to the gills. An ever-increasing, insatiable appetite for that elusive "it" propels this man. He doesn't know what "it" is, but he thinks if he can just acquire that one more possession, he will achieve "it."

Behind closed doors there are many fights and quarrels. He lives up to the limits of his income and beyond. He constantly refinances and borrows more. For him, Jesus Christ is not having much practical impact on his day-to-day living. His life revolves around "wood, hay, stubble." Eventually, this house of cards will come tumbling down.

2. Living "At" Your Means

This man wants more of the good life. He is not foolish enough to borrow for experiences or depreciating assets, but neither is he wise enough to save for a rainy day. He is stretched tighter than a kettle.

He loves to browse through the new car ads. He enjoys driving through what he considers his next neighborhood, eyes darting about to spot "for sale by owner" signs. He always studies the gadgets-and-gimmicks-for-sale magazines set out like mousetraps in the magazine pouch of every airplane.

This man perpetually daydreams about the next thing he wants. The more he thinks about these things, the less he thinks about God. He has heard God's Word, but the worries of this life and the deceitfulness of wealth have choked it and made it unfruitful. His preoccupation with things puts a strain on his relationship with his wife.

On Sundays he self-consciously removes a crisp twenty-dollar bill from his wallet, folds it over twice with a sharp crease, then slides it under the other offerings when the plate gets passed down his row. He feels guilty for not putting in more, but simultaneously resents being made to feel like he has a duty to put in anything at all.

He has worried about retirement, but that's all he has done. He has taken no positive steps to save for another day. He has twisted the meaning of the passage that says, "Take therefore no thought for the morrow" (Matt. 6:34 KJV). Soon he will have to decide: Does he start borrowing to relieve the pressure, or does he downsize his standard of living?

3. Living "Within" Your Means

This man recognizes that the Bible calls him to be a steward of what God has entrusted to him. He believes that everything he has belongs to God, who has entrusted resources to him for a season and for a reason.

He thinks about and plans for the future. Not only does he put money away toward a rainy day, but he has a well-conceived retirement plan. He started a college savings plan for each child when they were born. He is more generous than his resources suggest.

Several years ago he and his wife made a commitment to give 10 percent of their income to help finance the work of the church, though they didn't think they could afford it. They struggled at first, but quickly it seemed that they had *more* money to work with, not *less*. Actually, they didn't, but God changed their appetites.

The pleasures ballyhooed by the Madison Avenue pinstripers tempt them, too, but they examine themselves regularly, careful lest they should be hasty and miss the way. Notice that even in this brief description the emphasis has changed from "he" to "they." He and his wife work together as a team. In days gone by they quarreled relentlessly about money; now they hold hands when window-shopping at the mall like they did twenty years ago.

4. Living "Below" Your Means

This man, a rare breed in this generation, exercises unusual self-discipline. Though he could easily afford to drive a newer car or live in a more expensive neighborhood, he and his wife have deliberately decided to live a lifestyle lower than their income.

They do this as a response to the grace God has bestowed upon them and for the sake of His kingdom. Though they, too, from time to time feel the harsh blows of a world held hostage by sin, they are not so overextended that they cannot recover.

Together they have decided to teach their children to both tithe 10 percent and save 10 percent of every dollar they receive, believing this heritage will equip them as responsible citizens of the kingdom and the United States, respectively. They want their children to walk with God and not become materialistic.

· They do not want to be distracted by the worries, riches, and pleasures of this world. Though they use the things of this world, they have not become engrossed in them. They recognize that the world and its desires pass away, but the one who does the will of God lives forever. They have the gift of giving, and they would rather make eternal investments than spend up to the limits of their income.

Which of these four categories are you in today? Is that by design or default? What are the advantages and disadvantages of the approach you have been using? Do you need to rethink your lifestyle?

Four Ways to Earn Money

Sometimes the problem we face is not that we need to lower our lifestyle, but that we need to raise our income. Increasing our income is a long-term task. Let's look at the four ways a man can earn money and discuss how to improve the yield on each of those ways.

1. Labor

The principal way you earn money is by exchanging your time and labor for it. To increase your income through your labor, you must increase your productivity, hence your value or worth to the employer. No matter how nice a man you are, the skills you have carry only so much market value. You can't expect a raise because you are such a nice guy. You have to improve your performance through experience and/or training. The law of supply and demand is at work in the labor market. If you want a higher market value, then explore a career in a growing field with a short labor supply.

2. Other People's Labor

To build your own business can be a source of great pleasure. The life of the entrepreneur is not for everyone, but for those who own their businesses, the opportunity to employ others and earn a return on their labor constitutes an exciting, challenging way to increase income.

3. Rent

The best method of all to earn money is to rent money to others. Obviously, you have to accumulate some capital before you can take advantage of this method. Every man ought to have a goal of having enough money to save and invest in safety-oriented financial instruments.

4. Risk

To take some *calculated risks* may offer the highest returns. Forms of risk taking include starting your own business and making financial investments in real estate, stocks, or energy. This method is not for everyone. Generally, you need some capital, whether yours or OPM (Other People's Money), but there are also risks you can take that mainly require your time. You can try your hand at moonlighting projects like writing a book, creating software, perfecting an invention, or developing a business plan that you get others to fund.

Building a Budget

To seriously determine how much is enough, we must first know what we need. The man who wants to plan his finances should forecast his needs along these lines: a monthly/annual Operating Budget, an annual Capital Budget, and a Projected Long-Term Capital Needs Plan. It's not a bad idea to maintain separate checking/savings accounts for these categories. Let's briefly define each of them.

1. Operating Budget

Every family should know in advance what to expect for income and what to allot for each major category of expense. Trying to manage our finances without a clearly defined budget is like trying to bowl with a blindfold. If we don't know where the target is, we are likely to aim in the wrong direction.

The Operating Budget should include all regular, predictable monthly expenses. Each month should be estimated for a year in advance. Prepare this once each year. To ease the pain over one-time annual expenses, like property taxes and insurance premiums, you can write a check to your Capital Budget checking/savings account for one-twelfth of the cost.

Total the monthly numbers to see if your estimated income and estimated expenses match up. Also, calculate the annual totals. If expenses exceed income, you at least know in advance that you must make some cuts. Work at it until you at least begin with a balanced budget. If income exceeds expenses, then you can decide whether to invest, spend, or give away the extra money.

2. Capital Budget

Need a new car? Trying to save a down payment for a new home? Hoping to make an investment this year? Every family has capital expenditures that are large single-payment items. Make an annual list of these, and plan how you will fund them in advance. Don't borrow and pay interest when you can save in advance. You can schedule payments toward these items as part of your Operating Budget and make monthly escrow deposits into a Capital Budget checking/savings account.

3. Projected Long-Term Capital Needs

Worried about college tuition? Concerned about retirement income? Planning to move in a few years? The major long-term capital drains for most men are two: college educations and retirement. Every man should be thinking about and planning for these well in advance.

It is not fair to our wives to live at such a high lifestyle today that they would have to abandon it if we should die prematurely or become disabled. Ever wonder where that older waitress at your favorite breakfast diner came from? Why is she working at her age? Would you want your wife doing that? Would that be right?

Obviously, I have not covered everything that needs to be said about money. What I have tried to do is get you thinking. Check out a Bible-based financial planning course. My dear friend Howard Dayton founded Crown Ministries, which offers an outstanding twelve-week small group-study program (contact Crown Ministries, 407-339-6000). Ron Blue's book *Master Your Money* provides a wealth of financial planning ideas.[1]

Finding Contentment

As I walked by the glass wall of the conference room of our real estate business one day, I could see the side view of one of our salesmen talking across the table to a prospective leasing tenant.

Above the table, our man looked deeply and with great interest into the eyes of the prospective tenant, nodding at appropriate moments, showing every sign of patience and understanding.

However, below the table, and what the prospect couldn't see, my business associate's foot, leg, and knee were bouncing up and down at ninety miles an hour! Not only that, he had a pencil in his hand that he was tap-tap-tapping against his knee in perfect cadence to the bounce.

So what the prospect saw was Mr. Cool, Calm, and Collected. But what I saw were two very different men living schizophrenically side by side—one above the table and one below.

The pressure to make a living takes a toll. We put on a game face to reflect the appropriate behavior to make the deal. But below the surface we boil with anxieties, worries, fears, and doubts about where the money will come from to make rent. Most families are thirty days away from bankruptcy. This causes the breadwinner to run scared.

What would Jesus say to us today? He would tell us to be content with what we have. A lack of contentment leads to many disappointments. We can only eat one meal at a time, drive one car at a time, wear one suit at a time, sleep in one bed at a time, and love one woman. Everything else siphons off time that could be spent with a child, a wife, a friend, in prayer, in service to God.

The great secret of contentment is not getting what you want but wanting what you get. Jesus set the example for how we should live our lives. Study His life. Learn for yourself how Jesus would spend your money if He were you.

As I've already said, failure means to succeed in a way that doesn't really matter. So how are you doing?

QUESTIONS AND DECISIONS

1. Would you generally say that money has been your servant or your master?

2. Have you thought that if you just had enough money, all your problems would be solved? Why is that not true?

3. Read Ecclesiastes 5:10–12; Matthew 6:24; and Mark 8:36. Then comment on the following: "Poverty and prosperity are both great tests, but biblically speaking, prosperity is the greater test. Poverty risks the body, but prosperity risks the soul. All the benefits of money are temporal, while all the risks of money are eternal."

4. From your perspective, what is the purpose of money? How do you think that matches with God's perspective?

5. Review the section of this chapter entitled "The Top Ten Uses of Money." Would you add or subtract anything from this list? Which of these are areas of your strength? Of weakness? What decisions should you make to correct any weaknesses uncovered?

6. Review the four lifestyle choices under the section "Deciding On a Lifestyle." Which of these four categories are you in today? Is that by design or default? What are the advantages and disadvantages of the approach you have been using? Do you need to rethink your lifestyle?

Current Approach: _____

Desired Approach: _____

In the space provided, write down five or more changes you would like to see in your lifestyle:

Five Changes I Will Make or Begin to Make During the Next Ninety Days:

1. _____

2. _____

3. _____

4. _____

5. _____

7. Which of the four ways to earn money—labor, other people's labor, rent, and risk—would you like to more fully exploit? Do you have a plan? If not, set aside some time to think, and write down a specific action plan. Set some goals for yourself.

8. Have you lived on a budget? If not, how much of your financial problems would you guess relate to not having a financial plan? Are you ready to change? What should you do?

PART 3

•

THE SEASON OF

CRISIS

In the Belly of the Whale:
A Case Study, Part 3

A man's spirit sustains him in sickness,
but a crushed spirit who can bear?

—*Proverbs 18:14*

10 Oswald Chambers wrote that most men have their own morality well within their grasp. That coincides with my own experience.

Frankly, since becoming a follower of Jesus Christ in the early 1970s, I have never really struggled with choices between good and evil. Of course, I've made thousands of errors in judgment, but I have had my morality well in hand.

The problem with leading a moral life is that we can deceive ourselves into thinking that our good choices are also God's will. I learned the hard way that just because an idea is good and not evil does not necessarily mean it is "God." There is a huge difference between a *good* idea and a *God* idea.

Not knowing the difference between a good idea and a God idea got me into a heap of trouble. For the first ten years of my spiritual journey, I lived my life by my own best thinking. I believe it was God's will for me to be a real estate developer—a calling. However, when I would evaluate a business deal, I would first decide whether or not the numbers penciled out, and only after I had already decided what I wanted to do, I would pray and ask God to work it out: "Lord, if You will just make this deal work out, I'll split the profits with You, and we'll both be better off!" It was "plan, then pray." I never really gave Him the opportunity to lead my life. Instead, I asked Him to follow me.

Henry Blackaby, in his workbook *Experiencing God*, suggests that we "find out where God is working and join Him there." I'm afraid that in "our time" we are more likely to say, "Here I am working, God. Won't You come join me here?" Can you see how one approach puts God at the center while the other approach puts man at the center?

Hitting the Wall

Following this foolish formula, I built a Tower of Babel and made a name for myself. One day in mid-1985 we assembled our management team to discuss how to secure equity financing for one of our buildings. Instead, the discussion focused on a growing, vague feeling that our industry was getting ready to take a fall. Overbuilding was rampant. Greed, not market studies, fueled business planning. Lenders showed up at the door with wheelbarrows full of money. It was a time to get skittish.

Nevertheless, you don't turn a freighter on a dime. The average building project takes five years from conception through leasing it up.

The next year, 1986, three months after I made the commitment I have already mentioned—"I want to live the rest of my earthly life for the will of God"—my world came undone. The Tax Reform Act of 1986 was passed, and I was thrust into a season of crisis.

I woke up in the belly of a whale. Like Jonah, I had gone off in my own direction. Now God was going to turn me back, but not without a crisis. Like the great fish that swallowed Jonah for his disobedience, a time of darkness came over me for taking control of my life.

It was like the water main had broken. The giant hand of government reached over and turned off the spigot. Prospective tenants went on holiday. Suddenly, investors stopped returning phone calls. Lending sources dried up. The flow of capital ceased. All this didn't work too well for a freighter fueled by a constant stream of new capital. Like a jet that ran out of fuel in midair, we went into a nosedive.

One day a couple of months later, our lead lender "suggested" that we trim staff and expenses. I had never had a layoff. In fact, I had worked hard to create a family atmosphere in which we truly cared for one another. That all changed when I let the first seventeen people go.

At a meeting with the remaining headquarters staff I wept. I told them how I hoped this would be enough, but fortunately, I didn't make any promises. I told them I thought we had solved the problem. I was wrong.

Not Knowing How to Pray

Things became so dismal I didn't even know how to pray. I could not think of any specific meaningful prayer. The following Wednesday when I met with my weekly prayer partner, he asked how he should pray for me. I said, "Ken, all I can think of is to pray that God will grant me strength, courage, hope, grace, and mercy. If He grants me those five things, I can make it through."

In the meantime, we were scrambling to find a new source of capital. We visited Wall Street. Those men wore the grim, somber faces of morticians sizing up a prospect. We talked to regional securities firms. Those men spoke as darkly as their charcoal-gray suits. Finally, we found a company to help. We spent an entire year putting together a comprehensive equity package, only to be bounced by their chairman of the board minutes before we expected final approval.

At that point I felt doomed. I felt like someone had pushed me out of a perfectly good airplane at midnight on a black moonless night, blindfolded, without a parachute, not knowing how far I was from the ground. I was free-falling through the air, gaining speed, knowing I would splatter all over the ground any moment, but not knowing when. All in all, a pretty helpless state.

More Layoffs

At the next layoff I invited the "cut" associates to attend the meeting at which I would explain what was happening to the remaining associates. I had just read an article that said when a limb, like an arm, is dismembered, the arm still feels pain, just like the body. So I knew that everyone was hurting, and I wanted to be as humane and therapeutic as possible. But it really hurt. My knees wobbled, and my stomach churned as I walked into that room.

Except for a period in 1987 when I thought everything would work out, I had to live each day with the specter of going bankrupt from May 1986 to October 1993—more than seven years. It was as if I was under a giant sword of Damocles suspended by a slender horse hair, and I knew that at any moment that slender thread could snap and it would be over for me. Ironically, the most productive years of my personal ministry were simultaneously taking place.

It would have been easy to throw in the towel and give up. No one would have blamed me. The odds looked insurmountable. Yet, somewhere deep within me I sensed God was calling me to fight for survival and not give up. Don't misunderstand. I can't say I ever felt like I knew He would deliver me, but I can say I always sensed I knew I should never give up.

Thousands of times during those seven years, the pressure was too much. I simply couldn't visualize how to make it through one more day. Sometimes we couldn't pay our vendors on time. Sometimes we couldn't pay our mortgages on time. There were lender workouts. Vendor negotiations. More layoffs. The anxiety was devastating. It was embarrassing. It was humiliating. It was humbling.

Wanting to Give Up and Quit

Though I hated the agony of it all, I considered quitting only twice. One day I walked through the doorway to my office, and I remember thinking, *That's it. I just can't take it anymore. I quit.* Then I took another two or three steps, realized what I had thought, stopped dead in my tracks, and said out loud, "You can't quit. You hate quitters."

Another time, late in the process, I was talking to my attorney of twenty years on the phone. Everything could have been wrapped up after five years of crisis if not for one irascible investor. That investor hated my guts and would settle for nothing less than blood. In a state of utter exhaustion and depression I told my lawyer, "I can't take it anymore. The pressure has gotten to me. I just want to fold up our tent and quit. Let them do whatever they want. I don't care anymore. I just can't go on another inch. I am through. If they want to throw me into bankruptcy, so be it. I tried my best," and so on.

Tommy, my lawyer, wisely let me ventilate, then he said, "I understand how you feel, but if we quit now, you lose everything you've been working toward for these last six years. Why don't you let me worry about this and get it off your plate? Let me take it for a while."

Spared by Grace

I agreed. Two years later we settled with the investor, and I was able to completely avoid bankruptcy. By God's grace I was spared. It took seven years, but I was able to work completely out of all personal debts. It's interesting. I spent seven years piling up debt, and it took seven years to get out of it. In the Bible, seven is considered the "perfect" number. Today I owe no man anything "except the continuing debt to love one another" (Rom. 13:8). Praise be to God!

Even though God spared me from bankruptcy, I realize two things. First, if I had gone bankrupt, I would have deserved it. It was only the kindness of God's grace working in me to stay the course that resulted in deliverance. Second, there were no guarantees that I would be spared. Many wonderful men are forced into bankruptcy. There is no disgrace in declaring bankruptcy *if you have done everything humanly possible not to.*

Sometimes circumstances thrust us into a crisis. Other times we reap a season of crisis because of what we have wrongly sown, whether unintentionally or not. In this section we look at how a season of crisis comes about, and some suggestions to work your way back.

Burnout

It is a difficult and troublesome thing at such seasons for a soul not to understand itself or to find none who understand it.

—*St. John of the Cross*

11 It came as no surprise to anyone that a savvy, hardworking guy like Mark would rocket into the upper echelons of corporate management. Everyone congratulated him. He enjoyed the adulation.

In the months that followed, he realized that to be effective, he would need to travel extensively. For twenty-five thousand dollars he purchased an annual pass from a major airline that allowed him to travel anywhere he wanted, anytime he wanted.

Mark was a decent guy. He never drank. He never had an affair. He participated in religion. Yet his life was hollow—emptied out of any real satisfaction. Everything revolved around his job. Mark had allowed his career to become his mistress. Somewhere along the line he had acquired a distorted view of the Protestant work ethic. He was addicted to work.

Eventually, all the hours caught up with him. He continually felt tired. He felt guilty for not spending more time with his three children, all under the age of eight. He stopped reading his Bible. He stopped praying. He stopped caring. His sex life stopped. On three separate occasions chest pains sent shivers of terror through his mind. He was putting far too many hours into his career. He felt extremely unhappy. Mark knew he had to make some changes.

Several more months went by until one day he realized he was the only one who could make any changes happen. He sensed God was calling him to start his own consulting firm. When all the details were ironed out in his mind, he approached his boss, who turned out to be sympathetic. In fact, his boss promised he would become his first and biggest client.

With a few contracts in hand, Mark resigned from the corporate world to begin his own business.

Intent on rekindling his marriage, he took his wife to dinner for the first time in three years, and a few days later he asked her to lunch. As they sat at the lunch table nervously glancing at each other, she finally said, "You know, I don't really know who you are." He knew that it was true, and that he didn't know her either. Mark realized getting his life under control wasn't going to be as simple as waving a magic wand that instantly makes everything all right. This comeback was going to require some highly focused effort.

In the months that followed, Mark began to make himself vulnerable with other men he suspected were also addicted to work. As he would share his own story, he was amazed at how many men experienced the same symptoms as he did—little or no sex life, tiredness, and extreme unhappiness.

A Time of Crisis

Times of crisis come in many shapes and sizes. Nations struggle with geopolitical, military, and economic crises. Times of crisis crash in around us when tax laws change and stock markets plummet to the depths. Times of crisis seep into our lives from money, business, and debt woes. A crisis can result from problems with health, career, or family members going in separate directions. A crisis may be the outcome of a heart gone cold toward God.

Here are the most common areas where men feel the pinch of a crisis:

- work
- money
- marriage
- children
- health
- death of a loved one
- wilderness experience with God

If you find yourself in crisis, which of these areas are not working right? Where else are you hurting?

Some crises come suddenly; others develop long-term. Some can be resolved quickly; others take a long time. And some problems, like the death of a child or visiting arrangements for children living with an ex-wife in another state, simply don't have solutions—we have to learn to live with them. This is a difficult reality to accept in an optimistic culture that often believes anything can be fixed given enough hard work.

My *Webster's New Riverside University Dictionary* defines *crisis* as "a crucial or decisive point or situation." The Chinese have an interesting word for crisis. They combine two characters—*danger* and *opportunity*—together into one word. In this and the next chapter we will explore the dangers associated with this season, and we will also look at the opportunities.

Long-Term Burnout

Twenty to 30 percent of the people walking into doctors' offices are there because of feeling fatigued.[1] Some medical professionals estimate that up to 90 percent of all doctor visits result from stress.[2] In response to a perceived dramatic increase in stress-related health problems, Northwestern National Life conducted a landmark survey that revealed that two-thirds of the respondents suffered from exhaustion, anger, or anxiety. Thirty-four percent of all employees surveyed expect to burn out on the job.[3]

In this chapter we are going to zero in on one kind of crisis in particular, though not exclusively—*long-term burnout*. Long-term burnout leaves men drained—emotionally, physically, psychologically, and spiritually. It is not a momentary, fleeting, or sudden crisis. It is often a midlife thing, but not only that. Jim Conway's research for his book *Men in Mid-Life Crisis* revealed that men have midlife crises from age thirty well into their fifties.[4] Yet, I remember well a swollen-eyed man in his late sixties suffering from burnout. "I've lost my direction," he said.

Often the problem is that reality has set in. A man has had the thought, *It's just not going to happen the way I planned,* even though he can't quite accept it yet. Or as Jim Conway said, "I feel like a vending machine. Someone pushes a button and out comes _____." (Feel free to insert your own answers here. Smile.)

Symptoms

One day I was talking with several men about feeling burned out. Some of them were trying to decide whether they were burned out. Another man in the middle of a midlife reevaluation made the retort, "If you don't know whether or not you're in it—you're not!"

Feelings of high anxiety crash in at unpredictable times. The burned-out man becomes short-tempered and irritable. He feels friction at home, and guilt for depriving his family of time.

He is tired at the beginning of the day, not just the end. During the day, he becomes easily fatigued. He suffers from a loss of focus. He frequently finds his efforts ineffective. He often procrastinates even with important matters.

He finds himself frustrated with his performance, unhappy with his attitude, depressed by his circumstances, and confused about his direction. He is a prisoner of boredom, lacks enthusiasm, and is embarrassed by the whole doggone affair. On top of everything else, he often suffers from physical ailments such as headaches and neck pain.

The lingering feeling that something isn't right stalks him. His world appears to be coming unglued. And it doesn't look like anybody really cares. All summed and totaled together, it creates a crushing load. One day the man experiences a complete systems shutdown. He experiences a meltdown, an emotional burnout. He simply stops caring. But many times, he can't show it because he is a Christian, and as we all know, Christians aren't supposed to have problems. *Yeah, right.*

As a result, he feels trapped. He hates his job. His wife doesn't like him very much, and to be honest, the feeling is mutual. He is mad at God, and that just makes him feel worse and more guilty. Some days, he would like to pull the plug, chuck the whole thing, and run away to Maui where he would join all the dropout lawyers and take up boat-sitting.

But he can't because he has too much to lose; he is locked in. All of these feelings happen at the very point in life when he has accumulated enormous responsibilities. He has made wedding vows. He has fathered children. He has taken on a mortgage. He has borrowed for investments. Work, family, and all of life taste like soda crackers after a hot morning of yard work. He wonders, *What have I gotten myself into? I can't escape. I'm trapped.*

In the most severe form of burnout you may end up clinically depressed or even have suicidal thoughts. Twice a month I meet with the leaders of our men's ministry in my home. One morning a man described in icy, sober terms how he was considering suicide. That was certainly not the first time I had been with a man talking suicide (*many* men have this thought, though few consider it seriously).

I must tell you, however, that something in his cold, deliberate delivery sent shivers of fear throughout my body. He kneeled, we all touched him with a hand, we prayed, and by God's grace, he never had a suicidal thought again. But a quick turnaround is the exception. If things get this far, *it is serious.* (If that is where you find yourself now or in the future, take steps to receive medical help and professional Christian counseling without delay.)

Where are you? You may not be burned out, and that is good. On the other hand, you may be on the way, and you may know you are—or maybe you don't. Perhaps you have been through a meltdown before, or you may be in the middle of a burnout right now. One goal for this entire book is to help you avoid a burnout or, if you have already hit the wall, to come out the other side. Because Somebody does care. Jesus cares. He said,

> COME TO ME, ALL YOU WHO ARE WEARY AND BURDENED, AND I WILL GIVE YOU REST. TAKE MY YOKE UPON YOU AND LEARN FROM ME, FOR I AM GENTLE AND HUMBLE IN HEART, AND YOU WILL FIND REST FOR YOUR SOULS. FOR MY YOKE IS EASY AND MY BURDEN IS LIGHT. (Matt. 11:28–30)

Root Problems

How does a man get burned out? Whether you eat junk food or nutritious, healthy food, the difference is not immediately noticeable. In the same way, a season of crisis or burnout doesn't come suddenly. Burnout is the consequence of many choices made along the way. The crisis builds one day at a time, one choice at a time. These choices don't seem big at the moment, but when compounded and added to thousands of similar decisions, they inevitably lead to a crisis. We can choose our way, but not the results. Our choices have consequences.

Not all crises result from our choices, like certain health problems or calamities beyond our control, but the kinds of crises we want to talk about in this chapter do. They are crises within our control, crises for which we are responsible.

We make day-to-day choices based on our worldview, which consists of the answers we have given to life's most important questions. These "first principles" guide us in decision making in conscious and subconscious ways. The basic assumptions we make about the nature of God, man, the world, the devil, sin, eternal life, and salvation determine our foundation. And how we build on that foundation determines whether or not we will stand or fall in times of crisis. Jesus put it this way:

THEREFORE EVERYONE WHO HEARS THESE WORDS OF MINE AND
PUTS THEM INTO PRACTICE IS LIKE A WISE MAN WHO BUILT HIS
HOUSE ON THE ROCK. THE RAIN CAME DOWN, THE STREAMS ROSE,
AND THE WINDS BLEW AND BEAT AGAINST THAT HOUSE; YET IT DID
NOT FALL, BECAUSE IT HAD ITS FOUNDATION ON THE ROCK. BUT
EVERYONE WHO HEARS THESE WORDS OF MINE AND DOES NOT PUT
THEM INTO PRACTICE IS LIKE A FOOLISH MAN WHO BUILT HIS HOUSE
ON SAND. THE RAIN CAME DOWN, THE STREAMS ROSE, AND THE
WINDS BLEW AND BEAT AGAINST THAT HOUSE, AND IT FELL WITH A
GREAT CRASH. (Matt. 7:24–27)

Have you built your foundation on the sand or the rock?

We have already established that building a balanced, rewarding life
depends upon making right choices about career, family, money, and God.
What, then, are the poor choices that lead to burnout and crisis?

A tree is known by its fruit. When our lives display free-floating anger,
workaholism, preoccupation with material things, selfishness in relationships, and other rotten fruit, these are surface problems. We can, through
self-examination, discover *why* we do what we do. We can look at the roots
we have put down. We can look at the root problems.

In the rest of this chapter we will explore four root problems that lay
groundwork for poor choices. In the next chapter we will go one level
deeper still and look at *the* root problem that underlies it all.

A crisis, then, results from repeatedly making poor choices about *values*,
expectations, *purpose*, and *unresolved issues*. Let's look at each of these four
areas.

1. Values: What's Important? ~ based on what?

Our *values* answer the questions, "What's important?" and "What has
worth?" What are the principles, standards, and beliefs we hold to be
worthwhile? Values are what we consider important to us. Poor choices
about our values can lead to a crisis.

At the age of thirty-three, Mike finally understood the identity of
Christ, why He came, and what belief in Him means. The meaning of
Christ's death for his sins moved from his head to his heart, and he was
born again.

One day not long thereafter, while driving down a highway, Mike (real
name by request) was so overwhelmed by the presence of God that he had

to pull over to the side of the road. So overpowering was the experience that he finally said, "God, please stop. I can't take anymore."

A man in Atlanta spent time each week teaching him in the Word of God. "It was a time in my life that I was really growing," said Mike.

About two years later Mike was offered the statewide distributorship for a major running-shoe company. It was the break he was looking for. He had always wanted to run his own business. It represented what was important to him—what had value. He prayed for it and now thanked God for it.

Over the next ten years he fully devoted himself to building his business. He missed most of the growing-up experiences of his two daughters; he never really knew them. He traveled constantly, which led to an immoral lifestyle. To compensate for her loneliness, his wife turned to alcohol. Mike also began drinking. Eventually, it all led to a divorce. "My business became my god," he said. "I worshiped the goddess Nike."

After his divorce, Mike continued his immoral lifestyle. The more he drank and the harder he worked, the more lonely and empty he felt inside. In despair he began getting on his knees and trying to pray, but nothing would come out. He couldn't pray. Day after day he would try, but nothing happened. He had hit the wall. He burned out.

One day, wrenching in agony, he cried out, "God, where are You?"

In the next chapter we will look at the rest of the story. For now the question is, "How does this happen?"

We lose direction when we choose the wrong values. We have a problem when we buy into the values of our culture instead of the kingdom. We are all products of our culture to some extent. (Culture means the sum of a society's behavioral patterns including its art, beliefs, institutions, and all other products of its work and thought.)

Culture affects how we think, what we believe, amd even the type of language we use to express ourselves. We cannot, nor should we, escape from our culture. However, it is of paramount importance to understand our culture.

What's important in our culture in this generation? Careerism, individualism, consumerism, materialism, relativism, and pluralism top the list. We have a bad case of the "isms." Our purpose here is not to examine these "isms" but to remind ourselves that culture challenges us to take control of life and tolerate everyone and every belief.

Culturally formed values lead to pain. As a friend said, "We pursue God out of priority or pain." If we do not pursue the values of God as *priority*, then He will introduce *pain* into our lives. One way or the other, God is going to make sure we pursue His values. The pain that brings us back to God is grace.

What is important to you? List the top five in priority order. Based upon your answers, are you living by the values of the culture or the kingdom? What adjustments do you need to make?

2. Expectations: What's Due?

Our *expectations* show how we have answered the question, "What's due?" or "What can I expect?" Expectations are things we consider likely or certain to happen. We feel they are owed or due to us. In short, we expect them. Unrealistic or unmet expectations can lead to a crisis.

The problem we face is that our culture fosters high expectations, even rights. We end up thinking that to be happy, we need to hold down a particular kind of job; therefore, we need to earn a particular level of income; therefore, we need to live in a particular kind of house in a particular kind of neighborhood; and therefore we need to drive a particular kind of car; and all by a particular age. Why? Simply because that's what we are programmed to expect when we adopt expectations from our culture.

When we set our expectations too high, we take risks that cause us to alternate between pursuing significance one day and survival the next. Yesterday we dreamed of building an empire with streets paved in gold; today we freeze with fear over how to meet payroll.

The siren song of our age is that "you can have it all"; moreover, you *need* it all to be truly happy. When we buy into this idea, our goals, plans, hopes, dreams, and expectations come from the culture, not from God. We are living by our own ideas. We must remember that not every good idea is a God idea.

Unmet expectations can lead to tremendous disappointment, anger, and even depression. Maybe it's a marriage that isn't working the way it's supposed to, a career that seems stalled too soon, or a teenager making horrible choices.

For two years I have been pondering a sentence that I believe answers a lot of questions about life. I reproduce it here, but ask you to not read past it quickly. You may find it valuable to do as I have done and write it somewhere for long-term reflection. Here it is: *All disappointment is the result of unmet expectations.*

Think about it. Whether it's a promotion that didn't go through, a wife that isn't sympathetic to your pressures, or a child hanging out with the wrong group—*all* disappointment is the result of unmet expectations. Knowing this can help us reevaluate many of our expectations and lower some of them.

The Bible says, "Every good gift and every perfect gift is from above, and comes down from the Father of lights" (James 1:17 NKJV). Too often we don't show gratitude for the many blessings we do receive, and we become selfishly angered over the blessings we don't receive. Instead, we should receive everything with gratitude and humbly trust God when we don't get what we want.

How have your expectations led to disappointment?

3. Purpose: What's the Point?

Our *purpose* answers the questions, "What's the point? Why do you exist? What is your life all about?" and "What are you here for?" The wrong answer to these questions will lead to a crisis.

Charles Barkley said in a 1994 television interview that the purpose of his life—his reason to exist—was to win an NBA title.

There are three problems with this kind of thinking. First, he is searching for glory, not meaning. Second, that purpose is not big enough to last a lifetime. Third, he cannot control the outcome. Get ready, Charles. The demons of disillusionment are coming your way.

Dan set a goal of ascending into top management of a medium-sized company. He achieved his goal, but along the way he was unfaithful to his wife, who divorced him. To say our purpose is to build a certain-sized company (which I once said—I've seen those demons!), to live in a particular house, to make a certain income, or to achieve a certain position represents a foolish notion because it is not within our complete control.

The purpose of our lives ought to be based on the *quality* of our *character* and *conduct*, not on the *quantity* of our *circumstances* over which we have no or limited control. The only things we control completely, by God's grace, are our character and conduct. We control the character qualities of integrity, our love for God and people, and humility. We control how we conduct ourselves in speech, kindness, and diligence. Surely these will contribute to the quality of our circumstances, but not with a one-to-one correlation. A wrong orientation at this point surely leads to a crisis.

Is the purpose of your life big enough? Is it a purpose you can control? Who gets the glory?

4. Unresolved Issues

Most of us get so busy that we have *unresolved issues*. If we pretend certain problems will go away, we may be setting ourselves up for a crisis.

For some, our fathers may have never given us their blessing so we labor for their approval—even if they have already died.

By his nature, Bill's father was a highly critical, unhappy man. Even earning a Ph.D. didn't gain Bill much attention from his father. When Bill married, his father never quite accepted his wife, often severely criticizing her. After his father died, Bill regretted that he had never been able to talk through his feelings with his dad and be reconciled. His brothers shocked him further when they told him that their dad had written Bill out of his will and never told him.

After months of feeling depressed, Bill sat down one day and wrote his father a long letter. A few days later, he slid behind the steering wheel early in the morning and made the long journey to the next state where his father was buried. Bill spent several hours alone, grieving at the grave of his father. Finally, he placed the letter he had drafted on top of the cold tomb and set it on fire. He watched it burn, hoping to put his pain in the past. Today he would tell you that, to his constant regret, some kinds of pain never go away.

For some men, other key relationships go unreconciled in the pedal-to-the-floor race to keep on top of our responsibilities. Some unresolved issues relate to *tasks*, but by far the majority deal with *relationships*. We tend to take care of our tasks at the expense of our relationships. In the process we wound and damage the feelings of our loved ones. Remorse goes unexpressed. Forgiveness is not sought. Relationships break down.

What are the unresolved issues in your life? Better yet, *who* are the unresolved issues in your life?

Over the long term, making wrong choices in these four areas will lead to a crisis. The crisis will affect your career, your money, your family, and your relationship with God. Where have you been making poor choices? Which of these areas are root problems in your life? What decisions and changes do you need to make?

QUESTIONS AND DECISIONS

1. What has been the biggest crisis you have ever faced? How did it affect you?

2. Have you ever gone through long-term burnout? If so, how did you come back? If you have never been through a season of crisis, what factors do you think have spared you? Are you at risk, and if so, how? (If you are in the middle of a burnout, the parts entitled "The Season of Renewal" and "The Season of Rebuilding" contain some helpful suggestions.)

3. "A crisis results from repeatedly making poor choices about *values, expectations, purpose,* and *unresolved issues.*" Do you □ agree/ □ disagree? Explain your answer. Which of these areas are root problems in your life?

4. *Values:* What is important to you? List the top five in priority order. Based upon your answers, are you living by the values of the culture or the kingdom? What adjustments do you need to make?

5. *Expectations:* How have your expectations led to disappointment?

6. *Purpose:* Is the purpose of your life big enough? Is it a purpose you can control? Who gets the glory? Should you change your purpose?

7. *Unresolved issues:* What are the unresolved issues in your life? *Who* are the unresolved issues in your life?

8. Over the long term, making wrong choices in these four areas will result in a crisis. The crisis will affect your career, your money, your family, and your relationship with God. Where have you been making poor choices? How do you think the choices you are currently making will affect your future? What decisions and changes do you need to make?

The Dark Night of the Soul

It was a happy chance that God should lead the soul into this night from which there came to it so much good.

—*Saint John of the Cross*[1]

12 Over breakfast a man shared his life story with a friend. He started out with a highly focused plan, but his life meandered and fizzled into a fuzzy blur of endless meetings, unused adult male toys, meaningless relationships, and shrinking income. The friend, who was trusting Christ to guide his life, suggested several helpful ideas. Moisture collected in the corners of the man's eyes, and he said, "I guess I need a new paradigm."

To understand our crisis we must understand not only *how* we feel, but *why* we feel that way. In this chapter we'll examine *the* root problem that so often leads to a dark night of the soul, to being swallowed up like Jonah into the belly of a whale, and we'll begin to map out a new paradigm (system, road map, or model) that leads back to shore.

The Root Problem: Cultural Christianity

One morning as I was sitting in the rubble of my collapsed empire trying to discover where I had gone astray, a thought came to mind that I believe is the most important lesson I have ever learned.

I share it with you, hoping you will understand that, to me, these few words are as important as all the other words in this book combined. This is not an idea I have just dashed off, but it comes on the heels of several grueling years of self-examination. I believe it is the diamond—the Big Idea—that all that pressure produced for me. The more I meditate on these words, the greater their meaning and the wider their application. Please read them slowly several times until you have grasped not only their significance but their application to you personally:

There is a God we want, and there is a God who is. They are not the same God. The turning point of our lives is when we stop seeking the God we want and start seeking the God who is.

Does this make sense to you? As I said in chapter 2, Cultural Christianity simply means to seek the God (or gods) we want and not the God who is. It is clinging to our idols instead of smashing them to smithereens and hosing the glittery dust into the gutter where it belongs.

God is who He is. No amount of wanting Him to be someone or something else will change anything. Our task is not to change God but to be changed *by* God. Our task is not to reinvent God in our imagination but to discover the God who is already there. God will do what God will do. To think we can outsmart God is pure tomfoolery.

Here is a great problem: Men become Cultural Christians when they are not Biblical Christians.

The Dark Night of the Soul

The journey back from the world of Cultural Christianity to the kingdom of Biblical Christianity will often pass through what St. John of the Cross called "the dark night of the soul."

God will often lead a "soul" who has gone astray onto a path of "dark contemplation and aridity, wherein it seems to be lost." It is a time full of darkness and trials, constraints and temptations. Your season of crisis may well be a dark night for your soul.

In *The Ascent of Mount Carmel*, St. John of the Cross wrote, "When the will of a man is affectioned to one thing, he prizes it more than any other; although some other thing may be much better."[2] If our affections are on worldly things rather than on Jesus, we have not chosen the better. What must God do to break the stranglehold that the affections of the world have on a man?

In the wilderness God fed the wandering Israelites with manna. But they wanted more—they wanted meat. St. John of the Cross wrote, "They failed to find in the manna all the sweetness and strength that they could wish, not because it was not contained in the manna, but because they desired some other thing."[3] What must God do to make a man not want some other thing?

When a man is a Cultural Christian, he has divided his loyalties between God and the things of this world. For a man to become a Biblical

Christian, his desire for the things of this world must die. He must crucify, or mortify, the desires of his flesh. Unfortunately, few men can do this on their own. Hence, the dark night of the soul.

Before my own dark night of the soul, I remember hating my sin—that caldron of selfish desires boiling within. But I also remember being power-less to overcome it. There was too much "Patrick" in Patrick. The dark night of my soul was God's gracious gesture to turn me back to Him. It was His loving gift to help me mortify my flesh. He helped me crucify my ambition, purify my thought life, and correct my motives. (I wouldn't dare suggest I have attained anything near this, but at least I now desire it with all my heart.)

Do not chafe against the dark night of your soul. You may be on that path because you have been a Cultural Christian or because of some other reason. Whatever the reason, the dark night of your soul is God's kindness to empty your soul of self. Look to become detached from the world—to *attend* your worldly affairs without becoming *entangled* in them. Seek to abandon yourself to God. This dark night will lead you as surely as the brightest light.

Understanding Cultural Christianity

Like saltwater intrusion into a freshwater bay, Cultural Christianity pollutes Biblical Christianity slowly over time and with little observable notice. It is difficult to defeat an enemy you can't see and don't understand. For that reason, let's spend some time talking about Cultural Christianity. The heart of the problem of Cultural Christianity is twofold.

First, many men never understand what the Bible says. They have respect for the Bible but no knowledge of its contents. The Bible presents a detailed picture of who we are, who God is, and how we should live in response. In Biblical history, when the people of God did not study the Word of God, they always went in search of many schemes. Every man did what seemed right in his own eyes. Men called evil good, and good evil. The Bible says a man is the slave of whatever has mastered him (1 Peter 2:19). Better to be mastered by the Bible.

As the apostle Paul said, the trouble is that a little yeast works its way through the whole batch of dough (Gal. 5:9). What starts out as a tiny seed grows up into a huge tree. Its roots absorb all the nutrients from the soil, and its shade stops the sun from letting anything else grow. Cultural Christianity is *the* root problem.

Second, many men rebel against what they do know from the Bible and live by their own best thinking. Everyone has an opinion about everything. Ask ten economists for an opinion and you'll get twelve answers.

Does our opinion about the meaning of life, the nature of man, the character of God, and the way of salvation really make any difference if God has another opinion? I wonder why this doesn't occur to so many otherwise intelligent men.

The Self-Help Gospel

There are, of course, many gospels being preached today. However, the dominating good news preached in American culture today is the self-help gospel. The self-help gospel will always lead men to become Cultural Christians. Cultural Christians are self-made men.

The self-help gospel is a thin veneer of religiosity painted like camouflage to disguise a consuming desire for personal fulfillment. We could call it the "Get It Together with Jesus" movement. It is a blending of the human-potential movement and selected Christian values. It suggests that self-esteem and success, not salvation, are the purpose of faith.

According to a *U.S. News and World Report* cover story, 95 percent of Americans believe in God, 71 percent of college graduates believe the Bible is the inspired Word of God, 62 percent say they attend religious services regularly, and 46 percent describe themselves as born again.[4] This would be encouraging, except for what lies behind the statistics.

The article goes on to say that a series of recent studies found that today people are less committed to particular denominations, more eclectic in their beliefs, more tolerant of other views, more inwardly focused on their own private spiritual pilgrimage, and more concerned with their own needs. The tendency is not to accept the authority of the Bible and religious institutions, but to make up our own religion as we go. Many growing congregations multiply members by going light on theology and heavy on personal fulfillment. In short, many people follow a self-help gospel.

Statistically, it appears America has undergone a religious revival. On further reflection, however, we learn there is more to it. As the children of baby boomers grow up, their moms and dads want them to have religious and moral instruction. So the baby boomers are rejoining the church they abandoned when they went off to college.

In days gone by, a person had to confess faith in Christ before joining the church. Not so today. Because of low to no prerequisites for joining the body of Christ, many churches are top heavy with people who don't know God personally. On top of that, because of a low view of God in many churches, there is a plethora of Cultural Christians—some of whom we might call mature infants in Christ, and some don't even know Him at all. They know *about* God, but they don't know *Him*. By God's grace, let us pray that these statistical Christians will hear God's gospel and not just a self-help gospel.

Yes, we have seen a revival. However, it is not a *spiritual* revival, but a *demographic* revival. In truth, it is not Christianity at all. Oh, yes, it has a form of godliness, but it does not depend upon faith in the finished work of the historical Christ for redemption. In fact, redemption from sin and death often isn't even part of this new religion's message. Ron Nash said it well one day: "I don't mind if people want to make up a new religion. I just wish they wouldn't call it Christianity."

I don't believe that most men who become Cultural Christians, who follow the God they want, set out to do so. I know I didn't. Instead, our religious culture often encourages us to make up our God as we are swept along by the most current and popular teachings. Often we have not been challenged to personally study the Bible, to realize who Jesus actually is, and to follow Him wholeheartedly. What we need is a new paradigm.

Two Paradigms in Contrast

Paradigm One: The Self-Help Gospel

The self-help gospel is pure Cultural Christianity. Its ultimate purpose is personal fulfillment. It is to pursue the God we want.

Its followers become statistical Christians, mature infants, and inevitably end up burned out. Cultural Christianity focuses on man's mortal wound—how to build a better world.

For the Cultural Christian, faith becomes another item to be checked off on his "to do" list: Drop kids off at school, go to work, get saved, pick up milk on way home. One day this man will wake up in the belly of a whale.

Paradigm Two: The Gospel of the Kingdom

The gospel of the kingdom is Biblical Christianity. Its ultimate purpose is to usher in the kingdom of God. It is to pursue the God who is.

Its followers become disciples and stewards of Jesus Christ. Biblical Christianity focuses on mankind's eternal wound—how to save the world from sin, decay, and death.

For the Biblical Christian, faith becomes the plumb line against which every other area of life is measured. He devotes himself to a life of sacrifice, surrender, and service.

Which of these two paradigms best describes your life? Have you been living the life of a Cultural Christian or a Biblical Christian?

Suppose for a moment that ten years ago you took up fishing. For these ten years you have told everyone you meet that you are a fisherman. You own a fishing boat, though it has not been wet for eight years. You can hardly close your tackle box you have so much gear, but it has collected a thick coat of dust in your garage. Your fishing rod cost a king's ransom, but you can't remember what it feels like to lay a cast where you want it. You can't remember the last time you went fishing. Here's the question: If you don't do what fishermen do, are you really a fisherman?

To come out the other side of the dark night of the soul, a man needs a whole new paradigm. Do you need a new paradigm? Two steps in particular can help you crawl out from the belly of the whale that has swallowed you up—to pass through the dark night of the soul.

First Step: Accepting Responsibility for the Problem

The first step in turning around a season of crisis is to assume full, 100 percent responsibility for the problem. Forget the petty grievances against those who may have in some way accelerated your fall. Accepting responsibility paves the way for dealing constructively with your troubles.

Celebrity athletes blame their boorish behavior on the demands of stardom. Violent youths blame their problems on the family breakdown in the 'hood. Men who take office supplies home point out that everyone else does it too.

Consider this thought: "If a victim of privilege is not responsible for his actions, if a victim of poverty is not responsible for her misdeeds, if victims of addictions are blameless, if people who come from broken homes or dysfunctional families are not to be held accountable for their behavior . . . well, who is?"[5]

The S Word

When we live in a morally good way, we can hoodwink ourselves into thinking we are following Christ, even when we are not. In fact, the more righteous we are on our own without God, the greater the temptation to live our lives without depending upon Him at all.

The curse of the Cultural Christian is his *sincerity*. I'm convinced American churches hold millions of men hostage to their own sincerity. They are good men, but they are trusting in their own good deeds. Their intentions are noble. They are sincere, but they are sincerely wrong. And the "better" they are in their natural man, the tighter Satan has been able to draw the noose around their necks.

No, the S word is not *sincere*. The S word is *sin*. Cultural Christianity is, in a word, sin. To seek the God or gods we want is idolatry, and idolatry is sin—one of the Big Ten—the Ten Commandments. False worship is sin.

To talk about sin is not popular. Frankly, if we talked more about it, we would have fewer problems. When no one holds us accountable for how we live our lives, we live them however we want.

Once we have staged a pity party, it is time to acknowledge that not only is our crisis of our own making, but that we have sinned against God by living independently from Him.

It is not enough to feel sorry. What does that mean? You could be sorry that you got caught, sorry that you didn't get your own way, or sorry that you have to go through such a hard time. *Sorry is not enough. When we sin, the Bible calls us to repent.* To repent means to change directions, to begin thinking differently. It is to feel godly remorse.

If you offend your wife, you cannot be reconciled with her until two things happen. First, you must express remorse for hurting her. Second, you must indicate a desire to change and act differently in the future. Only then can forgiveness have meaning.

It is the same with God. When we have sinned against God, we must express genuine remorse and then repent, or pledge to act differently. There is a difference between *worldly* sorrow (merely feeling sorry for yourself) and *godly* sorrow: "Godly sorrow brings repentance that leads to salvation and leaves no regret, but worldly sorrow brings death" (2 Cor. 7:10).

We need to repent of our Cultural Christianity. We need to acknowledge our sin. We need to take responsibility for the way we have lived.

Second Step: Accepting Responsibility for the Solution

Under the leadership of Bill Hybels, the Willow Creek Community Church near Chicago grew from 125 people in 1975 to more than 14,000 today—one of America's largest. An internationally sought-after speaker, writer, and consultant, he was for five years the chaplain of the Chicago Bears.

This high-octane spiritual leader always kept his eye on two gauges on his dashboard. First, he kept his eye on the *spiritual* gauge by asking, "How am I doing spiritually?" He always kept this area of his life in tune. He also watched the second gauge closely, the *physical* gauge, by asking, "How am I doing physically?" He kept his body healthy. When these gauges said go, he would go as hard as he could.

One day while he was preparing for some messages, his mind went dry, and he found himself sobbing. He checked his gauges. No problem. Yet, he broke down several more times in the following weeks. He thought maybe he was in a midlife crisis.

After a period of self-examination, he realized he had a third gauge on his dashboard, the *emotional* gauge, which he had never noticed before. Now, when he thinks, *I don't care if I ever do that again*, he knows he's close to redlining his emotional gauge. When he hopes the important people in his life can exist without him, he knows his emotional resources are near empty. When he doesn't feel like doing his regular spiritual disciplines, he recognizes it as a warning sign.[6]

The second step in turning around a season of crisis is to assume full, 100 percent responsibility for the solution.

My parents instilled a strong work ethic in me. I love to work. Work is my hobby. I would rather work than eat, and I often do. As a result, I tend to run myself down emotionally. One habit I have gotten into helps. When I feel like throwing my hands up in the air, I will often quit and take the rest of the day off. Recently, I had enough and went to the movies— two in a row. Four hours later I felt like my engine was back down below redline.

The forgotten priority of our culture is rest. We excel at our tasks, but we find it extremely difficult to slow down. Rest is a priority of God. At its core, a long-term burnout is not only a spiritual problem but an emotional problem.

The Way Back

One day I was bringing my father-in-law up-to-date on my dark night of the soul. The pressure had drained me of all enthusiasm. Food didn't appeal to me. I walked and talked like a mummy. I was depressed. I figured I would never again be happy. I was drained of all joy. I was a wreck—an emotional, physical, and psychological burnout.

After I explained my situation and how I felt, he said, "Pat, two years from now your joy will return, and the enthusiasm you have always felt for your work will come back."

I remember two distinct thoughts colliding in my mind. First, *No way. I will never, ever again enjoy what I'm doing. It will never happen.* The second thought I had was, *Why does it have to take so long?*

What is the way out of a long-term crisis? The plain truth is that you will not find an easy way out. If you leave your car lights on overnight, your battery will run down. You can jump-start it and get it going, but the only way to bring the battery back permanently is to recharge it slowly. In the same way, when our emotional batteries get run down, we can jump-start our bodies with caffeine, nicotine, alcohol, or drugs; but the only way to make a permanent comeback is to recharge slowly. It takes time.

Another metaphor may help. Assume you have been a peak-performing athlete. You work out aerobically five days a week for fifteen years. Then you stop exercising altogether for several years. You decide to get back in shape. In your wildest dreams you would never expect that you could spend a whole day exercising and be back in top shape. Rather, you bring your body back slowly. In the same way, when we have let other areas of life slip out of shape, we must bring them back slowly. It doesn't happen overnight.

What about Mike?

What happened to Mike, who had made his business his god? Let's pick the story up again . . .

After his divorce, Mike continued his immoral lifestyle. The more he drank and the harder he worked, the more lonely and empty he felt inside. In despair he began getting on his knees and trying to pray, but nothing would come out. He couldn't pray. Day after day he would try, but nothing happened. He had hit the wall. He burned out spiritually and emotionally.

One day, wrenching in agony, he cried out, "God, where are You?"

In his breast he sensed the voice of God tell him, not audibly, but as an impression, "I want you to stop drinking."

Immediately he stopped, but after a week he was climbing the walls. He prayed again for strength and relief, and again, he sensed the voice of God telling him to go to Alcoholics Anonymous. He stood, walked to the phone book, and called the first AA chapter in the book. The man who answered the phone told him they had a meeting that started in fifteen minutes.

Though he couldn't place exactly where the address was, Mike climbed in his Porsche and started driving. As he pulled to a stop at a traffic light, his car broke down. *Oh, nuts,* he thought. *Now I'm going to miss this meeting.* He pushed his car to the side of the road, and as he looked up, he happened to see the shopping center across the street where the AA meeting was to take place. He abandoned his car troubles, walked across the street, and nervously stepped inside the meeting hall.

In the six years that have followed, Michael has reconnected with God through Alcoholics Anonymous. He abandoned his Cultural Christianity. He stopped backsliding. He made the commitment to become a Biblical Christian, to let God lead and direct his life to study the Bible and grow in his faith. But it took time. God is not an American who gets it done for us "yesterday." For Michael (he changed his name from Mike to symbolize his changed life) it was a dark night of the soul.

He was still extremely lonely, and he began to pray, "God, please give me a godly wife." By God's mercy and grace, today Michael is remarried. "It's such a blessing to look over and see my wife on her knees praying," he said. He also meets each week with another man for accountability to encourage and challenge each other in their walks with God.

"I pray for people now," he said. "I pray that God will heal them— emotionally and spiritually. We all need healing. I thank God that He did not abandon me. Instead, He healed me and continues to heal me—one day at a time. Thank You, God."

An Immediate Crisis Management Tool

God has anticipated your crisis, your dark night of the soul. He has prepared a healing balm for your wounds. The book of Psalms could easily be titled *The Burnout Book*. Whatever grief you are facing, God will meet you in the book of Psalms. Look especially at chapters 3–13, 22, 40, 42, 51, 56, 57, 60, 61, 63, 64, 73, 77, 103, and 107. One suggestion to help manage your rebound is to read several psalms every day. Pray them out loud to God. Let the words speak to your own heart and hurt.

There are many other issues to consider in getting out of the belly of the whale and passing through the dark night of the soul, which will be covered in the next part, "The Season of Renewal." In the meantime, why not read for renewal in the book of Psalms?

QUESTIONS AND DECISIONS

1. Are you in, or have you ever been in, a dark night of the soul? How would you describe it?

2. Read the following statement:

   There is a God we want, and there is a God who is. They are not the same God. The turning point of our lives is when we stop seeking the God we want and start seeking the God who is.

   Have you been seeking the God you want or the God who is? If it's the God you want, what has building on that foundation led to?

3. The problem of Cultural Christianity is twofold. First, many men never understand what the Bible says. Second, many men rebel against what they do know from the Bible and live by their own best thinking. Which problem has caused you to stumble?

4. "Men become Cultural Christians when they are not Biblical Christians." Have you been a Cultural Christian or a Biblical Christian?

5. To what extent have you been a Christian who is more interested in finding personal fulfillment, self-esteem, and success rather than in building the kingdom?

6. Do you need a new paradigm?

7. The first step in turning around a season of crisis is to assume full, 100 percent responsibility for the problem. Forget the petty grievances against those who may have in some way accelerated your fall. Accepting responsibility paves the way for dealing constructively with your troubles. "Godly sorrow brings repentance that leads to salvation and leaves no regret, but worldly sorrow brings death" (2 Cor. 7:10). Are you ready to accept full responsibility for your crisis? Do you need to repent of Cultural Christianity? If so, tell God in prayer.

8. The second step in turning around a season of crisis is to assume full, 100 percent responsibility for the solution. What steps do you need to take to "recharge your batteries?" What steps do you need to take to get back in shape?

PART 4

●

THE SEASON OF

RENEWAL

Restoration:
The Prodigal Returns

The danger is not lest the soul should doubt whether there is any bread, but lest by a lie, it should persuade itself that it is not hungry.

—*Simone Weil*

13 Occasional laughter punctuated the exchange of banter this particular Thanksgiving Day in the early 1970s. Mom, Dad, my wife, Patsy, and all my brothers were celebrating the safe return of my younger brother, Robert, from Vietnam.

I had left home to join the army in 1967 at the age of eighteen. Not long before I was to get out, Robert followed in my footsteps. Now, this day, we could relax and enjoy each other's company with lighthearted teasing, warm embraces, and Mom's incredible cooking. Our family had survived the Vietnam era intact. Not everyone's family could say the same.

As we sat down at the dinner table, we all bowed our heads, and my father began to pray the blessing. "Lord," he said, "I just want to say thank You. . . ." At that point he choked up, he couldn't finish his prayer, and he excused himself from the table. It was the first time I had ever seen my father cry.

Seeing him lose it, the rest of us got all choked up too. When he came back a couple of minutes later, I asked, "What was that all about?"

"I'm just so happy. You see, your mother and I didn't think we would ever see the family all together again."

There is no joy that exceeds the joy of a father who sees his son or daughter return after a long absence.

The Problem

Men who live by their own ideas end up in rebellion against God. Many times this is not by a sinister plot, but by simple neglect of their relationship with their Father.

When men move away from their Father, whatever the reason, their relationship begins to wax and wane like any other relationship would. He becomes more like a famous person they once met and followed for a while. If you met the president of the United States, joined his reelection team, helped his campaign, but never spoke to him or read about him again for ten years, would you *really* know him?

Ask, "How many years was it after you received Christ until you really started to do business with God?" and the majority of men in a typical group won't respond until you suggest eight, nine, or ten years. Herein lie a great problem and a great opportunity. There seems to be a pattern for men to receive Christ, but then live for a number of years without the full impact of His presence and power at work in their lives. They think because they have prayed a prayer, everything will turn out all right. They go off to pursue their dream.

The man who abandons God to pursue his own plans will not be abandoned by God. God is the hound of heaven. When our plans lead in a wrong direction, He will send reversals into our lives to humble us and turn our hearts back to Him.

In this chapter we will show how the man who has suffered *reversals* because of *rebellion* can experience *restoration* through *repentance*. The welcome lights never go out. The prodigal is always welcomed back.

Jesus regaled the crowds of saints and sinners that followed Him with a parable about a young man who went away but came back. The parable illustrates by analogy our relationship with our heavenly Father. By studying the four stages this young man went through, we can better understand how much God wants to restore us, indeed longs to restore us, when we go through a crisis. Let's explore these stages together.

Stage 1: Rebellion

JESUS CONTINUED: "THERE WAS A MAN WHO HAD TWO SONS. THE YOUNGER ONE SAID TO HIS FATHER, 'FATHER, GIVE ME MY SHARE OF THE ESTATE.' SO HE DIVIDED HIS PROPERTY BETWEEN THEM. NOT LONG AFTER THAT, THE YOUNGER SON GOT TOGETHER ALL HE HAD, SET OFF FOR A DISTANT COUNTRY AND THERE SQUANDERED HIS WEALTH IN WILD LIVING." (Luke 15:11–13)

A *rebellious spirit* marks the first stage of getting into a crisis. This rebellion can be outward and active, or internal and passive. In this story we can detect four ways a man rebels against his Father. Let's look at the clues left by four "smoking guns" in the passage above.

1. Impatience with God's Timing

The son didn't want to wait until his father decided to distribute the inheritance. He wanted it now. He said, "Give me my share of the estate." Why do we become impatient when God's timing isn't the same as ours? Let's be candid. The more power we possess to *not* wait, the harder it is to wait. If you have a persuasive personality, you are accustomed to getting what you want. If you can write a big check for an investment, why should you wait? If you have the ability to reason through a problem, why shouldn't you go ahead? Taking action before we sense God leading us, however, signifies rebellion.

2. Desire to Be in Control

The son wanted to leave town, to be on his own. He wanted to be independent of his father and in control of his own destiny. He was sure his life would be better off if he didn't have to live in the long shadow of his father's success: "Not long after that, the younger son got together all he had" and "set off for a distant country." We may run away from God like the prodigal son or Jonah did. But with all of our debts and duties, when we rebel, it's more likely we will stay where we are. Like a disgruntled employee who cripples productivity by becoming a bottleneck, we drag our feet in protest. We like control and pout when we don't get it. Or we don't want to trouble God where we are strong, so we don't consult Him in prayer or read the Bible for guidance. Generally, if we don't need to pray to make a good decision, we forget to.

3. Financial Irresponsibility

All that money went to the son's head, and he got swept away by a flash flood of opportunists. He found plenty of new "friends" to help him spend his fortune. "And there squandered his wealth." Actually, the prodigal son is much smarter than we are. At least he only spent all he had. In our culture we go into debt to finance our consumptive lifestyles. The modern sign of financial irresponsibility is a lifestyle of cultured squandering that doesn't save, doesn't tithe, and accumulates debt for things already consumed.

4. *Moral Lapse or Decline*

The son soon forgot his moral upbringing. He wasted his money on "wild [prodigal] living"—parties and prostitutes (Luke 15:30). Few men today make the same crass choice this young son made and have an out-and-out moral lapse. More likely, we slide into a state of moral decline by a thousand small choices strung out over the years, none of which by itself seems to matter much.

These four acts of rebellion on our part lead to the second stage.

Stage 2: Reversals

"AFTER HE HAD SPENT EVERYTHING, THERE WAS A SEVERE FAMINE IN THAT WHOLE COUNTRY, AND HE BEGAN TO BE IN NEED. SO HE WENT AND HIRED HIMSELF OUT TO A CITIZEN OF THAT COUNTRY, WHO SENT HIM TO HIS FIELDS TO FEED PIGS. HE LONGED TO FILL HIS STOMACH WITH THE PODS THAT THE PIGS WERE EATING, BUT NO ONE GAVE HIM ANYTHING." (Luke 15:14–16)

The son blew his bankroll and—notice that only after it was gone—then comes the famine. "After he had spent everything, there was a severe famine in that whole country." Isn't that the way life goes? The contingency doesn't strike until the contingency fund is depleted!

After a rebellious spirit has run its course, the second stage we go through is a *reversal* that grabs our attention. God sends a famine into our lives, and it's a severe famine! Why did God wait until the son had spent all? Perhaps He wanted to make sure the young man had no vestige of his own resources left upon which he could fall back and prolong his rebellion against his father.

Then, "He began to be in need." Curiously, at that point the young man turned to a foreigner rather than to his own father. His new boss sent him out to the fields to slop the pigs, and he was ready to eat pig food he was so destitute: "He longed to fill his stomach with the pods that the pigs were eating."

Why didn't he just go back home? Perhaps he was embarrassed to have been such a fool. Maybe it was pride. Possibly he was blinded by self-deceit. Or could he have been in a state of depression? More to the point, why don't you and I turn back after we start to be in want? When our sins, like those of the prodigal son, blind us, we often turn to everyone else but God.

To add insult to injury, notice that "no one gave him anything." What happened to all those "friends" who helped him squander his father's fortune? Suddenly, he became a leper. No one would touch him. Have you ever been through a period of reversals, gone to your friends for help, but no one lent a hand? Just on the law of averages someone should have helped, but nobody did. Amazingly, when God sends a famine or severe famine into our lives, many times our friends don't support us the way we think they should.

Stage 3: Repentance

"WHEN HE CAME TO HIS SENSES, HE SAID, 'HOW MANY OF MY FATHER'S HIRED MEN HAVE FOOD TO SPARE, AND HERE I AM STARVING TO DEATH! I WILL SET OUT AND GO BACK TO MY FATHER AND SAY TO HIM: FATHER, I HAVE SINNED AGAINST HEAVEN AND AGAINST YOU. I AM NO LONGER WORTHY TO BE CALLED YOUR SON; MAKE ME LIKE ONE OF YOUR HIRED MEN.' SO HE GOT UP AND WENT TO HIS FATHER." (Luke 15:17–20)

At this point we have a full-blown crisis. *Rebellion* has led to *reversals*. In the depth of his despair this young man comes to his senses. That he "came" to his senses implies that he had "left" his senses. Letting go of our good sense makes a crisis in the first place.

A self-made crisis, big or small, short-term or long-term, will drive us to our knees for a time of self-examination. Actually, a crisis is a gift from God that points us back toward Him. It is a gift because God doesn't let us utterly destroy ourselves. In the same way the pain from touching a hot burner on the stove top prevents a far greater injury, God uses the pain of a crisis to turn us back from paths of self-destruction. A crisis represents the unfailing love of a perfect Father to restore a wayward son. Our deep miseries invite us to again turn to the unfailing love of our perfect Father. Yet, often we don't turn until we are turned. It often takes a sanctified crisis to bring us back to our senses.

And come to his senses the young man did. Through his deep miseries, the young man realized he had sinned. In the depth of his despair it dawned on him that he would be far better off with his father, even if only as a hired hand. So, the young man humbled himself and planned to ask his father, "Make me like one of your hired men." He felt so unworthy to be called a son, a sure sign of contrition and repentance. This represents a good step. A friend of mine, Jim, said, "More and more I hate it when I sin." It is good to wrestle with and hate our sins. In the kingdom of God, <u>even the desire to repent comes from the Father</u>.

"So he got up and went to his father."

Have you done something that has separated you from the Father? If so, have you come to your senses? Have you examined yourself? Do you need to repent?

Stage 4: Restoration

"BUT WHILE HE WAS STILL A LONG WAY OFF, HIS FATHER SAW HIM AND WAS FILLED WITH COMPASSION FOR HIM; HE RAN TO HIS SON, THREW HIS ARMS AROUND HIM AND KISSED HIM. THE SON SAID TO HIM, 'FATHER, I HAVE SINNED AGAINST HEAVEN AND AGAINST YOU. I AM NO LONGER WORTHY TO BE CALLED YOUR SON.' BUT THE FATHER SAID TO HIS SERVANTS, 'QUICK! BRING THE BEST ROBE AND PUT IT ON HIM. PUT A RING ON HIS FINGER AND SANDALS ON HIS FEET. BRING THE FATTENED CALF AND KILL IT. LET'S HAVE A FEAST AND CELEBRATE. FOR THIS SON OF MINE WAS DEAD AND IS ALIVE AGAIN; HE WAS LOST AND IS FOUND.' SO THEY BEGAN TO CELEBRATE." (Luke 15:20–24)

If we subtitled Stage 3, "What the Son Did," we would then subtitle this final stage, Stage 4, "What the Father Did." The father did two things.

First, the father lavished his son with love. Why did his father spot him while he was still a great way off? Most likely, the father had been looking for him every day. He loved his son. Period. No conditions. He was filled with compassion for him. The Greek word for *compassion* means "to have the bowels yearn, to feel sympathy, and to have pity." This father actually ran to greet his son, threw his arms around him, and kissed him.

Second, the father restored his son. When the son tendered the little repentance speech he had been rehearsing, that was all the father needed to hear. He said, "This son of mine was dead and is alive again; he was lost and is found." He called for a celebration because his "dead" son was once again alive. He was lost but had found his good sense again.

It's ironic. While the son felt remorse, the father felt joy. Actually, *because* the son felt remorse, the father felt joy.

The Bible says there is rejoicing in the presence of angels over one sinner who repents (Luke 15:10). This must surely be the most joyful moment in the life of God.

Two Lessons

Two lessons jump out at us from the parable of the lost son. First, no sin is so egregious that God will not forgive us. No matter how far away from God you have been living, you can find your way back. If a young man who rejected his father's values, took half his father's wealth, debased himself in immoral living, and lost all his fortune on wild living can be restored to his father, so can we be restored to our heavenly Father through repentance. God comes running to meet us when we turn to Him in our hearts.

Second, you can break out of the downward spiral into crisis at any point. A full-blown rebellion means crisis, but full-blown repentance means restoration. You can stop the crisis of your own making any time you want.

Rescued from Rebellion

A man wrote me this letter:

> I would like to share with you a story about a man who was self-destructing. Being in real estate you know the passions, the money, the "art of the deal" behind the scenes without me adding detail.
>
> In the last year and a half I have been running out of control. I became successful at everything—I was respected, loved, admired and becoming moderately wealthy. I was a deacon, Sunday-school teacher, successful businessman, father, friend, and husband. In short, a Renaissance man with an attitude. I went from daily devotion to independence and my life became unbearable.
>
> My wife told me to pray for our family before I left for a Christian conference I recently attended. She told me I had better come back with some answers. We did not part pleasantly.
>
> Pat, I couldn't pray anymore. I had lost God, lost my way. I couldn't find my way back. Friday night, after the first session, I went to my room with a friend who sensed my despair. For two hours I poured out my miserable life.
>
> I thanked my friend and went to bed, but couldn't sleep. Like Jacob, I wrestled with God all night. Exhausted, I rolled out of bed at 4:30 A.M., went to the desk, and began to read a Christian magazine. Unmoved, I turned to the Scriptures, specifically Luke 9:23: "Then [Jesus] said to them

all: 'If anyone would come after me, he must deny himself and take up his cross daily and follow me.'"

I was moved. I understood—my disobedience, my independence, my rebellion was going to cost me everything. I fell to my knees and cried out to God. Like Peter on the water, I was about to sink. I wept and begged the Lord to take back the reins of my life. I re-surrendered to Him. I confessed and all the garbage inside of me came up. I did something I don't remember doing before. I repented. It was life-changing. It was real. I was free, cleansed, restored. In spite of my unfaithfulness, my arrogance, and my disobedience He remained faithful and wrapped His loving arms around me and loved me—He never stopped loving me! I knelt before His glory and praised Him.

A Prayer of Repentance and Restoration

If you have been suffering through a crisis of your own making and want to be reunited with your heavenly Father, you can do so right now through prayer. Express your despair, your remorse for sinning against God, your sorrow for hurting those you love the most, your sense of unworthiness to even be called His son, your pledge to change directions, and your willingness to be a servant.

Here is a suggested prayer. You may pray it word for word, you may paraphrase it, or you may want to pray in your own words. The important thing is the attitude of your heart.

Lord Jesus and Father God, I am perishing from hunger for You. My circumstances are in a shambles. Against You, O God, have I sinned. I despise my sins and repent of my rebellion against You. Forgive me, Lord, according to Your great mercy. Forgive me for the pain I have caused my loved ones, and show me how to restore those relationships. I am unworthy to even be called Your son. By Your grace, restore me to wholeness. Restore me to a right relationship with You and a right relationship with the people in my life. I surrender control of my life to You. I make a pledge of new obedience. Make me into a servant. Amen.

Does this prayer capture the desire and intent of your heart? If so, pray this prayer right now and allow God to begin the process of restoring you.

QUESTIONS AND DECISIONS

1. If you have been going through a crisis, which of the four stages discussed in this chapter best describes the state of your heart and mind now? Why?

   • rebellion
   • reversals
   • repentance
   • restoration

2. How have you been a rebellious man, now or in the past? (Mark appropriate spaces.)

   ☐ 1. impatience with God's timing
   ☐ 2. desire to be in control
   ☐ 3. financial irresponsibility
   ☐ 4. moral lapse or decline
   ☐ 5. other (*specify*): _____

3. Have you had friends who seemed to desert you in times of trouble? Do you think it could have been part of God's plan for your life? Will you forgive them?

4. What have you done that has separated you from the Father? Have you come to your senses yet? Have you practiced the art of self-examination?

5. What decisions do you need to make about your life based upon this chapter? Do you need to turn from rebellion? Do you need to acknowledge your reversals are the effect of your rebellion? Do you need to express repentance and ask God for restoration? Did you pray the prayer at the end of the chapter? If not, should you?

A New Message for Men

14 The following comments were made during a small group meeting earlier this week. They are typical of the comments Christian men everywhere are making:

- "I finally have peace in my career. I want to do more for Him."
- "I just turned forty. I've been in the [Christian] battle for twenty-five years. I find myself wanting to feel more significant."
- "My Christianity is like a savings account that has not produced a very good return."
- "Will you pray for me? My passion to serve the Lord is gone, and I want it back."
- "I only have one talent, but I want to be faithful with the one I have."
- "I burn with a desire to serve this generation."

The greatest yearning I hear today in my travels is that Christian men have an intense desire to make their lives count. However, there is a new sense in which men are thinking these thoughts. In the 1970s and 1980s, men wanted their lives to count in their work and families, and they wanted to achieve financial success. Although these desires have not gone away, today men want more. Today men want their lives to count for God.

After praying a prayer to receive Christ, many men have lived the best they knew how for five, ten, fifteen, twenty, or more years. But instead of being fulfilled, their lives are more empty than ever—even shallow. After searching for personal fulfillment and self-esteem, they realize they have gained neither. Christian men today are saying, "Hey! What gives? This isn't very satisfying. There must be more to life than this. There's gotta be!"

A Two-Story Kingdom

Francis Schaeffer wrote that life consists of a first story and a second story. The first story holds the lower order of man, earth, and created things. The second story contains God, heaven, and eternal things.[1] We live in a two-story kingdom.

Notice what the Scriptures say about the first and second stories. . .

SINCE, THEN, YOU HAVE BEEN RAISED WITH CHRIST, SET YOUR HEARTS ON THINGS ABOVE, WHERE CHRIST IS SEATED AT THE RIGHT HAND OF GOD. SET YOUR MINDS ON THINGS ABOVE, NOT ON EARTHLY THINGS. FOR YOU DIED, AND YOUR LIFE IS NOW HIDDEN WITH CHRIST IN GOD. (Col. 3:1–3)

[FROM NOW ON] THOSE WHO USE THE THINGS OF THE WORLD, [SHOULD LIVE] AS IF NOT ENGROSSED IN THEM. FOR THIS WORLD IN ITS PRESENT FORM IS PASSING AWAY. (1 Cor. 7:31)

The Problem

The problem is that for several decades we have been falling down the stairs into a Christian culture preoccupied with first-story issues—issues centered on this life and man.

Many of us have pursued a self-help gospel that never rises above the first story. First-story preaching and teaching only reach the level of exhorting men to be better husbands and dads, manage their time better, make better decisions, become better money managers, and be successful. Of course, these are good goals—we all need to do better in these areas. And it is better to meet these personal needs from a biblical point of view rather than send men to a secularized self-help seminar. But these represent an anemic victory if we neglect the greater second-story demands of authentic faith. The self-help gospel preached today is often too weak and sickly to even make it up the stairs to the second story—where God is.

Beyond that, this gospel often focuses on how to become successful enough to distance ourselves from the troubles of other people rather than on how to take the Bread of Life to people starving to spiritual death. We can easily become consumed by the goal of insulating ourselves from the aches and pains of a world held hostage by sin. We can yearn to live in a gated community that holds at bay the woes of the world. We end up preaching to ourselves "the gospel of the gated community."

Here is the core problem for men: The mainly economic man is not a whole man. There is no sustaining passion, no fire in the belly, of a man preoccupied only with issues of the first story. When we concentrate our energy exclusively on building a better life for ourselves, we put a ceiling on how much our lives can count. First-story faith is merely another synonym for Cultural Christianity.

So, where do we find satisfaction? How do we make our lives count? Where can we find sustaining passion, some fire for our bellies? Authentic satisfaction, a life that counts, a life that matters, a life that makes a difference—these we find only in the second story. The power of God is in the second story.

Drawbacks

What keeps men stuck in the first story? First, to be a successful man in today's economic climate demands a great deal of concentration. In the pressure cooker of commerce men forget to worship their Creator. Cash-flow problems crowd out calling. Men become so busy, they lose sight of their larger purpose.

Recently, a doctor friend of mine took early retirement. When I asked him why, he said, "My work consumed me. I have missed out on so much. It cost my marriage. So I said to myself, 'Stop the world—I want to get on!'" He had lost sight of his larger purpose.

Second, in many cases the culture has influenced the church more than the church has influenced the culture. Consequently, much preaching doesn't lift the spirits of men into the heavenlies. Rather, the focus remains earthbound. When men go to church, what they want, whether they can express it or not, is to hear a word from the Lord, to be brought into the presence of the living God through authentic worship, music, confessions, creeds, and the preaching of God's Word. Too often they never get out of the first story.

A New Message for Men

God has a message for men who have become Cultural Christians— for men stuck in the first story. I believe what God wants to say to us might be summarized this way: "I love you, but you can't be a Christian on your own terms."

I believe what the Lord wants to say to Christian men in these times is that we must move fully into the second story without abandoning the first.

God invites you to join Him in the second story, move some furniture upstairs, turn on the lights, throw open the curtains, and let your light shine before men. Let the world know that the second story of your life is occupied. He wants you to occupy the second story without moving out of the first. It is not an either/or proposition, but both/and. He wants you to occupy the whole house that He has built for you. To do less is to build wrongly on the right foundation. He doesn't want your life to be one-dimensional. Will you join Him there?

For the last several years I have encouraged men to ask the questions, "Who am I?" and "What is the purpose of my life?" I have also suggested men write out a Written Life-Purpose Statement to reflect their understanding of the answers they get to these questions. These are issues of identity, meaning, and purpose. They are critical questions. They are, and always will be, good questions.

Yet, I have come to see how we can make ourselves earth-bound and culture-bound by them. Although we should keep asking them, I have come to believe they have a man-centered (anthropocentric) thrust rather than a God-centered (theocentric) focus. They belong to the first story. However, by massaging the questions a bit, we can create an additional pair of questions that will bring us upstairs into the second story.

See if this doesn't make sense. Before we can successfully know, "Who am I?" we must first know, "*Whose* am I?" To correctly know, "*What* is the purpose of my life?" we must first know, "*Who* is the purpose of my life?"

"Whose am I?" and "Who is the purpose of my life?" These two second-story questions can help us climb up out of the morass of self-centeredness that has such a vise grip on so many men and so much of the church today. It can elevate us to serve the kingdom of God rather than the kingdom of self. As a Christian counselor friend of mine said, "The biggest problem I see today is that people are preoccupied with themselves rather than Jesus, and that's on both sides of the cross."

This second set of questions will lift the spirit of a man to new, lofty heights. They change his focus from finding within himself a basis for earthly self-esteem to looking into the Scriptures to learn how God designed him for dignity. They force him to dwell on high and holy matters. They elevate a man to a height where he can clearly see his God-given purpose and calling in the world and in the kingdom. The man who answers these questions will find he can *engage* the world without being *absorbed* by it—he can be "in" the world but not "of" the world.

Only when we begin relating to the issues of identity, meaning, and purpose with a "from above" perspective as well as a "from below" perspective will we find the elusive fulfillment we desire. Moreover, these questions have the potential to help us keep our eyes on Jesus, the author and perfecter of our faith.

To live a full-orbed life with and for God, we must ask ourselves not only, "Who am I?" but "Whose am I?" We must explore not only, "What is the purpose of my life?" but "Who is the purpose of my life?"

Let's briefly compare these questions.

"Who" Am I? Vs. "Whose" Am I?

The question "Who am I?" deals with our identity. The question "*Whose* am I?" deals with our identity *in relation to our Creator.* To know ourselves, we must also know something of the nature and character of the One who made us—what is His design, plan, and purpose for mankind?

When we change the nuance of this question from "who" to "whose," we force it upstairs into the second story. We relocate the focus from self to God.

The Bible says that you have been stamped with the *imago dei,* the image of God, and that He knit you together in your mother's womb. Acts 17:26 says, "He determined the times set for [you] and the exact places where [you] should live."

As said before, you represent God's crowning achievement. You are His most excellent creation. You are the full expression of God's creative genius. God was at His very best when He made you.

What should a man say in response to all this? Simply this: "I am who I am because of the grace of God. He has made me. I belong to Jesus. I am not my own; I have been bought with a price. I am a slave of Jesus Christ. I should no longer (and by God's conquering grace will no longer) live for myself but for Him who died for me and was raised again. I have been crucified with Christ, and I no longer live. The life I live in the body I live by faith in Him who loved me and gave Himself for me. For me, to live is Christ; to die is gain. Whatever was to my profit I now consider loss for the sake of Christ." (For further study see 1 Cor. 6:19–20; 2 Cor. 5:15; Gal. 2:20; Phil. 1:21; 3:7–8.)

We are who we are because of *whose* we are.

"What" Vs. "Who" Is the Purpose of My Life?

Most men I have known would prefer to "do" something for God rather than simply "be" with Him. This task-oriented approach to Christian faith can lead to a huge spiritual defeat.

To explore "*What* is the purpose of my life?" focuses me on the *task* God has for my life. Certainly, there is work to be done. On the other hand, to explore "*Who* is the purpose of my life?" focuses me on my *relationship* with Christ.

I would simply suggest that we cannot accurately answer the question, "*What* is the purpose of my life?" until we have correctly answered the question, "*Who* is the purpose of my life?" This simple additional question draws our attention to the truth that we must find our significance in a God-centered way instead of a self-centered way. We will find our true purpose only as it trickles down from the second story into the first story.

Let me further suggest that a better question than "What is the purpose of my life?" is this: "What is *His* purpose for my life?" Again, this small change relocates the emphasis into the second story.

An Organizing Principle

In 1991, I gave up day-to-day business responsibilities to devote more time to a calling I received in 1988 "to take God's message of love to a broken generation," and to the vision of "helping to bring about a spiritual awakening in America by reaching the men and leaders of our nation with Christ."

These are noble purposes, but within weeks I found myself evaluating how I was doing by using the same methods of measuring performance as I do in business. How many people were in attendance at that speaking engagement? What percentage of them indicated they gave their lives to Christ? How many books did we sell this month? Was it more than last month?

And I began to hate it. So I began to pray and ask God to give me some sort of organizing principle around which I could order my life. A few months later I was reading *The Letters of Francis Schaeffer*. I can't recall exactly what part I was reading, but I was prompted to put down the book, pick up my legal pad, and write, "I will commit myself to a life of devotion and study of God, then speak, teach, and write about what I am learning."

Eureka! I thought. *That's it! The key to staying on track is a life of devotion and study of God.* A life of devotion means to *love* Him more and more, and a life of study means to *know* Him more and more. To love and know God. These, then, should become the chief pursuits of my life, and everything else should proceed out of the overflow of what God is doing in my life spiritually. I realized that my relationship with Him must always be a higher priority than the work I do for Him.

This organizing principle—however one might word it—has application for each of us. In other words, every man should be committed to his relationship with Christ as his first priority. He should be committed to a life of devotion and study of God. Then, after he is filled up to the overflow with enough Jesus for himself and some left over to give away to others, too, he should do whatever it is he is called to do—practice law or medicine, fix plumbing, sell, manage, mow lawns, drive a truck, perform accounting, or do whatever.

In other words, in God's economy paying attention to our relationship with Him necessarily takes priority over the work He has called us to do. To begin a workday without some time for reflection and planning would lead to a day of wasted motion and fatigue. In the same way, if we do not spend time praying through our concerns and listening for the voice of God in Scripture, throughout that day we will not enjoy the guidance that comes from standing regularly in the presence of our Maker. We won't be the salt and light we are called to be if, through neglect, we lose our flavor and let our batteries run down.

What Is the Plan?

Until 1986, I always had a plan for my life. I knew where I wanted to go and what I wanted to do. When the Tax Reform Act of 1986 was passed, my plan went up in smoke. For six long years I had no plan whatsoever. I was in a crisis management mode, and I went from day to day, crisis to crisis.

One morning toward the end of this odyssey I had an unusual devotion in which the Lord *seemed* to say to me, "You have always had a plan for your life, haven't you, Pat?"

"Well, yes, Lord, I have."

"But now you have not had a plan for more than six years, have you?"

"Well, yes, that's right." Under my breath I was thinking, *Thanks a lot!*

"And actually, you have been able to get along quite well without a plan, haven't you?"

"Yes, yes, I have," I conceded.

"And if you had to, you could probably live your entire life without a plan, couldn't you?"

"Well, yes, Lord, I suppose I could," I responded begrudgingly.

Then, the point God had been trying to teach me for six painful years struck me like a thunderbolt. I realized that what God was trying to teach me is simply this: *He is the plan.*

Clarity swept over me. All the cobwebs disappeared. *He* is the plan. He is the *plan.* He is *the* plan!

If you will make Jesus the purpose of your life, He will show you what to do in response. He is the plan, and through a life of devotion and study of Him, you can learn what His real purpose for your life is.

The Challenge to Change Paradigms

Take a moment to review the comparison of first-story Cultural Christianity to second-story Biblical Christianity in figure 14.1 below. These two approaches to Christian life represent two radically different paradigms. Which one best represents your life today? Which one would you like to represent your life?

Fig. 14.1
Cultural Christianity and Biblical Christianity Compared

Note: For maximum effect, review twice. The first time compare columns line by line. On the second review, read down the Cultural Christianity column by itself, then down the Biblical Christianity column by itself.

Cultural Christianity	Biblical Christianity
First story only	Second story (without giving up first)
Man, earth, created things	God, heaven, eternal things
"This world"-oriented	"Kingdom of God"-oriented
The God we want	The God who is
The gospel of the gated community	The gospel of the kingdom of heaven
A passive Christianity	An active Christianity

Goals/Emphasis:	*Goals/Emphasis:*
Self-help	Ushering in the kingdom
Personal fulfillment	Pleasing God
To be something	To be used by God
Guidance	God
Support	Salvation
Help	Holiness
My will	God's will
"Jesus belongs to me."	"I belong to Jesus."
Christ exists for the sake of man.	Man exists for the sake of Christ.

In seventy brief years the Communist ideology captured one-third of the earth's territory and population. The Communists understood a great principle: If you make a small challenge, you will get a small response. But if you present men with a great challenge, they will do something heroic.

It is interesting that today's churches that do present men with a strong challenge to live by the whole gospel—the gospel of the kingdom—have learned they will accept the challenge, and as a result, they are growing. Most men, after all, are heroes. Most men want to be "all the way" Christians, not "statistical" Christians—Biblical Christians and not just Cultural Christians. They simply need someone to show them how.

I'm going to present you with a great challenge. I'm going to ask you to do something heroic, something that can turn the world upside "right"—something that will make your life count. If you have been living the life of a Cultural Christian, I'm going to ask you to become a Biblical Christian, to move some furniture into the second story without giving up the first, to make a commitment to abandon the self-help gospel for the gospel of the kingdom of God. Are you ready? If you are, talk it over with Jesus in prayer. You may pray the following prayer, or you may want to put it in your own words.

Lord Jesus, I need You in my life right now more than I ever have. I realize that I have been living the life of a Cultural Christian. I have been preoccupied with the ambitions of the first story. As a result, I have neglected the second story of my life with You. I have been seeking the God(s) I have wanted and not the God who is. I have sinned against You, and I am sorry. I ask You to once again forgive me by Your amazing grace and bring me back into a right relationship with You. Jesus, I belong to You. I want to live the rest of my life for You. I want my life to count, to make a difference. Yet, I want my life to count for You, not for me. I want You to be my closest friend. Help me to love You with all my heart, soul, mind, and strength. I know whose I am, and I know who is the purpose of my life. Pledging to remain aware of these things, I ask You now to reveal to me what Your purpose for my life is. I rededicate myself to serve and please You with all my heart. I ask You to once again take control of my life and make me into the kind of man I know You want me to be—make me into a Biblical Christian. Amen.

If this prayer expresses the desire of your heart, pray it now. Move upstairs and turn on the light. He is the Light of the World.

At this point, I hope you feel a fire burning in your belly to do something significant for God. You yearn to be used. To build in a right way, we must know what it is that God wants built. What God wants to build is the kingdom of God, not the kingdom of self. We'll talk more about that in upcoming chapters.

QUESTIONS AND DECISIONS

1. "I want my life to make a difference. I want my life to have mattered." Do these statements represent how you feel? Explain your answer.

2. Life consists of a first story and a second story. When men get stuck in the first story, they put a ceiling on how much their lives can count. Have you been stuck in the first story? If so, how?

3. How do the demands on your time pull you toward the first story?

4. How does the church often tend to leave men in the first story instead of lifting them up into the second story?

5. "God loves you, but you can't be a Christian on your own terms." Do you □ agree/ □ disagree? To what extent have you been a Christian on your own terms?

6. Answer the four following questions:

   • "*Whose* am I?"
   • "*Who* am I?"
   • "*Who* is the purpose of my life?"
   • "*What* is *His* purpose for my life?"

   Were you able to answer all four questions? If not, which one(s) gave you trouble and why?

7. Do you have some sort of an organizing principle you use to determine how you spend your time, what your priorities are, and how you are doing? If so, what is it? If not, what would be a good organizing principle for your life? Write out a draft in the space provided.

   _____

   _____

   _____

8. Did you pray the suggested prayer (pages 148–149)? If so, what do you hope will happen as a result?

A Letter from God:
A Time of Reevaluation

15 A man felt great anxiety about the direction of his life. *I wish God would write me a letter and tell me what to do,* he thought. Actually, God has written a letter to us for guidance. We call it the Bible.

If God chose to write us a letter today, what might be some of the things He would want to say? Using what can be gleaned from the Scriptures, it might go something like this.

Dear son . . .

It is almost your time. The chariot of fire and the horsemen of Israel will soon be coming for you. Perhaps you can hear their hoofbeats pounding. I cannot tell you exactly how much longer you have. That is not My way, but trust Me, the time is short.

I am writing because I want you to stop and take stock of your life. I want you to look closely at the way you have lived your life. I want you to make changes based on a new commitment to My larger purposes for your life and the world—while you still have time.

I am going to give you some things to ponder. Do this in a quiet place either early in the morning or late at night, when it is still and quiet. Don't be in a rush. Give yourself plenty of time. Think it over.

You have wanted success. Success is elusive, isn't it? That's because you have been living by your own ideas. I do want you to be successful, but on My terms, not yours. You measure success in the quantity of your possessions and achievements. I measure success in the quality of your character and conduct. You are interested in the success of your goal. I am interested in the success of your soul. True success is to satisfy your calling, not your ambition. Live as a called man.

Do you still love the world, My son? Most men do. Have you become engrossed in the affairs of this world? Most men are. What will it profit you to gain the whole world yet forfeit your own soul? You have wanted to be something; it will go better if you want to be used.

Men pursue Me out of priority or pain. It's amazing how pressure and pain refocus priorities. From now on, try to make decisions based upon your priorities, not your pressures, okay?

He is successful who is found faithful to do the will of God. Are you seeking to know and do My will? Or are you succeeding in a way that doesn't really matter to Me? Would you be willing to live the rest of your life in obscurity if that is My will?

I made you with dignity. I created you to be significant. I have put in you the spark of divinity. You are My crowning achievement. You are the full expression of My creative genius. You are My most excellent creation. I was at My very best when I created you. Do you understand and believe what I have just said?

On the other hand, you must recognize your insignificance—not in dignity—but in the grand scheme of the cosmos I have made. Man is a mere vapor that appears for a little while, then vanishes. He is a speck of dust, a flea, a worm, an insect, as dust and ashes, like water spilled on the ground. In the kingdom of heaven, you are a little lower than the angels, but in the created cosmos, you are but a tiny speck. Have you been guilty of thinking more highly of yourself than you ought?

Be careful not to overemphasize either your significance or your insignificance. If you think too highly of yourself, you will lose your humility and brokenness before Me and think there is nothing you cannot do. Are you a humble or proud man? Answer carefully. Or if you think too little of yourself, you will not love yourself and your neighbors. You will be afraid to try something bold. At the end of their lives most men wish they had been more bold. Do you love yourself? Do you love your neighbors? Do you need to be more bold for Me?

What are you, man, that I am mindful of you? You will never be good enough for Me to love you. Rather, I love you because I made you. I want you to live with Me forever. In this world you will have trouble, but remember, through Christ Jesus I have overcome the world.

Even though the whole world is a prisoner of sin, you don't have to be a prisoner of sin. Does sin have a stranglehold on you? Are you walking in your flesh or My Spirit? You will always have the flesh, but you also have My Spirit. It's your choice, but ask Me and I will help you.

The enemy, My son, is death. But death has no more dominion over you. Death has been swallowed up by victory if you truly put your faith in My Son. He is the door. In Him is life if you accept that His innocent blood was shed for your sins and that by surrendering to Him in faith you are saved because of My grace and kindness—not because you are good, but because I am merciful to those who humble themselves before Me. I am, remember, holy, holy, holy. You must be born again. As one of your own said, "Born once, die twice. Born twice, die once." Have you given yourself completely to My Son, Jesus, the best you know how? Do you have any area you are unwilling to yield? Let Me encourage you to surrender all to Me, or at least say you want to be willing to surrender all. I will help you.

Because I have not yet crushed Satan completely underfoot, there is pain. I allow the same suffering to strike the believer and the unbeliever alike. This futility will in the meantime make you groan, but I have given you My Spirit. I have done this so that My creation may be liberated from its bondage to decay and death. You see, when the way is hard, men turn to Me, though I am not far from anyone. I realize this leaves you wounded. Where do you need to be healed? What is your wound? Call on Me in the day of your trouble, and I will help you. There is a balm in Gilead.

Remember this: Satan is a defeated foe. Yes, he roars about like a hungry lion. On the other hand, My Son made a public spectacle of all demonic powers, having triumphed over them on the cross. Greater am I in you than the devil who is in the world. If you will resist the devil, he will flee from you. You need not fear him, unless you take him too lightly. Pray to be delivered daily from evil. If you don't, remember that Satan will try to attack you at the point of your strength. If you are a good businessman, he will tempt you to pour yourself into your work. If you are a good churchman, he will tempt you to give yourself to the service of God at the expense of your family, and so on. Are you giving Satan too much credit or not enough? Have any of your strengths become weaknesses?

By the way, no matter how sincerely you pledge new obedience to Me, you will still stumble every day. I am as quick to restore you to right relationship with Me as you are quick to ask. Do this daily. Don't let things build up between us. Be humble about this, and accept it as part of your lot in life. Is there anything for which you need forgiveness? Confess it, repent, and I will restore.

The biggest problem I see in your life is that you have spent your whole life looking for something worth living for. It would be better if you found something worth dying for. Give your life to that, and I will give you joy, no matter how hard the path becomes. What is the cause you would be willing to die for? Better still, who is the one you would be willing to die for? How, then, should you reorder your life?

You have been satisfied to know *about* Me; I want you to *know* Me. I want you to spend time with Me every day. Listen carefully. In the same way your relationship with your wife or a close friend will shrivel up unless you talk frequently, there is no way you can walk with Me if we do not communicate. Forget the idea of only a daily quiet time. I want to be with you all the time. I want to be your closest friend. Pray without ceasing. Meditate on My Word day and night. Do you really know Me? Are you spending enough time with Me so that we are really close to each other?

Make a distinction between fame and immortality. You have always craved recognition. You have wanted to be remembered. There are three places you can be remembered—in the record books, in the history books, and in the Lamb's Book of Life. Are you flirting with fame at the risk of eternal life with Me?

I want you to reflect carefully on what I am about to say. Success that really matters depends upon a few key areas: having a close moment-by-moment walk with Me, finding fulfilling work, modeling a life of integrity, living within your means, maintaining your health (My temple), establishing loving relationships, living a life of good deeds, and coming to live with Me when you die. Also, for those who marry, it is important to develop a strong marriage, be a good provider, help children become established, and pray for family members to come to saving faith. Do you get it? Do you see what's important? Which of these areas do you need to reemphasize?

Your central flaw, son, has been your preoccupation with self. Are you preoccupied with finding personal fulfillment? Don't feel too bad;

most every man does the same. It's part of fallen human nature. During this period of self-examination, I want you to reflect on the larger reasons I have put you where you are. I want you to consider not only how to become a better man, but also your duty to your country, society, and culture.

I am looking for men who are willing to penetrate their arenas—whether business, the trades, government, education, medicine, law, the arts, media, entertainment, military, sports, science, or religion—and represent Me there. I need men who will witness for Me among the idols of the world. Are you doing your part to tend the culture and build the kingdom of God? Go into the arena I have given you and be faithful there. Use your skill, cling to your integrity, and whatever you do, don't be ashamed of the gospel. In My economy being a strong witness will not hurt you one iota, but it may make My kingdom come on earth, as it is here in heaven.

I am looking forward to having you with Me. I will give you a new country, a new capital city, a new home, and a new body. You and I will dwell together. We do things differently here. There are no tears. No death or crying or pain.

Like a dazzling jewel box, this city of pure gold, as pure as glass, beckons you, "Come." I have arrayed precious stones like the sparkling, twinkling colors of the rainbow. You will be able to run your hands across the cool smoothness of the twelve pearly gates.

I am the temple, and the city needs no light because I am the light. It is never night. Nothing impure will ever enter here, nor will anyone not written in the Lamb's Book of Life. The air smells fresh with the fragrant aroma of righteousness.

Down the middle of the great street of this celestial city flows the river of the water of life, clear as crystal, flowing down from My throne and the Lamb's. I invite you to stand ankle deep in the refreshing river and feel the cool, healing waters of life swirl around your feet.

Come eat of the fruit from the tree of life. Luscious fruit beckons you to be satisfied. Pluck off a leaf and pinch it. The oozing salve of the leaf is for the healing of the nations.

You will join with the saints from all the ages—Moses, Joshua, David, Daniel, Isaiah, Jeremiah, Elijah, Elisha, Ezekiel, Peter, James, John, Paul, Timothy, Luke, and throngs of lesser knowns—to sing in My heavenly choir. And there will be in that choir people from every tribe, every language, and every nation. These people were purchased by the blood of the Lamb. You will be My servant, and you will reign forever and ever.

What changes should you make in the brief time you have remaining? How would you live if I told you that you have only one year left on earth? One month? One week? One day?

Live your life in the shadow of the cross. Soon, My son, you will see me face-to-face.

Eternally yours,
Your Heavenly Father

QUESTIONS AND DECISIONS

Early in this letter it was suggested that you ponder the questions posed in a quiet place, either early in the morning or late at night, when the world stands silent and still. For your convenience the forty questions in this letter are reproduced below. If you need to do business with God, set aside some quiet time to reevaluate your life and answer these questions in self-examination. Do this prayerfully. Pray with a pencil—"A pencil is one of the best of eyes." Write down your answers. Francis Bacon said, "Writing maketh an exact man." Also, write down what specific action you will take as a result. Don't be in a rush. Give yourself plenty of time.

1. Success is elusive, isn't it? _____

2. Do you still love the world, My son? _____

3. Have you become engrossed in the affairs of this world? _____

4. What will it profit you to gain the whole world yet forfeit your own soul? _____

5. From now on, try to make decisions based upon your priorities, not your pressures, okay? _____

6. Are you seeking to know and do My will? _____

7. Or are you succeeding in a way that doesn't really matter to Me?

_____

8. Would you be willing to live the rest of your life in obscurity if that is My will? _____

9. I was at My very best when I created you. Do you understand and believe what I have just said? _____

10. Have you been guilty of thinking more highly of yourself than you ought? _____

11. Are you a humble or proud man? _____

12. Do you love yourself? _____

13. Do you love your neighbors? _____

14. Do you need to be more bold for Me? _____

15. What are you, man, that I am mindful of you? _____

16. Does sin have a stranglehold on you? _____

17. Are you walking in your flesh or My Spirit? _____

18. Have you given yourself completely to My Son, Jesus, the best you know how? _____

19. Do you have any area you are unwilling to yield? _____

20. Where do you need to be healed? _____

21. What is your wound? _____

22. Are you giving Satan too much credit or not enough? _____

23. Have any of your strengths become weaknesses? _____

24. Is there anything for which you need forgiveness? _____

25. What is the cause that you would be willing to die for? _____

26. Better still, who is the one you would be willing to die for? _____
_____

27. How, then, should you reorder your life? _____

28. Do you really know Me? _____

29. Are you spending enough time with me so that we are really close to each other? _____

30. Are you flirting with fame at the risk of eternal life with Me? ___

31. Success that really matters depends upon a few key areas. Do you get it? _____

32. Do you see what's important? _____

33. Which of these areas do you need to reemphasize? Walk with God, work, integrity, living within means, maintaining health, relationships, good deeds, salvation, and (as applicable) marriage, provider, establishing children, praying for saving faith for family? _____

34. Are you preoccupied with finding personal fulfillment? _____

35. Are you doing your part to tend the culture and build the kingdom of God? _____

36. What changes should you make in the brief time you have remaining? _____

37. How would you live differently if told you have only one year left? _____

38. How would you live differently if told you have only one month?

_____

39. How would you live differently if told you have only one week?

_____

40. How would you live differently if told you have only one day?

_____

Defining Moments

16 She taught the city's children of privilege in a wealthy, manicured neighborhood that stood in sharp contrast to an adjacent slum area. She kept to herself and tried not to venture out into neighboring areas.

One evening as she walked down the street, she heard a woman crying out for help. Just then a dying woman fell into her arms. Seeing that her condition was critical, she rushed her to the hospital. When the staff observed that the ill woman was poor, they were told to take a seat and wait. She sensed this woman was going to die without immediate medical attention, so she left and went to another hospital. Again, they were told to wait.

After the nurses and doctors still didn't come, she took the dying woman to her own home where, later that night, she died in the school-teacher's arms.

This young teacher decided that would never happen again to anyone if she could help it. She decided to devote the rest of her life to easing the pain of those around her so they could live, or die, in dignity.

The city was Calcutta. The woman was Teresa. It was for her a defining moment.[1]

Defining a Defining Moment

Each day we make hundreds, even thousands, of decisions. We decide whether or not we will interrupt a staff meeting to take a phone call. We decide whether or not to make a follow-up phone call to find out if the prospect will buy or not.

There is another category of decision, however, that we might call a defining moment. Most men make only two or three truly major decisions in the course of a year. Some of these major decisions are so significant that we might term them defining moments. Why is that?

Defining moments are monumental decisions that change the course or direction of a life. They represent choices with a five-, ten-, or twenty-year horizon, or they may last for a lifetime. They are defining moments because of their impact, because the consequences are so great, or because the wrong decision carries a high price tag. They are experiences, decisions, and choices we make at major junctions in life.

A defining moment is a watershed experience that shapes a man's character and determines the direction of his life. Defining moments determine destinies. They reveal our identity and character—who we really are. They often represent signposts that mark the transition from one season to another.

Examples of Defining Moments

An example of a defining moment might be that moment your wife told you that you had changed, that you had become a different person to live with. Or perhaps you never shared your faith before, but an associate comes right out and asks you to tell him about why you are different. Maybe God is calling you to a midlife career change.

The Bible is replete with examples of defining moments. Though sold into slavery by his brothers, twenty-one years later Joseph was able to say to those brothers, seeking food during a famine, "You intended to harm me, but God intended it for good, . . . [for] the saving of many lives" (Gen. 50:20). It was a defining moment.

As the ministry of Jesus burgeoned, the ministry of John the Baptist shrank. Was Jesus ruining his vocation? John said, "A man can receive nothing unless it has been given to him from heaven. . . . He [Jesus] must increase, but I must decrease" (John 3:22–30 NKJV). It was a defining moment.

His business empire crumbled. All his children perished together in a disaster. To this, Job said, "The Lord gave, and the Lord has taken away;/ Blessed be the name of the Lord" (Job 1:21 NKJV). It was a defining moment.

Jesus asked His disciples who people were saying He was. Then He asked them who they thought He was. Peter answered, "You are the Christ, the Son of the living God" (Matt. 16:13–16 NKJV). It was a defining moment.

The Problem

Many defining moments result in men laying down their lives to serve others or display strong character, but sometimes men miss their moment.

When Richard Nixon was reelected to office in 1972, he immediately fired everyone on his staff. Bob Haldeman instructed them to prepare their letters of resignation. The troopers who labored so hard to reelect the president were stunned.

Following reelection, Nixon moved from the White House to Camp David for several weeks while putting together his new team. Harry Dent, special counsel to the president, was surprised to get the first call to Camp David. He boarded Marine One and made the short trip with Vice President Spiro Agnew—the only person Nixon could not fire.

Harry Dent was further surprised when he was invited to meet privately with Nixon—even before Agnew. What was to be a brief meeting turned into a two-hour session. Nixon wanted Dent to stay. Dent wanted to go home. After ten minutes of discussion on that subject, Dent spent the rest of their time imploring the president to deal with Watergate and to consider his place in history. As he poured out his heart, he shook the president.[2]

Looking back, Harry now realizes he missed his moment. For two hours he had the complete favor and attention of the president of the United States. Yet he chose to speak to the president about his place in history rather than his place in eternity. On the other hand, this incident became a powerful motivator for the rest of Harry Dent's life. Even a missed moment can become a defining moment.

Sometimes men miss more than their moment—they choose to do wrong. You've never fooled around before, but you're tired, you're out of town . . . You've never signed personally on a note before, but this deal really looks good . . .

Again, the Bible brims with examples. When Jesus told Pontius Pilate, "For this reason I was born, and for this I came into the world, to testify to the truth. Everyone on the side of truth listens to me." Pilate replied, "What is truth?" (John 18:37–38). It was a defining moment.

From the roof of his palace, David spotted the very beautiful Bathsheba bathing. He had a choice to make—to lust after her beauty or to look away. David gave in to temptation, committed adultery, and killed her husband (2 Sam. 11). It was a defining moment.

When God gave Jonah the task of going to Nineveh to preach against it, Jonah ran away from the Lord and headed to a different city. He ended up in the belly of a great fish (Jonah 1). It was a defining moment.

As covered in the chapter, "Restoration: The Prodigal Returns," "The Season of Renewal" includes turning back to God after a crisis of our own making. Also in this season are those occasional defining moments that, choosing rightly, put us firmly on the straight path or, choosing wrongly, can land us in a ditch.

As we have already seen, there are many types of defining moments. For the rest of this chapter, let's look at four "most" defining moments:

1. Control: To answer the question, "Who's in charge?"
2. Character: To decide you will take the blows.
3. Confidence: To accept God's love on God's terms.
4. Calling: To discern and accept His calling.

As we proceed, ask yourself, "How would the Holy Spirit have me respond?" Then, at the end of the chapter, you will have the opportunity to consider some choices.

Defining Moment #1: Control

I met a sharp young businessman on a plane. He prayed to receive Christ, but a few weeks later said, "I just can't give up control." Another man, a stockbroker, wouldn't attend our large Bible study, but wanted to meet privately. He had to be in charge—to do it his own way. Today he is divorced.

Every man must answer the question, "Who's in charge?" It is the issue of who has control. The kingdom of God is not about "praying a prayer" and then everything will turn out all right. Rather, the kingdom is a turning from self to God, a total release. It is to say, "I will go anywhere You want me to go, be anything You want me to be, do anything You want me to do." Obedience to God is the trademark of a Biblical Christian. It is how we demonstrate our love for God.

If you have not made the decision to receive Christ as your Savior, every other decision you make will be different from what it would have been if you had. If you have salvation and know it, but wrestle against putting Christ in charge of your life, every decision you make will be at risk. Personally, I had been a follower of Christ for twelve and a half years before I settled once and for all who would be in charge of my life. It's a tough surrender to make. The irony, of course, is that surrender ends not in defeat but in victory.

Have you settled the issue of who's in charge? Have you really turned from self to God? Released totally? Said you will go anywhere, be anything, do anything? Made a commitment to obey God?

Or do you have your life all planned out?

Here is the issue: Whether you know Christ already or not, will you say to Jesus, "Take control of my life; make me the kind of man You want me to be"? This issue is a defining moment.

Defining Moment #2: Character

Todd was the president of his high-school class. He played first team on the basketball squad, and his dream was to play college ball.

After the Christmas break during Todd's senior year, the coach never played him again. No explanation was given. The Lord gave Todd the grace to sit on the bench. He never complained. He never even asked the coach why, though many parents of other players were asking.

Week after week, sitting in the stands, the father of another player gained a profound respect for Todd as he quietly observed Todd's character. Two years later, when this high-powered businessman needed a key execu-tive assistant, the first call he placed was to Todd. Today Todd attends college full-time and pays his tuition by working for this man part-time in a career field he loves.

Todd didn't get to play college basketball—the basketball scouts never saw him play. Yet, Todd did find a rewarding career field. That's because a different kind of "scout" saw the character with which he *didn't* play. In a way, Todd did get a scholarship after all.

Every man must decide whether or not he will take the blows. This is the issue of suffering and hard times. They are defining moments.

To suffer is to be in God's school. The hard blow is a hammer that shapes our character on God's anvil.

Sometimes God's agenda is *correction*. We suffer for doing *wrong*. We experience discipline and punishment. God wants us to know that, yes, He does love us but, no, we can't have our own way.

Other times we suffer *persecution*. We suffer for doing *right*. We experi-ence confusion, and we don't know why. But we do know that God is good. We can trust Jesus. As Mother Teresa said, "Your sufferings are the kisses of Jesus."

Have you settled the issue of whether or not you will accept God's gracious blows? You can try to ward off life's blows if you want, or you can decide to stop chafing against the wisdom of God. Get in touch with the Father, not in resignation, but in submission. Know that His love is a Father's love. This decision is a defining moment. We will go into further depth on the issues of suffering in part 6 of this book, "The Season of Suffering."

Defining Moment #3: Confidence

The Bible says eternal life is a free gift. You and I know there is no such thing as a free gift. Everything has a price. Right? So our response is to discount this news, though we long to believe it. We even take the action of placing our faith in Jesus, hoping it is true. Yet, a residue of doubt remains.

This is the issue of assurance of salvation, or eternal security. It is the problem of uncertainty about God's love, forgiveness, and salvation. *It can't be that easy,* we think. *There must be more to it.* Or we have faith, we believe, but we still feel we are not good enough or worthy. So we think, *I've been so bad. I need to do something to continue to earn His favor.*

A typical way of dealing with this issue is to make a list of rules we can keep to try to be holy: Attend church, read the Bible, pray, serve on committees, and do a host of good deeds. Go here, go there, don't go there, say that, don't say that, don't look at that. Look, talk, and walk a certain way.

This is salvation by *performance.* The problem is that we will always find there is one more thing we can do.

Another typical way of dealing with this issue is to beat our breasts and constantly confess every peccadillo we can think up: "Lord, forgive me for not smiling at that older woman I passed in the grocery store aisle yesterday."

This is salvation by *confession.* The problem is that we will always find there is one more thing we can confess.

We can relax. Although eternal life is a free gift to us, it was not a free gift for Christ. He did pay a price for our eternal life. He gave His life. He accepted the judgment for sins that should have been ours. So it's not a free lunch after all. Read this next sentence slowly: Everything that needs to be done for you to be good enough in the sight of God has already been done by Jesus. Do you believe this by faith? Believing this by faith, and knowing more about how the Bible confirms this doctrine, is the key to eternal security.

Until we settle the issue of our eternal security, we will timidly perform and confess from a sense of duty. Our good deeds will lack the power that comes from knowing that our salvation is true.

When we accept that Christ has paid the whole price for our free gift on Calvary's cross, we will overflow in obedience and good deeds from a sense of gratitude. But, as Richard Niebuhr wrote, "If I have no confidence that the power that manifests itself in nature is God, I will accept nature's bounties without gratitude and its blows without repentance."[3]

Have you settled the issue of where you will spend eternity? Let the knowledge that God loves you move from your head to your heart. The longest distance in a man's life is the twelve inches that stretch between his head and his heart. Everything that needs to be done for you to be good enough in the sight of God has already been done by Jesus. This issue is a defining moment.

Defining Moment #4: Calling

Nine out of ten men I spend time with have the same question on their minds: "What does God want me to do? What is His will for my life?"

As followers of Christ, we must commit ourselves to discern and accept God's calling on our lives. This is the issue of letting ourselves be equipped and sent wherever God wants. This is the issue of our vocation and service. God has a job for each of us to do. Otherwise, why wouldn't He just beam us up when we receive Christ as Savior?

Those times when God changes His calling on our lives are defining moments. An unsettled period often precedes a change in calling. It is a time of equipping and reequipping. It is a season of working some things "into" our lives, and working some things "out of" our lives. Inevitably, God allows a lag time between the calling and the sending to break down wrong thinking and actions, and to rebuild others.

You cannot discover this calling if you are consumed by your own agenda. According to the pattern of the Bible, He probably wants you right where you are, but with a whole new orientation.

Have you settled the issue of your calling? Are you going in His direction or your own? This decision is a defining moment.

This issue is so important that we will devote all of chapter 22, "Discovering Your Calling," to help you explore your calling, vocation, service, and purpose in greater depth.

Suggestions

We cannot manufacture defining moments, but we should always have our antennae up for defining moments that come our way. We should have a sense of occasion for the monumental decision that might change the course of our lives. Give five-, ten-, or twenty-year decisions time to gestate. Don't make a choice until you have peace. God is not the author of confusion. Satan, however, is.

Personally, I write down defining moments and keep them in a biographical file entitled "Calling Journal" on my computer. I find that if I don't write them down, I tend to forget them. Writing them down gives me a powerful reference tool to look at when I get confused about what I'm supposed to be doing.

You may want to consider keeping a record of your defining moments. You could keep a file in your drawer or on your computer labeled something like "Calling Journal," "Defining Moments," or "Biographical Information." Then you will have benchmarks or signposts that you can look back on and refer to when God's will seems unclear.

John bumped into Marilyn at an eyeglasses store. He had not seen Marilyn for seven years when their sons had been close school friends.

She spoke first. Actually, John didn't recognize her right away. She had cancer the last time they had seen each other, and her emaciated body told him that she obviously still did.

John remembered the coat that Marilyn's son had outgrown and given to his boy. His son had long since outgrown the coat, so John wore it. Frankly, the only time he ever thought about Marilyn was when he put on that coat.

As they parted after a warm conversation, Marilyn added, "Come see me." John explained how his wife, Maureen, had a virus, but they would visit as soon as she was well.

A month went by until one Saturday morning John woke up with Marilyn's phone number going through his head. He didn't call. He thought, I'll call after church tomorrow. After church the next day, his son encouraged him to call. He finally called, but the person who answered the phone said she had been taken to the hospital.

John was relieved. *It will be a lot easier to visit her in the hospital,* he thought. *Boy, am I a coward.* He procrastinated for another hour, then went to a store where he bought a bird-of-paradise flower, and headed for the hospital.

When he arrived at Marilyn's room, he noticed a stir. Her husband came out to greet him and said, "Thanks for coming, John. Marilyn died an hour ago."

Later, as John recalled this story, he said, "And then he hugged me. Like I deserved it or something. I feel like such a slug."

This event became a defining moment for John. Never again would he put off until later what he sensed the Lord wanted him to do now.

Earlier in this chapter I suggested that you ask yourself, "How would the Holy Spirit have me respond?" What have you been putting off? Don't put off any longer what the Lord is telling you to do. Defining moments can make us or break us. The choice is ours.

QUESTIONS AND DECISIONS

1. *Control:* What keeps us from letting God be in charge of our lives? Have you settled the issue of who's in charge? Have you really turned from self to God? Released totally? Said you will go anywhere, be anything, do anything? Made a commitment to obey God? Or do you have your life all planned out?

2. Are you ready to say to Jesus, "Take control of my life; make me the kind of man You want me to be"? If yes, tell Him so now in prayer.

3. *Character:* Are you presently on God's anvil? What is your situation? Why do we resist being in God's school? Have you settled the issue of whether or not you will accept life's blows? Talk it over with Jesus in prayer.

4. *Confidence:* What happens when a man is unsure of his salvation? Have you settled the issue of where you will spend eternity? Let the knowledge that God loves you move from your head to your heart. Everything that needs to be done for you to be good enough in the sight of God has already been done by Jesus. If you have not settled this issue, is there any reason not to go ahead and settle it right now by faith through prayer?

5. *Calling:* Have you settled the issue of your calling? Are you going in His direction or your own? What decisions do you need to make?

6. Four biblical defining moments were mentioned in this chapter:

   - Joseph's decision about *how to respond to the wrong done to him by his own family:* "You meant it for harm, but God meant it for good."
   - John the Baptist's decision about *how to respond to the decline of his ministry:* "He must increase, but I must decrease."
   - Job's decision about *how to respond to the loss of his family and business:* "The Lord gave and the Lord has taken away./ Blessed be the name of the Lord."
   - Peter's decision about *how to view Jesus Christ:* "You are the Christ, the Son of the living God."

What are the defining moments before you? Are any of these four applicable? If so, why not talk them over with the Lord in prayer and settle these issues?

7. Is there anything else you have been putting off? Does it carry the weight of a defining moment? What is it? What should you do?

PART 5

●

THE SEASON OF

REBUILDING

The Summer of My Sin:
A Case Study, Part 4

17 It was a long, hot summer.

Over the last twenty-one years I have grown spiritually to the point that I am in the third major phase of my spiritual pilgrimage, as I mentioned in chapter 2—"The commitment to the God who is."

In this chapter I would like to share with you some of the most personal aspects of my life and make myself very vulnerable. As I write this book, I look back on this past summer as a season of renewal and rebuilding. It was a season in which God smashed many ideas I held about myself, my future, His character, and His plan. Over a five-month period He chastened, healed, restored, renewed, and rebuilt several key areas.

At the beginning of the summer I thought I was walking closely with my Lord. Indeed, I was. But I had no idea of how powerfully my flesh had deceived me. What follows are some lessons I've just learned at a deeper level.

"Don't Try to Make Up for Lost Time"

In 1991, I responded to a new calling in my life to move from real estate to ministry. Although I still have business interests, I have no day-to-day operating responsibilities.

For the next couple of years I worked extremely hard to become established in my new calling. One day I was standing around talking to one of our men's ministry leaders, and he made a statement that startled me. He said, "Pat, don't try to make up for lost time." *Zap!*

Suddenly, I realized that I was working so hard because I felt I should be producing at a certain level because of my age and experience. It was as though I had assumed God made a mistake by having me in business for twenty years, so I was going to help Him get me where I needed to be by working extra hard.

Since that day, I have pondered my friend's statement over and over again. God doesn't make mistakes. All the years you and I have spent and invested to this point, whether wisely or not, form part of a unique plan God has for our lives. There is no such thing as a wasted past. The past is one of the ingredients God uses to produce the character of Christ in us. When God calls us in a new direction, He will equip us to accomplish everything He intends without our having to "make up for lost time."

"You Don't Trust Me"

A month later I presented the keynote message for the Orlando Mayor's Prayer Breakfast here in my hometown. That kind of invitation just doesn't happen! Actually, it only came about because the scheduled speaker, Tom Skinner, couldn't come because he was ill.

As you can appreciate, I wanted to do a good job in my own hometown. I spent more than thirty hours preparing, and I completed six different drafts of my message. I simply couldn't make up my mind. At 6:30 the evening before the prayer breakfast, I asked Patsy if I could go over my sixth message with her.

Two sentences into the message I knew it was pointless—I still didn't have the right message. I became angry with God. I had worked my mind numb. As I was getting more and more worked up, the Lord revealed the problem to me. It was as though what He wanted me to understand was this: "You don't trust Me."

"O Lord, will I ever learn? I do trust You. I also trust the equipment You gave me." Notice the number of times the word *I* occurs in the preceding paragraphs. I had focused on my self-sufficiency instead of trusting the Lord and listening for His message to those people. In utter exhaustion I prayed and went to bed. I rose at 3:30 A.M., and one hour later I completed the seventh message *I* had prepared, but the first message from the Lord. I went straight from my study to the podium and gave a well-received message.

The lesson for me is this: Many times we become frustrated with God when all He is trying to do is remind us to depend upon Him, and not our own strengths and abilities.

The Motive for Good Deeds

Not long after that incident another one of our men's ministry leaders hit me in the solar plexus with a devotional based on Matthew 6:1, which says, "Take heed that you do not do your charitable deeds before men, to be seen by them. Otherwise you have no reward from your Father in heaven" (NKJV).

He challenged us to consider why we wanted to serve as leaders, why we attended our weekly Bible study, even why we attended seminars and did our quiet times. It was very convicting, and during a time of prayer, I repented. *To repent* means "to change direction."

Unfortunately, sometimes we can't change direction until we know the direction in which we are already going.

The next day I got wind that I was going to be asked to take a lesser role in a citywide rally in another city that was part of an ongoing ten-year plan for which I had the original vision. The year before, I had been a keynote speaker. This year they wanted to demote me to emcee. There is a world of difference between acting as a master of ceremonies and delivering a keynote message!

When I heard the news, I went ballistic! *I've paid my dues! I spent years and years doing emcee work!* For forty-five minutes I ranted at the chairman of the mission. I even halfheartedly threatened to not attend at all, admittedly the height of immaturity, and an act that would have damaged the continuity of the program. Finally, he suggested we give it a rest and discuss it again the next day.

The following day I called him on the phone from an airport. "Tom, I would like to apologize for the way I acted yesterday and ask for your forgiveness."

"You don't need to apologize," he offered.

"Yes, I do. Yesterday I showed you what I was capable of doing in the flesh. Today I would like the opportunity to show you what I can do by the Spirit. First, let me say that I will definitely be there. You can count on me. I would like you to put in writing exactly what you and the Executive Committee would like me to do, and then I will respond."

What devastated me the most about this incident was how quickly I collapsed into such a despicable display of flesh. God was showing me where I needed to change direction.

The flesh. I discovered something significant. The Bible says the flesh is *deceitful*. The Bible says the flesh is *wicked*. The Bible says the flesh is *weak*. However, the flesh is *most* deceitful, *most* wicked, and *most* weak when disguised as piety. The only thing worse than flesh is pious flesh.

Through self-deceit, I had constructed a mirror that reflected what I wanted to see. It was a warped image. God smashed my mirror, and I was surprised to learn there was a mirror behind the mirror. This second mirror gave a true reflection of who I am, and I didn't like what I saw at all. Once the distorted mirror was shattered, I could see in the second mirror behind it how I had misjudged my motives, my pride, and my ambition.

If there is any one most important lesson I have learned lately, it is this: The sins of our piety far exceed the sins of our immorality. The problem is that we do our sins of immorality in our own name, but we do our sins of piety in the name of Jesus.

God used this regrettable incident to reveal that my motives were not pure. I was not acting as a servant—I was trying to be a star. I was not motivated by wanting to serve Christ—I was trying to make a name for myself. I had started out with the idea of wanting to be used. Instead, I was acting like I wanted to be something. I was guilty of wanting to be seen. I had to ask myself, "What is the motivation for my good deeds?"

We worked it all out. I did everything they requested. Lately, I've been more sensitive that maybe my motives for doing good deeds need watching after. I do know this: As far as is possible, I have given up working out of my own righteousness.

Dietrich Bonhoeffer had this to say in his classic book, *The Cost of Discipleship:*

> [Jesus] says, "Take heed that ye do not your righteousness before men, to be seen of them." . . . Jesus warns us to take heed. He calls a halt to the innocent spontaneous joy we get from making our Christianity visible. He calls us to reflect on what we are doing. . . . If we want publicity in the eyes of men we have our reward. In other words, it is immaterial whether the publicity we want is the grosser kind, which all can see, or the more subtle variety which we can only see ourselves. Our old man must die with all his virtues and qualities, and this can only be done where the disciple forgets self and clings solely to Christ. . . . "I live; yet no longer I, but Christ liveth in me" (Gal. 2:20).[1]

Pride

Ninety percent of the business deals that don't work out fail not because of the terms but because of the relationships. Men get their pride wounded. They feel slighted. They feel they are not given enough attention or respect. They don't feel appreciated. They become jealous. They don't want to give up control or power. They think their prestige will be diminished. So the deal fails on ego rather than on lack of merit.

The greatest threat to each of us is pride. It is the most ingrained weakness in character and the most difficult to recognize.

This past summer I found myself feeling jealous of the platform speakers at a conference I was attending. "Where in the world did that come from?" I asked myself. God allowed me to fall into the abyss of pride that I might learn humility.

It may be difficult for you to understand how I could be jealous of a platform speaker—if you're not a platform speaker. But each of us can become jealous of men one, two, or three steps ahead of us in our own career field. Who's going to be more jealous of the number-one lawyer in your city—the 250th best lawyer or the second-best lawyer? The number-two man will, because number two hundred fifty has no chance of competing with him. But (in the flesh) number two will always have his eye on number one.

Andrew Murray wrote,

> The spirit of Him who washed the disciples' feet makes it a joy to us to be indeed the least, to be servants one of another. The humble man feels no jealousy or envy. He can praise God when others are preferred and blessed before him. He can bear to hear others praised and himself forgotten, because in God's presence he has learned to say with Paul, "I am nothing" (2 Corinthians 12:11). He has received the spirit of Jesus, who pleased not Himself and sought not His own honor.[2]

I have felt the bitter taste of jealousy and envy. Every man has. I can understand what Andrew Murray says. His words have personal meaning to me. Lately, God has been showing me that I need to be a servant, a slave of Christ. I need to guard against and forsake all human pride.

What to Do with Leftover Pain

What do we do with leftover pain? After I had worked through the sins of my summer, I was left with the genuine hurt of not being invited to give a major address at the citywide mission, of having fallen prey to pride, and of not trusting the Lord completely. There were other hurts as well.

When I became right with God, I had to ask, "What do I do with this leftover pain?" The Bible says, "[These sufferings are] for your benefit, so that *the grace that is reaching more and more people* may cause thanksgiving to overflow to the glory of God" (2 Cor. 4:15, emphasis added).

Pain, then, is the grace of God that is reaching more and more people to the glory of God. In other words, our sufferings touch other people's lives, and our witness in those sufferings causes them to turn to God. Pretty neat, don't you think?

Pain has purpose. Pain is the greatest teacher. Pain produces growth. Pain focuses us. God uses pain to point us in a new direction. God uses pain to make us more sensitive to others, to comfort them, to remind us not to rely on ourselves, to send us back to the foot of the cross.

Pain is the grace of God that shows me *who* I am, *whose* I am, *what* is the purpose of my life, and *who* is the purpose of my life.

I learned that we should not be hasty to rid ourselves of leftover pain. Instead, we should search for the message. What is God trying to teach us? For whom else is our lesson intended?

"Conquered by Grace"

I told my wife, Patsy, that until further notice, if I should die, she should put on my tombstone, "Conquered by Grace."

Man is a rebel. I am a rebel. I did not come willingly to the cross, but Christ regenerated my heart. He put in me the desire to know Him: "No one can come to Me unless the Father who sent Me draws him; and I will raise him up at the last day" (John 6:44 NKJV). When I came, I came willingly, but not until He had immersed me in the warmth of His marvelous grace. He conquered my rebel spirit by His grace.

Over and over again, the Spirit of the living Christ overcomes my willful, prideful flesh. How I thank Jesus for His immeasurable grace poured out upon me! He spilled His blood so that I might live.

In the years that have followed my initial conversion I have had dozens of additional conversion experiences. I am always surprised to learn there is yet another area of my life that I thought was yielded to God, but was not. As God reveals these weaknesses and sins, one by one, I am grateful that He also gives the conquering grace to work them through.

As a matter of my upbringing, I tend to lead a moral life—usually by depending on God, but sometimes by relying on my own strength. Living a clean life only tends to disguise the more subtle sins of piety that are born in the flesh. I get sucked into sins like doing my good deeds to be seen by men, wanting to be something instead of wanting to be used, and so on.

Yet, every time I stray I soon hear the gentle voice of Jesus calling for me above the din of all those supposedly crucial activities. Jesus comes looking for His lost sheep, His prodigal. One might think I would be happy to see Him, but actually, I don't usually think I have wandered away. I really do want to control my own life. I really do not want to be dependent on someone else. So Jesus has to make my circumstances so uncomfortable that I call out for relief. This pain is grace. He conquers me by His grace.

I have been conquered by grace, and I am being conquered by grace. The Lord Jesus continually pours out His grace and mercy to me, a sinner. We will never fully arrive until Christ returns. The portion of the kingdom we have is only a foretaste of the coming kingdom.

We belong to Jesus. We have been bought with a price, and we are not our own. With Paul, we should say, "I have been crucified with Christ; it is no longer I who live, but Christ lives in me; and the life which I now live in the flesh I live by faith in the Son of God, who loved me and gave Himself for me" (Gal. 2:20 NKJV). We who belong to Jesus should no longer live for ourselves but live for Him who died for us and was raised again (see 2 Cor. 5:15).

God has a purpose for our lives. He wants to rebuild and renew us so we can both know and do His will.

The New Paradigm:
Four Crucial Conversions

"Conversion is to give as much of your self as you can to as much of God as you can understand, and to do so every day."

—Bishop William Temple

18 A man talked out of jumping off the ledge of a high-rise office building may have just had his life saved, but he still needs a lot of work to make him whole again.

Every man saved by Jesus was on a suicide mission. He was headed toward destruction. But once saved from the ledge he stills needs to solve the problems that drove him there in the first place. There is a difference between *salvation* and *sanctification*.

Salvation takes place in an instant of fully yielding the control of our lives to the saving grace of our Lord Jesus Christ, who is the atoning sacrifice for our sins. *Sanctification*, however, is the lifelong process of each day becoming more like Jesus.

If you don't know what sanctification means, you should. Look it up in the dictionary. It should be a central concept in the life of every true believer. It is a God-centered idea, not a man-centered idea.

Paradigm "Shift" or "Different" Paradigm?

When a man gives his life to Jesus in our culture, we immediately begin to teach him to pretend that he has it all together. We socialize him to pretend that he doesn't have any more problems. Actually, a newly committed or recommitted man ought to rethink everything he has been taught about what Christianity is.

Is it a paradigm "shift" we need to make, or do we need a completely "different" paradigm? Different ones of us will necessarily come to different conclusions. But let me suggest that biblical Christianity—building the kingdom—is a radically different model from what many of us have become accustomed to in today's culture.

The Paradigm Is Jesus

Jesus said, "I am the way."

Jesus is our example.

Jesus set the example for how we live our lives.

The paradigm is Jesus.

Jesus is the object of our faith.

Biblical Christianity is Jesus.

A friend called me to talk about the head of a local ministry in which he had been helping. The man he was calling about is the most loving man I have personally ever known. He said, "I'm having some problems with _____." He briefly went on to elaborate.

I said, "The problem you are having is that he is too much like Jesus."

Biblical Christianity is not a business. It is medicine for people sick unto death. It is healing by the Great Physician. Too often we want people to think in the narrow categories of American, Aristotelian, linear logic—we want to chart Jesus on a graph. We can't do that. He won't let us.

When we build on Him, we find a whole different way of life. We find a good explanation of it in 2 Corinthians 5:14–18:

> FOR CHRIST'S LOVE COMPELS US, BECAUSE WE ARE CONVINCED
> THAT ONE DIED FOR ALL, AND THEREFORE ALL DIED. AND HE
> DIED FOR ALL, THAT THOSE WHO LIVE SHOULD NO LONGER LIVE
> FOR THEMSELVES BUT FOR HIM WHO DIED FOR THEM AND WAS
> RAISED AGAIN. SO FROM NOW ON WE REGARD NO ONE FROM A
> WORLDLY POINT OF VIEW. THOUGH WE ONCE REGARDED CHRIST IN
> THIS WAY, WE DO SO NO LONGER. THEREFORE, IF ANYONE IS IN
> CHRIST, HE IS A NEW CREATION; THE OLD HAS GONE, THE NEW
> HAS COME! ALL THIS IS FROM GOD, WHO RECONCILED US TO
> HIMSELF THROUGH CHRIST AND GAVE US THE MINISTRY OF
> RECONCILIATION.

Let's look more closely at some of the ingredients.

- We are compelled by Christ's love.
- We no longer live for ourselves but for Him.
- We have a whole new way of looking at people.

- We are new creations in Jesus.
- The old nature is gone; a new nature has come.
- We are reconciled to God.
- We have been entrusted with the ministry of reconciling others to God.

This faith is no simple paradigm shift. Biblical Christianity is a radically different paradigm. It is a whole different way of living. Why don't our lives look like this?

We don't look like this model of Biblical Christianity because we have unfinished business. We have not crucified everything on the cross. We have whole tracts of our lives unconverted. And why is that? We have not been willing to let God control us completely. We have not been willing to give up the world completely. And why is that? We have been preaching a gospel not worth making a sacrifice for. A small challenge has led to a small response.

Jesus calls men to a radically different way of thinking and living. It is an altogether different paradigm from what many of us have been led to believe.

On the other hand, the way of Jesus is not to be feared. Jesus will never force you to be someone you don't want to be. Recently, some friends went to Africa as missionaries, easily the worst fear of every new convert. Yet, they went to Africa because they *wanted* to go. Jesus put the desire in their hearts to go. He will not ask you to do something without also giving you the desire.

Conversion

Easily the most difficult challenge of Christian living is the conversion from the old life of "the flesh" to the new life in "the Spirit." In fact, we relapse, but we can be encouraged that it occurs less frequently the longer and closer we walk with Jesus. So the challenge is to increasingly walk in the Spirit and not in the flesh.

Bishop William Temple said, "Conversion is to give as much of your self as you can to as much of God as you can understand, and to do so every day." *Conversion* means "to transform, to change from one use to another."

Conversion from the old life of the flesh to the new life in the Spirit necessarily takes place over an entire lifetime. We are not called upon to wear size ten shoes when we have grown only to size four feet. The more we know, however, the better the quality of life with Christ.

A man should not be discouraged if he wants to be a size ten Christian, but wears only a size four boot right now. God grows us at the pace He deems best for us, knowing every motive of our hearts and every weakness that must be overcome.

A man in the rebuilding season of life must yield areas to the sufficiency of Christ. This yielding is a growing commitment. Four areas in particular that need to be converted to the ways of the Spirit of Jesus deserve special attention: the *heart*, the *head*, the *calendar*, and the *wallet*. Let's take each of these in turn.

Your Heart

A man married the love of his life. He worshiped the very ground she walked on. He spent every waking moment serving her. From sunup to sunset, thoughts of how to make her happy consumed him.

Because he diligently worked so hard to provide for her, he spent most of his time away from her. The harder he worked to serve her, the happier he was, but the less time he actually spent with her. She, on the other hand, missed the time they once spent together when they first met. He believed she was someone very special, but as the years rolled by, he couldn't say that he really knew her.

Perhaps the single greatest risk of walking with Jesus is that we would lose our first love. What starts out as a wonderful love relationship is reduced to an endless repetition of religious tasks and activities—all of which are intended to please Him. Yet, what He wants most is not what we can do for Him. He wants us. He wants a relationship. He wants us to talk with Him and spend time with Him in much the same way as our wives do.

It is not enough to give Jesus your life. You must also give Him your heart.

How do you give your heart to Jesus? Give priority above all else to your personal relationship with Jesus. Become the lover of Jesus. Give Him your affections. This is the decision to let your heart be converted. Have you given your heart to Jesus?

An irony about serving God exists. If we love Him with all our hearts, then we will serve Him with all our might. Yet, we don't love God because we serve Him; we serve God because we love Him. In other words, serving

God with the totality of our strength and being will not bring us to love Jesus. Rather, out of our overflow of loving Him, His love compels us to do something wonderful for Him because of the rich deposits of gratitude building up in our hearts.

A caution is necessary. Devotion to God is paramount, but this alone may lead one to become what we could call an emotional hearer. Devotion must be accompanied by knowledge.

Your Head

One day one of my son's coaches called to cancel practice because he was sick. Wanting to express genuine concern and an evangelistic witness, I said, "I'm sorry to hear that. I'll pray for you."

A few weeks later I had to call him to cancel for my son because he was having some lower-back pain. After I explained what steps we were taking to get him better, he felt compelled to return the favor I had shown him. He said, "I'll pray for him and keep my fingers crossed!"

He wanted to cover all the bases! What he was essentially saying was this: "I'll pray in case there is a God who hears, and I'll cross my fingers in case it's all up to chance." All bets were covered! Obviously, he was making a harmless social gesture, but it does illustrate how many people simply don't know any better because they don't have enough knowledge about God.

Biblical Christianity is a thinking man's religion; it is a religion of the mind. It consists of specific truths, and these truths are knowable. We make choices based upon what we know. It is, therefore, crucial to know what we believe and why. It is essential to the work of God's kingdom to think rightly.

It is not enough to give Jesus your heart. You must also give Him your head.

How do we give our heads to Jesus? We give our minds to Jesus by developing a Christian worldview. Unfortunately, the Christian worldview has competitors, such as Islam, Judaism, naturalism, New Age, and so on. These competing ideas are floating around in the culture, and we must learn to distinguish among them and how they influence us.

Have you developed a Christian worldview, or are you stuck in a gospel that looks more cultural than biblical? Perhaps you would like to join me in saying, "Lord, I confess my culture. Relieve me of the burden of my culture. Help me to think biblically. Help me develop a Christian worldview. Let me see Jesus. Amen."

If you need to spend some time developing a Christian worldview, let me encourage you to talk to your pastor or an employee of a Christian bookstore for recommended reading.

Your Calendar

One day I was invited to have lunch with a wealthy retired Christian businessman. During the course of lunch, I asked him, "What do you do with your time?"

"I do whatever I want to do," he replied a bit too quickly. I remember thinking at the time that he probably had not thought deeply about the responsibilities of Christian wealth.

What was he really saying? He was making a statement about how he runs his life—about how he had dealt with the issue, "Who's in charge?"

In describing his own relationship with Christ, author Gary Smalley paints a far different picture of how he spends his time. Each day when he awakens, he takes his empty cup, gets in line, and goes to meet with Jesus. Then during the day, he empties out his cup serving others. The next day, he gets up, takes his empty cup, once again stands in line, and starts all over again.

It is not enough to give Jesus your heart and your head. You must also give Him control over your time.

How do you give your calendar to Jesus? If your heart and your mind have truly been converted, your calendar will follow. You convert your calendar by telling Jesus, "I will go anywhere You want me to go, do anything You want me to do, and be anything You want me to be." This is the decision to convert your time to Christ. Why not tell this to Jesus right now?

Your Wallet

As alluded to earlier, most of my early life was devoted to thinking about the next thing I wanted to acquire. Unfortunately, this current era is not much different.

I would like you to reflect carefully on what I am about to say. *Our Christian culture tends to teach that we own our money and should give some of it back to God. The Bible, however, teaches that God owns everything and allows us to keep up to 90 percent of it, for which we remain responsible as stewards.*

Biblical Christianity is a whole new orientation to money. If your heart has been converted, the question is, "Has your wallet been converted too?"

What will happen if we yield control of our money to Jesus? The Bible says, to paraphrase, "Where your wallet is there will your heart be also." If we give our money to Jesus, He will draw us closer still into the safety of His pasture. He will release us from our bondage to money. He will set us free to serve Him financially with gladness.

It is not enough to give Jesus your heart, your head, and your calendar. You must also give Him control over your money. Have you ever said to Christ, "I not only give you control of my heart, but I give you control of my finances"? If not, perhaps there will be no better time than this moment. Why not tell Him you will do it?

A Conversion Prayer

You may want to express your desire to convert areas of your life to God in prayer. Use your own words, or you can pray this prayer:

Lord, I want to go all the way. I want to be sold out to Jesus. I will go wherever you want me to go, do whatever you want me to do, and be whatever you want me to be. I want to be out-and-out for Christ. I want to be committed to the gospel of the kingdom. I want to be converted in my heart, my head, my calendar, and my wallet. Make me a new creation. Rebuild and renew my life. Put in me a new season for your praise and glory. I want to give as much of myself as I can to as much of you as I can understand. In Jesus' name I pray, Amen.

QUESTIONS AND DECISIONS

1. How have you been socialized to pretend you have it all together?

2. What is the difference between salvation and sanctification?

3. Comment on the following statements:

   - The paradigm is Jesus. He is the object of our faith. Biblical Christianity is Jesus. He is our example.
   - Biblical Christianity is not a business. It is medicine for people sick unto death. It is healing by the Great Physician. Too often we want people to think in the narrow categories of American, Aristotelian, linear logic—we want to chart Jesus on a graph. We can't do that. He won't let us.

4. What areas of your life are unconverted? What frightens you about the thought of giving those areas to Jesus?

5. *Your heart.* Have you fully given your heart to Jesus? Decide to give priority above all else to your personal relationship with Jesus. Become the lover of Jesus. Give Him your affections.

6. *Your head.* Have you developed a Christian worldview and way of thinking, or are you stuck in a gospel that looks more Cultural than Biblical? If you would like to, pray, "Lord, I confess my culture. Relieve me of the burden of my culture. Help me to think biblically. Help me develop a Christian worldview. Let me see the way of Jesus more clearly. Amen."

7. *Your calendar.* Have you surrendered your time and calendar to Christ? You convert your calendar by telling Jesus, "I will go anywhere You want me to go, do anything You want me to do, and be anything You want me to be." If you are prepared to do so, tell this to Jesus right now.

8. *Your wallet.* Have you ever said to Christ, "I not only give you control of my heart, but I give you control of my finances"? If not, perhaps there will be no better time than this moment. If you are prepared to do so, tell this to Jesus right now.

Restoring Relationships

If we could read the secret history of our enemies, we should find in each man's life sorrow and suffering enough to disarm all hostility.

—Henry Wadsworth Longfellow

19 The Problem

At the office I can always tell if someone's phone call relates to a task problem or a relationship problem.

If it is a task problem, the person picks up the phone, talks for three minutes, then hangs up, smiling—mission accomplished.

If it is a relationship problem, though, the person answers the phone, and soon his shoulders begin to slump. Keep watching and you will see a deep furrow slowly spread across his forehead. You can feel the weight of the call, even though you're not in on the details. Thirty minutes later the person slowly replaces the receiver in the cradle, heaves a deep sigh, and looks around for the aspirin bottle.

The difference between solving a task problem and a relationship problem is about twenty-seven minutes, depending on how badly the relationship has deteriorated.

Of all the areas that suffer from poor choices, the one area that suffers most is our relationships. Even though we get into right relationship with God through recommitment, we are not automatically in right relationship with one another. The second most important thing to God is that we get into right relationship with one another.

Jesus put it this way: "A new command I give you: Love one another. As I have loved you, so you must love one another" (John 13:34). After saying the greatest commandment is to love God, Jesus said, "And the second is like it: 'Love your neighbor as yourself'" (Matt. 22:39).

The apostle John wrote, "Dear friends, let us love one another, for love comes from God. Everyone who loves has been born of God and knows God. . . . Dear friends, since God so loved us, we also ought to love one another. . . . And he has given us this command: Whoever loves God must also love his brother" (1 John 4:7, 11, 21).

Each day when you arrive home, your wife and kids hear a first signal that you are about to reenter their orbit. Maybe it's the sound of your tires squealing on the driveway, the garage door going up, a barking dog, or the door slamming shut as you step inside. When she hears you coming, what does she feel inside? Does she feel a flood of warmth and anticipation flow through her heart, or does she tense up? When they realize "Dad's home," what do your kids think? Is it a time of great joy, or is it a time of not knowing what to expect? Do you bring life, love, and encouragement home with you?

On this journey we make some poor choices. The lingering effects of our poor choices are most keenly felt at the point of our relationships. It is also the most difficult area to rebuild; a broken relationship is not easily repaired. Once faith and trust have been broken, the road back is rocky. Wounded loved ones end up feeling bruised, hurt, fragile, and tender. It takes a tender, sensitive, loving man to restore a tender relationship.

The closer to the center of our lives we get, the greater the stakes if we create broken relationships. The nucleus of our relationships is the family. With this in mind, this chapter focuses on family relationships. However, the same principles readily apply elsewhere too. The responsibility for restoring tender, bruised relationships falls to the man as the spiritual leader of his home. It is not enough to provide for physical well-being of our families; we must also be tender with them. Let's look at four characteristics of a tender man:

1. A tender man *initiates healing*.
2. A tender man *listens attentively*.
3. A tender man *expresses remorse* and *seeks forgiveness*.
4. A tender man *perseveres* when reconciliation is not immediate.

Let's look into each of these crucial steps for healing damaged relationships.

1. Initiate Healing

A man's daughter away at college started living with a boy. It drove him crazy. He cut her off financially and was so angry that he wouldn't speak to her. Their relationship continued to deteriorate. He was deeply offended by what she did, and embarrassed too. He took it as a slap in the face of all the upbringing he had poured into her life. Later, after he cooled down, while he didn't want to approve of her behavior, he did long to give her a hug and say, "I love you." Yet, his pride was wounded, so he did nothing.

The Bible says, "Therefore, if you are offering your gift at the altar and there remember that your brother has something against you, leave your gift there in front of the altar. First go and be reconciled to your brother; then come and offer your gift" (Matt. 5:23–24).

The Bible says that reconciliation should precede worship. If we have broken relationships, the Scriptures command us to go and be reconciled first—before we worship. Said another way, we cannot worship God acceptably if we are at odds with someone.

The verse says, "If you are offering your gift at the altar *and there remember that your brother has something against you,* leave your gift," and go and be reconciled. Please notice something extremely important: The verse doesn't give regard to who is at fault. Your wife may erroneously hold something against you. You think she's wrong. It doesn't matter if you are right or think you are in the right. God says, "Go and be reconciled."

In other words, whether you are right or wrong doesn't matter. What matters is that the relationship is not right. If you know the relationship isn't right, right or wrong, you must initiate reconciliation. And all the more if you know you are in the wrong. It takes a tender man to initiate healing a tender relationship. Is there someone with whom you need to initiate healing?

2. Listen Attentively

Just twenty months after Stephen's father died, Stephen's mother became deathly ill.

In the days that followed, eight of her nine children came to pay their last respects. One daughter, however, underestimated how serious her mother's condition had become.

Every day Stephen's mother asked about her daughter, "Has anybody called her? Does she know I'm sick?" She had nightmares because her daughter didn't come. Finally, she passed away. Her daughter never came. Stephen said, "I was filled up with so much anger toward my sister that I could not pray and be healed."

Over the years other offenses had built up too. You could cut the family tension with a knife. Two of his sisters had the idea to convene a weekend family gathering to hash things out. All the brothers and sisters found the idea agreeable, and they set a date.

After starting with a meal together, they were given the chance to say whatever was on their minds—how much they hurt and why, and how others had made them feel. There were some emotions, some anger, and some shouting, but nothing out of control.

They listened carefully to each other. Because they heard each other, each one felt led to apologize, express remorse, and forgive each other. Their gathering became a healing weekend that brought the family back together again.

To rebuild relationships requires active listening. How does a doctor heal the body? By asking questions and listening attentively to the patient. He cannot heal without careful listening.

Why do two employees end up in a conflict? Because they don't listen carefully and really hear each other. How do you resolve a conflict between two employees? By helping them to calm down enough to hear each other. Actually, you don't resolve the conflict. You mediate so that they can resolve their conflict.

You must understand the other person's point of view. He may not be acting rationally, but there are reasons why he does what he does. It takes a tender man to listen attentively. Is there someone to whom you need to listen more attentively?

3. Express Remorse and Seek Forgiveness

If your wife has asked you for years to help with small chores around the house and for years you have given her a hard time, she harbors resentment against you for not being a team player.

If you decide because of reading this chapter or because of some other reason that you have not done right by her and want to set things straight, how would you go about it? Would you tell her, "I'm sorry," and expect everything to turn out right?

I'm sorry and *I forgive you* are key words in healing any relationship.

However, to be sorry is enough to begin healing, but it is not enough to finish the job. The question is, "Sorry about what?" For all she knows, you could be sorry you couldn't get her to stop asking for your help.

When we hurt somebody the same way over and over again, each additional offense adds another brick to a wall building up between us. However big or small the wall, that wall represents a history.

To bring down the walls that build up between us, we need to initiate healing, listen attentively, and give the offended party an opportunity to express the grievance, anger, hurt, and pain. Then we must express genuine remorse or regret.

For remorse to be sincere, one must make a pledge to change. Without a willingness to change there is no evidence of true remorse, or repentance. Is there someone to whom you need to express true remorse?

It is by forgiving and asking forgiveness that relationships are healed. Until someone says, "I'm truly sorry. Please forgive me," there is a stalemate. Until the offended party says, "I forgive you," healing can't take place.

Forgiveness is a damp cloth wiped across a blackboard of recorded grievances that erases even the trace of the offense.

Our relationship with God depends upon our willingness to forgive those who sin against us. Immediately after teaching the disciples how to pray, Jesus told them, "For if you forgive men when they sin against you, your heavenly Father will also forgive you. But if you do not forgive men their sins, your Father will not forgive your sins" (Matt. 6:14–15). Forgiving is not optional.

Jesus said, "If your brother sins, rebuke him, and if he repents, forgive him. If he sins against you seven times in a day, and seven times comes back to you and says, 'I repent,' forgive him" (Luke 17:3–4). Mark Twain is reported to have said, "Forgiveness is the fragrance the violet sheds on the heel that crushed it."

Is there someone from whom you need to seek forgiveness? Is there someone you need to offer forgiveness from whom you have been withholding it? No matter how egregious the offense, the rule of Jesus is to forgive.

4. Persevere

A number of years ago I was talking on the phone to one of my brothers. We got into a dispute, and before I knew it, we were yelling at each other. In utter frustration I returned the phone to the receiver quite a bit more forcefully than recommended.

Later, I felt terrible over the things I had said but didn't know exactly what to do. It had been a really bad scene. After prayer, I had an idea.

I wrote out a note in which I apologized and asked for his forgiveness. I loaded my family into the car, went by the bakery, and bought a box of fresh-baked chocolate chip cookies, then drove to his apartment. Unfortunately, his car wasn't in the lot.

After I had knocked enough times to make sure he wasn't there, I put the note and the cookies between the screen door and the door to his apartment.

I never heard from him.

It took several years and much prayer before our relationship began to recover. That's one of the prices of hurting each other. Sometimes the wounds don't heal overnight.

A tender man will persevere when reconciliation is not immediate. We cannot control the other person. We can control ourselves. We can only continue to respond in the Spirit. Is there someone you have given up on? Is there someone you need to redouble your efforts with and persevere with?

Dealing with Conflict

Obviously, if we can avoid conflict in the first place, our relationships will be far better off. But conflict is part of life, so knowing how to deal with conflict is a critical part of living together.

Some time ago our kids, like all kids, were fighting too much in the mornings getting ready for school. My reaction to all of this was the typical male overreaction, which got us nowhere. Finally, I figured the best thing I could do was to sort out my thoughts and feelings in writing, and then have a family meeting to see if we could iron things out calmly. Here is the text of what I wrote:

To: Patsy, Jen, and John:
   I would like us to calmly discuss the following issues and any others you think we should talk over.
   1. I have feelings too. I feel like no one cares how I feel when these hurtful words are spoken.
   2. I don't think it is right to say hurtful things. Wisdom dictates that people use self-control and not say everything that comes to mind.

3. It's not right. To say "I can't stand you" is just plain wrong, no matter how you look at it. No amount of talking can justify this. No amount.

4. I don't feel like you two kids are "fighting fair."

5. I am concerned about your long-term relationship with each other.

6. I feel like the attention always shifts from the issue to how I seem to be handling (or mishandling) it. So, the focus shifts from the *issue* to the *process*. I may have some problems in processing, but that doesn't get at the heart of the issue. I'm not the one starting these conflicts!

7. There is a right way and a wrong way to deal with interpersonal tensions. To scream at the other person and to say something hurtful or to ignore the other person and walk away are wrong ways. What is the right way? I'm not sure I have the answer, but these ideas seem to be at least part of the solution:

To avoid conflict:

- Pray for and act out a Christlike attitude. Ask yourself, "What would He do?"
- Don't expect to always get exactly what you want—it's a family.
- Don't be petty. Let offenses go.
- Be more concerned about the relationship than getting your own way.
- Don't lose your temper. It does not bring about the righteous life God desires.

To resolve conflict:

- Again, don't lose your temper. It does not bring about the righteous life God desires.
- Try counting to ten.
- Try walking away, suggesting you discuss it later after you cool down.
- Don't attack the other *person;* stay focused on the *issue.*
- Don't try to hurt the other person intentionally.
- Instead, talk about what you want to happen and your own feelings.
- Try to understand the other person's point of view.
- Be quick to apologize.

In one short meeting, we changed the entire texture of our mornings. Are there elements here that could be applied in a family meeting of your own?

Families that work well expect some conflict and have thought through some ground rules for dealing with it.

Conclusion

It is true that relationships often take more time than tasks. It is true that relationships often cause more conflict than tasks. It is true that relationships talk back, and sometimes we have to compromise. Somehow, though, we must get hold of the idea that Jesus puts the premium on relationships, not tasks. The only "new" commandment Jesus gave during His earthly ministry was that we love one another as He loved us. This love is the glue that can keep us together and the oil that can keep us from rubbing each other the wrong way.

QUESTIONS AND DECISIONS

1. Which of the following four steps to restore broken, tender relationships are strengths for you? Which are weaknesses? What is a specific action you can take right now as a result of this chapter?

   1. A tender man *initiates healing.*
   2. A tender man *listens attentively.*
   3. A tender man *expresses remorse* and *seeks forgiveness.*
   4. A tender man *perseveres* when reconciliation is not immediate.

2. Is there someone with whom you need to initiate healing? What should you do?

3. Is there someone to whom you need to listen more attentively? What should you do?

4. Is there someone to whom you need to express true remorse? What should you do?

5. Is there someone from whom you need to seek forgiveness? Is there someone you need to offer forgiveness from whom you have been withholding it? What should you do?

6. Is there someone you have given up on? Is there someone you need to redouble your efforts with and persevere with? What should you do?

7. "Families that work well expect some conflict and have thought through some ground rules for dealing with it." Do you ☐ agree/ ☐ disagree? Explain your answer. Have you developed ground rules of your own?

Three "Private" Spiritual Disciplines

Unless in the first waking moment of the day you learn to fling the door wide back and let God in, you will work on a wrong level all day; but swing the door wide open and pray to your Father in secret, and every public thing will be stamped with the presence of God.
—Oswald Chambers[1]

Once upon a time I was an avid fisherman. Then I caught "the big one"—a nine-pound, thirteen-ounce smallmouth bass. (I had it stuffed to prove I did it.) After that, fishing never turned my crank like it did before. Here's how it happened. . . .

It was a warm, muggy Memorial Day morning. My wife and two small children took advantage of the holiday and slept in. Not me, though. I was out on the lake early. Ordinarily, my little johnboat would slip across the water at the slightest breeze, but this still day it sat like it was frozen in concrete. I hit the battery-powered trolling motor and glided another few yards around the shoreline.

I positioned myself about fifty feet from shore—the perfect distance to cast the oil-colored plastic worm on a weedless hook that I was using for bait. On each cast I carefully selected what looked like the place I would wait for a worm if I were the Loch Ness Bass.

On my first pass around the lake I didn't get a single strike. I had just passed by our dock when I heard the water ripple slightly on the other side of my boat. As the good hand of Providence would have it, I was just completing working my plastic worm in from the shoreline. Bored, I gave it a little flick of the wrist. I was surprised to see the worm land on the other side of the boat precisely where the water had rippled.

Immediately, something akin to King Kong with fins grabbed my bait and started to run. My heart stopped beating. The reel whirred wildly as my line ripped through the water. *Could this be my day?* I wondered.

Now, the number-one rule for catching bass is that you let the fish run with the bait. If you try to set the hook too soon, the bass will simply spit out the bait and, with it, the hook. What you want to do is make sure the fish feels no resistance so that it will think it has the worm, no "strings" attached. You want that bass to get lulled into a false sense of confidence—to feel safe enough to swallow the whole bait. So you let it run, count to ten or twenty real slow, then give a strong yank, and set the hook. After that, all you do is reel her in—there's no way for her to get off the hook.

That's how I caught my big one. And that's exactly how Satan works too. He lets us grab the bait, but he doesn't try to set the hook right away. Instead, he lets us run a while until we lull ourselves into a false confidence. Then, just when we are sure it's safe, he sets the hook, and it's too late. All that's left is to reel us in. Have you ever felt like Satan had you hooked? Have you had the helpless feeling of being reeled in, and there was nothing you could do about it?

A Spiritual Battle

Actually, there is something we can do about it. We can constantly realize that we are in a spiritual battle. We have an enemy who wants to defeat our Christian faith—an enemy who wants to distract us, discourage us, disillusion us, and defeat us. That's why the apostle Paul made frequent use of the military image: "Endure hardship with us like a good soldier of Christ Jesus" (2 Tim. 2:3).

We won't win the spiritual battle, though, if we identify it as a worldly war. The Bible says, "For our struggle is not against flesh and blood, but against the rulers, against the authorities, against the powers of this dark world and against the spiritual forces of evil in the heavenly realms" (Eph. 6:12). Our enemy is the devil.

Nor will we win if we fight with the wrong weapons. If your dog had fleas, you wouldn't try to get rid of them with a shotgun. You wouldn't try to get the chinch bugs out of your lawn by using dynamite. You wouldn't try to repel a charging pit bull with a flyswatter.

Too often we try to win the daily battles we fight with worldly weapons—working harder, positive thinking, better planning, et cetera. However, a spiritual battle can be won only with spiritual weapons. The weapons God offers us in the Bible—the armor of God—are often referred to as "the spiritual disciplines." Many of them are referred to in the passage immediately after Ephesians 6:12 cited above:

THEREFORE PUT ON THE FULL ARMOR OF GOD, SO THAT WHEN THE DAY OF EVIL COMES, YOU MAY BE ABLE TO STAND YOUR GROUND, AND AFTER YOU HAVE DONE EVERYTHING, TO STAND. STAND FIRM THEN, WITH THE BELT OF TRUTH BUCKLED AROUND YOUR WAIST, WITH THE BREASTPLATE OF RIGHTEOUSNESS IN PLACE, AND WITH YOUR FEET FITTED WITH THE READINESS THAT COMES FROM THE GOSPEL OF PEACE. IN ADDITION TO ALL THIS, TAKE UP THE SHIELD OF FAITH, WITH WHICH YOU CAN EXTINGUISH ALL THE FLAMING ARROWS OF THE EVIL ONE. TAKE THE HELMET OF SALVATION AND THE SWORD OF THE SPIRIT, WHICH IS THE WORD OF GOD. AND PRAY IN THE SPIRIT ON ALL OCCASIONS WITH ALL KINDS OF PRAYERS AND REQUESTS. WITH THIS IN MIND, BE ALERT AND ALWAYS KEEP ON PRAYING FOR ALL THE SAINTS. (Eph. 6:13–18)

As you can see from the text, some of these weapons, or "disciplines," are offensive, while others are defensive.

What Is Spiritual Discipline?

The Bible exhorts us to discipline ourselves to be godly. Paul wrote the key instruction about spiritual discipline: "Have nothing to do with godless myths and old wives' tales; rather, train yourself to be godly. For physical training is of some value, but godliness has value for all things, holding promise for both the present life and the life to come" (1 Tim. 4:7–8). *Train yourself to be godly.* In this short phrase lies a priceless truth: Godliness doesn't just happen; you've got to pay the price.

Training is the avenue to excellence in any field. The ingredient that NBA greats Larry Bird, Magic Johnson, and Michael Jordan had in common was that they were willing to pay the price in practice and preparation for the game that others were not willing to pay. William De Vries, who installed the first artificial heart, said, "The reason you practice so much is so that you will do things automatically the same way every time."[2] Buz Braman, shooting coach for the Orlando Magic, says the goal of practice is to build up muscle memory so you can repeat in the game what you did in practice. In the same way, we achieve spiritual excellence by paying the price, by practicing what we are not good at so we will do things automatically, and by building up our "faith muscle" memory.

Unfortunately, for most of us the tendency is to not be disciplined. In the Garden of Gethsemane, Jesus told His disciples to watch and pray. When He returned, He found them asleep. He said, "The spirit is willing, but the body is weak" (Matt. 26:41). I believe there is not a single man who truly knows Christ who doesn't want to walk with and please God, but in our flesh we are weak. To overcome our weaknesses, we must exercise spiritual discipline.

So what is the purpose of spiritual discipline? Ultimately, the Bible says that we are to become like Jesus. We are to be transformed into His likeness. We do this by emulating Him. If Jesus was anything, He was godly. Spiritual discipline helps us to be godly like Jesus.

Sometimes we must substitute discipline for a lack of natural interest. For example, you may be too tired to toss a baseball with your son, but it may be exactly what you ought to do. So you deny yourself and put on your glove. In the same way, we don't always feel like emulating Jesus. Yet, we forge ahead, pick up the Bible, and study it. Spiritual discipline means simply this: *Do what you don't want to do, and you will become what you want to be.*

The Bible offers us the principle of spiritual discipline and also specific disciplines by which we can become godly.

What Are the Spiritual Disciplines?

If a farmer tills, plants, waters, and harvests but never puts anything back into the soil, eventually, the soil will give out. In the same way a farmer needs to put something back into the soil, so the believer needs to put something back into his relationship with God. The spiritual disciplines are the means by which we keep our relationship with the Lord fertile.

The purpose of this chapter and the next is to help you understand what the spiritual disciplines are and why you need them, and to help you develop a practical plan for the study of God's Word, prayer, fellowship with other believers, and accountability that will lead to spiritual growth, personal holiness, obedience, personal ministry, and a Christian lifestyle.

Spiritual disciplines are means of grace God has given to us by which we are connected to Him moment by moment in personal relationship. A strong relationship with anyone correlates to the amount of time and energy invested in the relationship. To build or rebuild a vital, moment-by-moment personal relationship with Christ requires an investment in certain spiritual disciplines, or spiritual activities.

There are historic spiritual disciplines that have down through the ages become the tried, tested, and proven means of grace through which God makes Himself known to us. By understanding and employing these disciplines, we follow God's plan for us, gain weapons for the spiritual battles we will fight, and gain the temporal blessings God desires to give us.

Figure 20.1 (shown below) maps out what have traditionally been considered as the spiritual disciplines. As you can see, some of the disciplines occur as public activity that takes place in community with other believers. Others we do on our own in private. To explore each of these disciplines is beyond the scope of these chapters. However, we will discuss three important *private* tools of spiritual discipline in this chapter and three important *public* means of spiritual discipline in the next chapter. Let me encourage you to delve into further study by reading any of the excellent books listed at the bottom of Figure 20.1.

Figure 20.1
The Spiritual Disciplines
1. *Public*
   Confession
   Worship
   Guidance
   Celebration
   Fellowship
   Lord's Supper
   Christian Conference (Accountability)

2. *Private*
   A. *Inward*
      Prayer
      Meditation
      Study
      Journaling
      Fasting
      Silence
      Singing

B. *Outward*

Withdrawal	Engagement
Simplicity	Service
Solitude	Evangelism
Submission	Stewardship
Frugality	Accountability
Chastity	Spiritual Direction
Secrecy	Affirmation
Sacrifice	Watching

These spiritual disciplines represent a synthesis of those mentioned in three books that are recommended for further study: Richard Foster, *Celebration of Discipline* (San Francisco: Harper and Row, 1978); Dallas Willard, *The Spirit of the Disciplines* (San Francisco: HarperCollins, 1988); and Donald Whitney, *Spiritual Disciplines for the Christian Life* (Colorado Springs: NavPress, 1991).

Notice the variety of spiritual disciplines. Think of them as conduits, pipelines, or roads to get in touch with God. You will not use them all, most likely—at least not all the time. When you want to get in touch with someone, you can phone, send a fax, a letter, an express mail letter, E-mail, or a messenger. In the same way, the spiritual disciplines are many different ways to help us communicate with and worship God.

Different disciplines have different levels of importance—call it a hierarchy of importance. Obviously, Bible study, worship, and prayer are generally more important than, say, journaling or silence.

The spiritual disciplines are *spiritual exercises* that bring us into contact with God. They help us to become more like Jesus. They help us attain godly character.

Spiritual disciplines are *gifts*, not *requirements*. They are *graces*, not *laws*. You may think, *Oh no, not another list of things to do!* The spiritual disciplines are not simply more things to do. They are not a series of duties or mechanical steps to perform by rote.

Spiritual disciplines are *means*, not *ends*. They have no value in and of themselves. They offer the practitioner no spiritual superiority over someone else.

Spiritual disciplines do not save us. We attain no merit for our salvation through our works or sufferings. Salvation is the free gift of God by faith.

Spiritual disciplines, though, are the means to pursue godliness in response to our salvation, but not to gain any merit or advance any cause.

The Christian walk is a beautiful journey when we walk His way. Walk it any other way, and it can be a desperate thing. Christ has given us great freedom. Freedom in Christ, though, is the liberty to do what we *ought* to do rather than what we *want* to do.

Just how important are the spiritual disciplines? It is hard to get off track if you do spiritual disciplines. It is impossible to stay on track if you don't.

Let's look at three private disciplines that every man should employ.

1. Study of the Bible

On the Via Dolorosa in the Old City of Jerusalem, the significance of a nondescript store run by Ferridah Hana could easily be lost amid the menagerie of garish hawkers stationed along that historic road. I met Ferridah Hana on a pilgrimage to the Holy Land.

Known as the Mother Teresa of Israel, this Arab Christian, Ferridah Hana, supports six hundred orphans out of her tiny shop. From her income she has started two orphanages and a children's hospital. In her store she sells love beads, so named because it can take a little disabled child an entire day to put a single bead on the string. She also takes in abandoned Muslim widows without families and teaches them to sew for a living.

One day she was sitting in her store visiting with two American men. Into her shop came two other Americans, rude men who talked loudly about how filthy the Arabs were in that quarter of the Old City, not knowing Ferridah, whose shop is spotless, was an Arab.

One of her American visitors began to get up to give his rude fellow countrymen a piece of his mind. Ferridah reached over, put her hand on his shoulder, and gently pressed him to sit back down. Then she said, "You Americans are so interesting. You take your Bible literally, but you don't take it seriously."

The Bible is God speaking to man. The Bible communicates the truth of God to men in search of ultimate reality. The God who is, is revealed in Scripture. The Bible, then, is the starting point of a life with God. He is rich who dwells upon God's Word. Psalm 19:7–11 says this:

THE LAW OF THE LORD IS PERFECT,
　　REVIVING THE SOUL.
THE STATUTES OF THE LORD ARE TRUSTWORTHY,
　　MAKING WISE THE SIMPLE.
THE PRECEPTS OF THE LORD ARE RIGHT,
　　GIVING JOY TO THE HEART.
THE COMMANDS OF THE LORD ARE RADIANT,
　　GIVING LIGHT TO THE EYES.
THE FEAR OF THE LORD IS PURE,
　　ENDURING FOREVER.
THE ORDINANCES OF THE LORD ARE SURE
　　AND ALTOGETHER RIGHTEOUS.
THEY ARE MORE PRECIOUS THAN GOLD,
　　THAN MUCH PURE GOLD;
THEY ARE SWEETER THAN HONEY,
　　THAN HONEY FROM THE COMB.
BY THEM IS YOUR SERVANT WARNED;
　　IN KEEPING THEM THERE IS GREAT REWARD.

A friend in the publishing business tells me that only 30 percent of college graduates ever read a book again after graduation. Reading and studying have largely been replaced by watching television and videos. For the Christian, however, reading and studying open the door to communication from God.

Frankly, after more than twenty years of following Christ, I find I no longer read my Bible. My Bible reads me. On its crinkly pages I *see myself—* my motives, my ambitions, my longings, my pain, my sufferings, my sins, my hope, my joy. As the rustling pages turn, I *see God—*His love, His forgiveness, His birth, His death, His resurrection, His sovereignty, His holiness, His character.

I love my Bible. I love the Bible because I don't have to worry about receiving flash updates or corrective bulletins. I don't have to worry about a factory recall. I don't have to be concerned about whether or not a retraction will appear in tomorrow's version. I love my Bible because it is true, and truth doesn't change. In a world awash with change, I'm glad to have an anchor, a solid rock upon which to build my life.

Have you ever read the Bible cover to cover? Do you know how to use a concordance to find verses about topics of interest to you? Why not consider making a commitment to study God's Word as an exercise of spiritual discipline?

For example, you could read a chapter a day from the New Testament. Or at your Christian bookstore, you can purchase a one-year plan to read through the Bible. Personally, each year I read through *The One-Year Bible* in a different version—it only takes twenty minutes a day (and that's if you read it slowly). If you want accelerated growth, read your Bible with a pen and pad nearby. Write down questions about passages you don't understand. Then ask your pastor or a Bible teacher what God meant in those passages.

Whatever plan of reading and studying you use, the important thing is to have some plan. Otherwise, inertia will take over. The best plan is the one you will use.

How important is Bible study? Can you think of any other way to become a Biblical Christian other than by studying the Bible? I can honestly say that I have never known a man whose life has changed in any significant way apart from the regular study of God's Word. Do you want your life to change? Study His Word.

2. Prayer

One day I was trying to decide if I should send a copy of a letter I received from President Clinton to our ministry partners list. It didn't feel right. I talked it over with a man in our office but couldn't get closure. As I was concluding the conversation, I said, "Well, I'll keep praying about it." Just then it hit me that I had been thinking about it, but not actually praying. There is a huge difference between thinking and praying. I prayed, and immediately the answer came—don't send it.

When a friend of mine became deathly ill with cancer, another friend asked me how he was doing. "He's a very sick boy," I said. "I guess the only thing we can do is pray."

"No," he corrected. "The thing we *can* do is pray." What gave his statement added authority was that he offered this advice just six months after his own wife of twenty-six years had died from cancer.

Another friend was going through a crisis at work. He said, "I've tried everything I can think of. I guess I'll pray."

Why is prayer the last thing we do and not the first? Why don't we pray more? First, we pray last or don't pray at all because we don't believe prayer *really* works. If we *really* believed God hears and answers our prayers, we would pray all the time. If we *really* understood prayer, it would be the principal habit of our hearts. It would be our first resort, not our last.

Second, prayer is hard work. One day I was in the car with Bill and Vonette Bright. At the time Vonette was the chair of the National Day of Prayer—she even got Congress to make it a law! I nearly ran off the road when she said, "Prayer is hard work. Sometimes I find it hard to concentrate. My mind wanders." Well, I already knew that was true for me! I just couldn't believe it was true for one of the world's most famous prayers! What an encouragement! Misery loves company. Prayer *is* hard work. Sometimes it's hard to stay focused. Besides that, no one holds us accountable to pray.

✓ God wants us to pray. Prayer is man speaking to God. Prayer is how we communicate with God. Prayer changes things. However, God doesn't answer petitions that are not presented. If we go about solving our challenges in our own strength, we rob God of the glory He wants for Himself. He would rather that we come humbly before the throne of His grace so that He can give us mercy and help in our times of need.

✓ Prayer changes us. Prayer breaks strongholds. Prayer determines the destinies of men, their families, their communities, and their nations. Only an army of men on their knees can turn the destiny of America back to God. It's time for you to get on your knees and fight like a man!

What is your prayer life like? Is prayer a significant part of your life? Do you sense a close, personal communion with Jesus when you pray? Or is your prayer life more limited, mechanical, and unrewarding? Here are a few suggestions.

Catchwords

Personally, I get bored unless I change things around periodically. One helpful idea for your prayer life is to use a list of catchwords. I keep such a list written on the inside front cover of my *One-Year Bible*. When I pray during my daily quiet time, I let my eyes stop on each word and see if it triggers something to pray over. It keeps my prayer life fresh and focused.

For example, one of my catchwords is *comfort*. One day when I see this word, it brings to mind how hard yesterday was when that deal fell apart. Another day it brings to mind Jesus saying to me, "Come to me, all you who are weary and burdened, and I will give you rest" (Matt. 11:28). Another time I am overwhelmed by a sense of God's love and peace welling up in my chest through the Holy Spirit.

Here is a partial list of catchwords I use (somewhat grouped, no order implied):

- objectivity, truth, no self-deceit
- worship, praise, love, trust, glorify, enjoy
- impure thoughts, selfish ambitions, wrong motives, unrealistic expectations
- negative attitudes, hurtful words, touchy feelings, critical spirit
- insight, wisdom, guidance, vision
- comfort, rest, fellowship, encouragement, healing
- power, life change, sanctification
- strength, courage, hope, grace, mercy
- humility, obedience, fear of the Lord
- will of God, calling, use gifts
- creativity, imagination, passion, excellence, integrity
- filled/walk in Spirit, grateful, joyful, faithful, available, teachable
- consecrated, unhardened heart, servant
- dependent, not relying on self, abide, delight, disengaged
- safety, blessing, promises

You may want to come up with a list of your own and give this a try. Each day when you look at this list, your changing current circumstances will bring to mind different thoughts to pray about. Let God use catchwords to bring specific prayer requests to your mind.

Writing Down Prayers

Pray with a pencil. The advantage of writing down your prayer requests is that you get to see and remember God working. It's amazing how often I forget to thank God for answering requests that I don't write down.

In the front of my *One-Year Bible* I have written my specific long-term prayer requests. These include important people in my life—saved and unsaved, different projects, and the list for my kids already mentioned.

For short-term prayer items I use Post-its and stick them in blank spaces next to my long-term requests.

If you don't already write down your prayers, why not give some method of writing them down a try? Then you can be sure to praise God for His answers.

3. The Quiet Time

In our culture we have a device called "quiet time." A quiet time is a routine period, usually at the beginning or end of the day, in which five, fifteen, or thirty minutes, or an hour or more is set aside to read and study God's Word, pray, and possibly perform some other spiritual disciplines. (For example, sometimes I like to sing hymns [it's the only place I dare to!], journal, or read devotional materials.)

Actually, the Bible calls for continual prayer and Bible meditation: "Pray continually" (1 Thess. 5:17); "Pray in the Spirit on all occasions with all kinds of prayers and requests" (Eph. 6:18); "His delight is in the law of the Lord,/ and on his law he meditates day and night" (Ps. 1:2).

The quiet time, then, is an accommodation to an overly busy culture. Nevertheless, the concept of setting aside a regular time to be with the Lord can greatly enhance any man's walk with God. In fact, without it, it is questionable if you can really have an ongoing relationship with Christ.

My pastor says, "The quiet time frames the entrance into the Christian life." Through its gate, we enter into communion and relationship with the living God. It is not the test of spirituality, but it is the key.

Why is it important to have a quiet time? <u>A fundamental principle of our national defense policy is that we defend against *capabilities*, not *intentions*. Enemies say one thing and do another. We cannot trust Satan's lies.</u> He wants to destroy you. And he has the capabilities to do so.

Each day we must resupply ourselves for the spiritual battle. To run out of spiritual food, ammunition, and strength can be catastrophic. During the Korean War, the United Nations troops pursued the enemy deep into the north of the Korean Peninsula. Unfortunately, they pursued faster than their supplies of food, ammunition, winter clothing, and engineers could keep up. They arrived at the Yalu River tired, their supplies thinned out, and unprepared for winter. The Chinese Communist army, fresh and ready for winter, crossed the Yalu River and drove the United Nations forces all the way back to the thirty-eighth parallel in a crushing defeat.[3]

That turning of the tide from victory to defeat carried implications still felt. Today the thirty-eighth parallel separates Communist, atheistic North Korea and the highly Christianized South Korea. One can only wonder what would have happened to the freedom of all Koreans if only the United Nations troop commanders had not pursued faster than supplied.

It is important not to "pursue faster than you can be supplied." To spend time "with God" supplies us with the spiritual strength and guidance we need to do work "for God."

How much time should you devote to a daily quiet time? If you don't already have a quiet time, why not consider giving five minutes a day to read one chapter of the New Testament and say a prayer like the Lord's Prayer? Later, if you want to increase the time you spend, fine. But start with a realistic goal. The best length of time is the one you will actually do. Don't bite off more than you will really do.

In Yosemite Park you can see grass growing out of the rocks up high. A tiny seed, by applying consistent pressure, works its roots into the rock and finds life. No matter how hard your circumstances, if you will apply consistent pressure, if you will have a daily quiet time, those roots will take hold for you.

How often should you have a quiet time? Shoot for five days a week (allow for early morning meetings, glitches, etc.). You wouldn't expect to eat once or twice a week and be healthy. Neither can you feed your spirit only one or twice a week and expect spiritual health.

Next we will look at three "public" spiritual disciplines to help you walk in the footsteps of Jesus.

_____

QUESTIONS AND DECISIONS

1. Do you regularly think of life as a spiritual battle? Why or why not? Has your thinking changed as a result of reading this chapter?

2. Explain in your own words what a spiritual discipline is. If you need to, look back through the chapter.

3. Do you read the Bible on a regular basis? If so, describe what you do, how long, how often, and how consistently. If not, do you think you should? What would be a good plan for you?

4. Would your wife consider you to be a man of prayer? Why or why not? Do you want to make any changes in the way you pray?

5. "In our culture we have a device called the quiet time. Actually, the Bible calls for continual prayer and Bible meditation. The quiet time is an accommodation to an overly busy culture." Do you ☐ agree/ ☐ disagree? Explain your answer.

6. "The concept of setting aside a regular time to be with the Lord can greatly enhance any man's walk with God. In fact, without it, it is questionable if you can really have an ongoing relationship with Christ." Do you ☐ agree/ ☐ disagree? Explain your answer.

7. Do you have a quiet time? If so, are you satisfied with it? If you don't have a quiet time, should you begin one? Why or why not?

Three "Public" Spiritual Disciplines

"Superficiality is the curse of our age. . . . The desperate need today is not for a greater number of intelligent people, or gifted people, but for deep people."

—*Richard Foster*[1]

We have all known men like this . . .

In the early morning darkness they migrate like lemmings from neighborhoods in which they don't know their neighbors down impersonal expressways to catacombs of commerce where they scurry about like rats in a maze.

At lunch they leave jobs in which they hardly know their co-workers to work out at a health club with other overweight men they've never met. After working late and forgetting to call home, they leave customers whose names they easily forget to arrive home after dark for a warmed-over dinner with a wife they barely know.

On Sunday they arise and travel to a church with kids they never spend much time with to hear a sermon with a bunch of people whose names they have long since forgotten from a pastor to whom they've only said hello. They rush out the door to watch football games for which they will never remember the score.

Their lives look thin as cardboard. They are the generation of cardboard men who live, eat, and sleep cardboard lives.

The tragedy of this scenario is that many times we, too, get caught up in a daily grind of unthinking routines. How do Christian men end up living cardboard lives? We live in an anonymous age. It is a dangerous age. Without public spiritual disciplines we, too, can find ourselves looking a little thin.

Men in Community

A man cannot be successful by himself.

One of the greatest losses to men in this generation has been the privatization of our faith. We have been taught that faith is personal, a private thing. We have been taught to separate our public life from our private faith.

As a result, men often walk their spiritual walk alone. They don't have any Christian friends, at least below the level of news, sports, and weather. So they become vulnerable to failure.

Women move about like sheep in the safety of groups, while men wander alone like proud lions through enemy territory. But the Bible says we are all sheep, men and women alike. We think we are like the fierce lion. We are really like Mary's little lamb. To wander alone is neither wise nor safe. We all, like sheep, can go astray.

If you are walking your walk alone, you are like a lone sheep culled out from the safety of the flock by a wily wolf. The devil has used this "faith is a private thing" teaching to make you vulnerable and keep you apart from other men.

A man can be successful only when he lives in community with other believers. Public spiritual disciplines done in community keep us from falling prey to the sins of anonymity. In this chapter we will limit our discussion to three potent forms of public spiritual discipline: _the accountability group, Bible studies,_ and _the church._

1. Accountability

I would like to suggest that many men are very confused about how to balance their priorities. Indeed, many men don't even know what their priorities should be—much less how to balance them. Some issues in life can't be handled by self-examination and the study of God alone. Sometimes we need a friend to help us see a thing more clearly.

We have been led to believe we should play our cards close to the vest. Here are other words of advice from our society: "Don't tell anyone anything that he can use against you"; "People who share their problems are weak"; "You can't depend on anyone but yourself"; and "Don't let anyone know your personal business."

The truth for the Biblical Christian is this: There is _power in vulnerability, strength in numbers,_ and _safety in visibility._ The most successful Christians I know have some accountability built into their lives. The Bible puts it this way: "Plans fail for lack of counsel,/ but with many advisers they succeed" (Prov. 15:22).

If you gain only one "take away" idea from this book, I hope it will be that you will decide to form an accountability group if you are not already in one.

I believe *no man can stay on track with his God, his family, his friends, his morality, his money, and his vocation unless he has an accountable relationship with other men.*

In *The Man in the Mirror* I explained what accountability is and how to do it, so I won't repeat myself here, except to say that an accountable relationship between two, three, or four men in which they give each other permission to ask the hard questions can be of immeasurable value. Accountability means *to be regularly answerable for each of the key areas in your life to qualified people.* (For further study refer to *The Man in the Mirror,* chapter 23, "Accountability: The Missing Link").

Why don't more men have accountability for private lives? Two reasons in particular are significant. First, *fear.* Why are we afraid? We fear a loss of reputation. As people say, confession is good for the soul but bad for the reputation. We assume that if other men really knew what we are really like, they wouldn't accept us. Of course, that other man feels the same way.

Men fear betrayal. One fellow said, "When men share out of their depths, we don't give them a Christian response."

"Yes, we do," said another. "We nail them to a cross."

We fear that accountability will be like a powerful light shined on our blemishes. It can wound our human pride.

Second, *false confidence.* We don't think we really need to be account-able. We think we can make it on our own all by ourselves. We think there are better uses of our time so we don't make accountability a priority. We don't realize how weak we really are.

What is needed in an accountable relationship? For an accountable relationship to work, we must be *vulnerable, confidential,* and *confrontational.*

Vulnerable means to open up. We need to give each other a break—we are all weak. False confidence comes easily, and a faithful brother can point out wrong thinking, but not if we don't open up.

Confidential means you can be trusted. In the good old days they made footballs out of pigskin. Guess why? Pigs don't have pores. In other words, they don't leak. Accountability partners don't leak.

Confrontational means willing to ask the hard questions. John, a Christian, was distraught because his friend Tom, a Christian, had taken up with a crowd of men from work who drank too much and cussed too loud. He was willing to risk his friendship, and he told Tom that if he didn't stop cursing in front of him, he didn't want to have anything to do with him anymore. Tom came to his senses and stopped.

Perhaps you have been through a tough time because no one confronted you. I doubt that anyone reading this book is "glad" that no one confronted him before he made a tragic mistake. The last thing Satan wants us to do is be our brother's keeper. That's because it's the very thing we need to do.

I have rethought one important area of accountability since I first wrote on the subject in *The Man in the Mirror*. I have come to believe that men should be in an accountable relationship of *four* men. Let me hasten to say that four is not a biblical number, but it is a practical number. Lyman Coleman, a pioneer in the small-group movement, favors groups of four.

The problems with two-man accountability groups are many. Two men can lead each other astray. The mind has not escaped the domino effect of the Fall. Our minds do not always think clearly. One dominating man can persuade another man that his sinful action is somehow justified. In fact, he can even lead his friend into the same sin. The chances of four men all being led astray into the same wrongful thinking or behavior is much more remote.

Two men may stop holding each other accountable in favor of fellowship. Relationships are thicker than blood. When two men become extremely close after meeting for a long time, there is a tendency to overlook the shortcomings of your partner—even though holding each other accountable is why you started to meet in the first place. Four-man groups can better guard against this tendency.

In a two-man accountability group one man may not have the courage to ask his partner a hard question about something that is conspicuously questionable to him. There is strength in numbers. In a group of four, the other three men can find strength in their numbers to question or even confront a brother on an issue.

If only two men meet and the other drops out, it spells the end of accountability. Feelings may get hurt. In a four-man group if a man loses interest, the other three men have a better opportunity to bring that man back into the fold than one man acting alone. If they cannot, together they can keep meeting and invite a new fourth on board.

Certainly, many two-man accountability groups can and do work. However, the odds are against it. Forming a four-man accountability group that meets weekly or biweekly is a sure-bet formula for finding and maintaining seasons of success. Incidentally, don't use an accountability group as an excuse to be less open with your wife. A chief purpose of accountability should be to lead you to greater closeness with your wife, not less. ✓

2. Bible Studies

As mentioned in the last chapter, a man's life won't change apart from the regular study of God's Word.

Most men do not have the time, interest, or aptitude to do the close work to really dig out the meat of a passage. Also, private study of the Bible can lead to error. Finally, it is easy to lapse if you try to study only on your own.

A good men's or couples' Bible study, in the community but preferably originating from your church, is a tremendous way of accomplishing several goals at once:

- to learn God's truth through Bible study
- to be discipled by a more experienced person
- to have role models to observe and emulate
- to have counselors to bounce ideas off of
- to group with other men or couples for fellowship
- to carry one another's burdens
- to be accountable by asking one another the right questions
- to have a sounding board for understanding biblical concepts

If you are not already in a Bible study, give prayerful consideration to this community spiritual discipline of personal growth.

Bible studies and accountability groups have the same end in mind—to make men into spiritual leaders and disciples—but they approach discipleship from very different angles. It takes time to study the Bible. It takes time to hold one another accountable. Personally, I think it would be quite difficult to accomplish both at the same time. The risk is to not do either in enough depth to really change lives.

3. Church

A navy man once told me that in his experience when a navy vessel is in port less than 5 percent of the crew attends church. When out at sea, the number doubles to 10 percent. Once, however, when a destroyer in their fleet was sunk, 100 percent of the crew attended services.

If we are not careful, we can end up using the Emergency Broadcasting System of Christianity. Unless we have a felt need, we don't worship God. We err when we put the emphasis on *us* not God. Besides, whether we feel a need to worship God or not, we do have a real need to do so.

The Greek word for church, *ekklesia,* appears ninety-five times in the New Testament. *Church* means the body of believers, not the buildings where the believers assemble.

It is the group with whom we baptize our babies, marry our children, bury our dead, receive comfort in crisis, accept meals in sickness, partake of the Lord's Supper, learn about the character of God, become trained in doctrine, commune with Christ, fellowship with other believers, become discipled in the way we should walk, develop a personal ministry, honor God with our tithes and offerings, bring unsaved friends, hear the preaching of God's Word, express our spiritual gifts, raise our children in spiritual instruction, and take vows for which we are accountable.

Have you ever really considered the depth of the role your church plays in your life and the life of your family? Read that last paragraph again, slowly this time, pausing to give thanks to God for your church.

Do you think it is possible to be a "Lone Ranger" Christian? How many of the above functions can you do on your own?

We live in an age in which the *individual* is held in higher regard than the *institution.* Baby boomer and baby buster lack of loyalty to institutions in general has spilled over into the church. In fact, many churches don't even require formal membership anymore. This is neither safe nor healthy.

It is a regrettable fact that in our generation, the culture has had more influence upon the church than the church has had upon the culture.

Though 94 percent of Americans say they believe in God, an amazing 80 percent of them expect to arrive at their religious beliefs independent from any church.[2] But where else would we find a more dependable guide for determining what we believe?

A great need today is that Christians revalue the church—that they recognize the importance of membership (including commitment, loyalty, and accountability) in a vital body of believers. Those who have worked around Christians who try to make it on their own without commitment to a local body of believers, as I have, are weary of being asked to pick up the broken pieces of lives shattered by lack of accountability.

Jesus Christ is the head of the church: "And he is the head of the body, the church" (Col. 1:18). We should belong to a church because He wants us to. The Bible puts it this way: "Let us not give up meeting together, as some are in the habit of doing, but let us encourage one another—and all the more as you see the Day approaching" (Heb. 10:25).

Finally, if you have a men's ministry in your church, be sure to support it (if not, should you start one?). The relationships you build when you don't necessarily need anything will be a blessing when you do.

Supporting a local church through membership—not merely attendance—represents the most significant of the public spiritual disciplines. (For additional suggestions on how to select a church, see my book, *Two Part Harmony*, pages 228–31.)

If we truly love Christ, we will want to be around His people.

QUESTIONS AND DECISIONS

1. What percentage of your life is anonymous? How much do you live a secret life? Does it concern you? Why or why not?

2. "A man cannot be successful by himself." Do you ☐ agree/ ☐ disagree? Explain your answer.

3. Comment on the following: One of the greatest losses to men in this generation has been the privatization of our faith. We have been taught that faith is personal, a private thing. We have been taught to separate our public life from our private faith. How do you think this has affected the ability of men to live up to their faith?

4. Are you in an accountability group? If yes, is it working? What changes should you make for it to be more effective? If no, are you ready to enter into an accountable relationship with some other men? What's your next step?

5. Are you now or have you ever been involved in a men's or couples' Bible study? What are/were the benefits to it? What were the downsides? If you are not presently in a good Bible study, why not consider joining or forming one?

6. Are you part of a vital church fellowship? If yes, are you a contributing member (time, treasure, talent)? Why or why not? If no, do you agree making a commitment to a local body of believers is biblical? What should you do? Will you do it?

Discovering Your Calling

I tell you that this sweet and loving gaze of God insensibly kindles a divine fire in the soul which is set ablaze so ardently with the love of God that one is obliged to perform exterior acts to moderate it.

—Brother Lawrence[1]

22 A couple of years ago Dave recommitted his life to follow Christ—a "no regrets, no retreat" surrender to Jesus. Though he didn't actually hear any words, he sensed the Lord saying, *You believe in Me.*

Hungry to grow in the knowledge of God, he and his wife enrolled in a thirty-four-week Bible study program offered by their church. He devoured everything they threw at him. He also continued to attend our TGIF Men's Bible Study. At the end of the thirty-four weeks, he sensed the Lord saying, again without words, *You know Me.*

In the process of growing in the Lord, Dave sensed a deeply felt desire— almost a drive—to not only *know* God, but to *do* something for Him as an expression of his gratitude. Eventually, he felt consumed by a desire to serve the Lord. He began exploring personal ministry options, yet none of them worked out. Week after week went by. Weeks turned into months. He began to get discouraged. He began to wonder if it was all a bunch of emotion on his part. He began to doubt. Second thoughts crept into his mind.

One day Dave was earnestly praying about not finding a suitable avenue to serve Christ. As he was pouring out his heart, his hurt, his desire, and his doubt to the Lord, he again sensed the Lord speaking to him, *You don't trust Me.*

Wow! thought Dave. *He is right! I have stopped trusting Him to show me what He would have me do in His good timing. Instead, I have taken charge of my life again.* Another lesson learned.

By divine "coincidence," the lesson at the next Friday morning Bible study centered on providing for our families by discipling them (1 Tim.

5:8)—to make our families a personal ministry. Dave felt like someone had hit him with a ball-peen hammer. It finally sank in what the Lord was wanting him to do. He realized that before he tried to save the world, he had better devote some time to his own family.

Curiously, shortly after Dave made this adjustment, the Lord began to shape a new idea in his mind for how to reach his peers at work. Lately, Dave spends a lot of time networking with other Christians in his career field, talking over the best ways to have an evangelistic witness, especially at trade shows. He also has begun to see intrinsic value in the work he does—that it is part of his calling.

The exact strategy has not yet surfaced, but Dave thinks God has clearly given him a vision for serving Christ, both in his family and in his occupation.

The Problem

There is a myth that states, "As long as we do it honestly, everyone is free to pursue his own self-interests." Sometimes this is called *principled self-interest.* Actually, this is a form of capitalism, but it is not Christianity.

The Christian is not free to pursue his own self-interests. The Christian has been bought with a price. He is not his own. He belongs to the King. He is called to deny himself, take up his cross, and follow Jesus.

God has a plan for your life. It is a calling, not just a career. It includes all of your life—your vocation, your family, your church, your community, your country, and your ministry.

What Is a Calling?

God reveals four types of calling in Scripture:

- The call to *salvation:* a divine summons to eternal life.
- The call to *sanctification:* a growing commitment to follow God's blueprint for godly living.
- The call to *suffering:* an expectation of opposition, trouble, and tribulation that we should consider joy.
- The call to *service:* personal tasks from God joyfully performed as a response to His kindness, mercies, and grace.

It is this fourth calling—*the call to serve the Lord*—upon which we will focus in this chapter. In the last two chapters we focused on the spiritual disciplines to help a man in his *walk with God*. Now let's turn our attention to helping a man discover his *work for God*.

In the Bible the call to serve God is a man's vocation. Calling includes all the tasks we do, not only in ministry but also in our work. In fact, for men of the Bible their work was a crucial part of their calling. Abraham served the Lord as a rancher. David served the Lord as a shepherd and king. Daniel served the Lord as a statesman. Jeremiah served the Lord as a prophet. Paul served the Lord as a tent-maker and evangelist. Peter served the Lord as a small businessman and disciple-maker. Their work and their service were one and the same.

It would be good to recover the idea that the work we do is as much a part of our calling as is a personal ministry.

Frequently Asked Questions

Once that fire to serve the Lord starts to burn in a man's heart, he bumps up against some obvious questions:

- I want to serve the Lord, but what can I do?
- Wouldn't I have to be a minister to serve the Lord?
- I have the desire to serve God, but how do I go about it?
- What kind of personal ministry can I do?
- Is my work part of my calling?
- Why is it taking so long to get in gear?
- What is God's will for my life?
- What does the Bible say about all this?

Let's explore the answers to these important questions.

What the Bible Says . . .

The Bible offers a comprehensive overview of a man's call to serve, so let's begin there. Here is a brief snapshot that will give you a firm base upon which to build your own personal calling.

- *God made us to serve Him:* "For we are God's workmanship, created in Christ Jesus to do good works" (Eph. 2:10).
- *God has already determined what He wants us to do:* "good works, which God prepared in advance for us to do" (Eph. 2:10).

- *God wants each of us to bear much fruit:* "This is to my Father's glory, that you bear much fruit, showing yourselves to be my disciples" (John 15:8). In fact, fruit proves we are His disciples.
- *Some are called to speak, some to serve, and some to both:* "If anyone speaks, he should do it as one speaking the very words of God. If anyone serves, he should do it with the strength God provides" (1 Peter 4:11).
- *The ultimate purpose of our service is to bring glory to God:* ". . . so that in all things God may be praised through Jesus Christ. To him be the glory and the power for ever and ever. Amen" (1 Peter 4:11).
- *The earthly purpose of our calling is to faithfully serve others:* "Each one should use whatever gift he has received to serve others, faithfully administering God's grace in its various forms" (1 Peter 4:10).
- *God calls us to be faithful, not successful:* "Now it is required that those who have been given a trust must prove faithful" (1 Cor. 4:2). In the exercise of our gifts it is not incumbent upon us to be successful. It is required that we be faithful. Faithfulness will lead to success, but on God's terms, not as seen through the eyes of the culture.
- *God gives each of us different spiritual gifts:* "We have different gifts, according to the grace given us" (Rom. 12:6). Spiritual gifts are unique spiritual abilities given by God to help us in serving Him. (For a full discussion of this topic, see my book, *The Rest of Your Life*, chapter 18, "Developing a Personal Ministry.")
- *We each serve God as part of a larger body:* "Just as each of us has one body with many members, and these members do not all have the same function, so in Christ we who are many form one body, and each member belongs to all the others" (Rom. 12:4–5). It's important to fit in with the larger picture of what God is doing in the world. All of us working together form a beautiful mosaic of loving service.
- *The Bible equips us to do good works:* "All Scripture is God-breathed and is useful for teaching, rebuking, correcting and training in righteousness, so that the man of God may be thoroughly equipped for every good work" (2 Tim. 3:16–17).

Career as Calling

When I stepped away from day-to-day business to devote myself full-time to the ministry of helping men and leaders think more deeply about their lives, I thought I would wake up the next day feeling more spiritual—somehow holier. It never happened.

Then I supposed that when I looked into the mirror, I would see the faint outline of a halo. Oh, I didn't think anyone else would ever see it, but I thought for sure that I would. It never happened.

I thought my walk with Christ would soar to new heights since I was now working directly for Him all day. It never happened.

I dreamed about how, once in ministry, I would never again have to go through that one day a week when I wanted to chuck the whole thing. It is true. I no longer want to chuck the whole thing one day a week. Now I want to chuck it two days a week!

Actually, I feel no more called to making investments in men and leaders than I did to making investments in land and buildings. I am no more passionate about what I do now than about what I did before.

The Bible makes no distinction between *sacred* and *secular*. For the Christian, all of life is spiritual. Francis Schaeffer put it this way:

> There are certain things which are given as absolutely sinful in the Scripture, and these things we as Christians should not do. . . . But then everything else is spiritual. The painting of a picture, the work of a good shoemaker, the doctor, the lawyer—all these things are spiritual if they are done within the circle of what is taught in Scripture, looking to the Lord day by day for His help . . .

> One thing you should very definitely have in mind—that is that *a ministry such as teaching the Bible in a college is no higher calling intrinsically than being a businessman or doing something else* (emphasis added).[2]

Many men who sense the desire to serve God welling up within them assume they must now do something else. This is rarely the case. For 99 percent of us, God probably wants us right where we are (1 Cor. 7:17, 20, 24). Generally, a man should keep doing what he already does, but differently—with a whole new orientation to pleasing Christ.

Your occupation is part of your call to service. Faith is not a private thing to be kept in a compartment. Instead, on the job your faith should season every action and word so that God will receive praise, glory, and honor. You don't have to force the word "Jesus" into every conversation, but His presence should be conspicuous to anyone giving it a moment's thought. People will decide whether Christianity is true or not based upon how you do your work when you think no one is looking.

Having a Personal Ministry

No man I have ever known has been more faithful to minister to men than Owen. For twenty-three years Owen has led a Monday noon Bible study in downtown Orlando. He has helped start several new churches. Yet Owen leases commercial real estate for his occupation.

"Why don't you go into the ministry?" someone asked.

"I am in the ministry. God has called me to business," he explained.

We are not called to earn enough money so we won't be bothered by the troubles of other people. We are called to be agents of the kingdom who bring life where there is death, light where there is darkness, and hope where there is despair.

Not only does God want us to serve Him in our work, but He wants us to serve Him by intentionally investing our lives in others. When God called and sent individuals in the Bible, He sent them to turn the hearts of people to God. Our callings revolve around the Great Commission and the Cultural Commission (or Cultural Mandate).

Build the Kingdom *and* Tend the Culture

Lyle, who owns his own business, went through a spiritual renewal. He says, "The Lord has shown me that my business *is* my ministry. I pray each morning for the business to glorify God. It's interesting. People are talking and acting differently. I am thinking about starting a Bible study at the office for anyone who wants to attend. And I have made it my goal to expose every vendor, employee, and key man to Jesus Christ." He also is having a leavening influence on his community by producing excellent work. He has become salt and light.

Jesus put the Great Commission like this: "Therefore go and make disciples of all nations, baptizing them in the name of the Father and of the Son and of the Holy Spirit, and teaching them to obey everything I have commanded you" (Matt. 28:19–20). *God calls us to build the kingdom.*

The Cultural Commission, which says we must manage the world as God's stewards, comes from Genesis 1:28: "God blessed them and said to them, 'Be fruitful and increase in number; fill the earth and subdue it. Rule over the fish of the sea and the birds of the air and over every living creature that moves on the ground.'" *God calls us to tend the culture.*

The question might well be asked, "The earth and all that is in it are going to melt anyway. Why invest any labor at all into 'meltables'?"

The two great themes of the Bible are *creation* and *redemption*. In recent generations we have put the emphasis heavily on redemptive tasks—building the kingdom, winning people to faith, fulfilling the Great Commission. (Whatever corrections we need to make, let's not stop doing this!)

However, in the last few generations we have neglected our creation tasks—tending the culture, preserving society, fulfilling the Cultural Commission (or Mandate). Perhaps the reason we have not invested in meltables is that we don't tend to see any redemptive value in creation tasks like commerce, the trades, law, medicine, government, and the arts. But that is to make a separation between sacred and secular where God does not. Besides, look at the slough of problems we have in culture. Where is the leavening influence of Christian men?

Let's be realistic. Most of us will spend most of our time at what have been erroneously called secular jobs. Most of our time on a day-to-day basis is spent in work that tends the culture rather than in work that wins the lost. These jobs are creation tasks, not redemption tasks—though we may end up sharing our faith with co-workers. More of us need to recognize that our work is our calling, and serve as though serving Christ, not men (Col. 3:23).

To devalue creation tasks is to say our work doesn't matter to God. That's simply not true. Since Adam began tending the garden, man's work has been a holy calling.

Actually, God never calls any man to either redemptive tasks or creation tasks. Rather, God calls us to both build the kingdom and tend the culture. Further, we often get this backward—we tend to build the culture and tend the kingdom. This won't do. We need an aggressive approach to both the evangelistic gospel and the social gospel.

God is building His kingdom, a family of people to live with Him eternally. Whatever we do, and wherever we do it, we must always think to serve with this eternal perspective. Frankly, many men have forgotten why Paul made tents. Their work has become an end in itself.

The Underground Railroad helped forty thousand slaves escape to Canada. On a Family Channel program about this exodus, a young white man named Ross took a special interest in a slave named Thomas. Thomas asked him, "Why are you doing this, Mr. Ross?"

"Ever since I was a boy I wanted to be in this cause," he answered. "But now that I'm involved, it's more than a cause. It's about people."

Remember why you do what you do. All callings, done well, will point men to Christ. Put yourself in a position to meet lost men. It is a devil's scheme to get men so churched that they don't know any lost men.

The Nature of the Call to Service

The call to service develops in three phases: *calling, equipping,* and *sending.*

When God calls, He rarely sends right away. Instead, we go through a season of equipping in which we encounter delays, uncertainties, and hardships. Sometimes this equipping period lasts a long time. I know this is not an idea that we in our culture find appealing, but usually the bigger the calling, the longer the equipping. Why is that? We can learn why from Moses, Abraham, and Joseph.

Delays

God gave a young, virile Moses the vision that he would be the deliverer of his people held as slaves in Egypt. Moses lived in Pharaoh's household, but remained true to his faith. One day he killed an Egyptian he found beating a fellow Jew. Surely that was the beginning of the vision to serve God. But there was too much "Moses" in Moses. So God sent him into the Midian wilderness for forty years for a time of equipping—a time of working some things into and out of Moses's life.

When God was ready to send Moses, we find a much humbler man. In fact, the Bible says Moses was the most humble man who ever lived. That's what forty years in the wilderness will do for you.

Equipping takes so long because sending demands so much. God is faithful to build into the life of the one He sends all that he will need. This takes time. Never ask God to send you until you are ready to go.

Uncertainties

God called Abraham to leave his native country and "go to the land I will show you" (Gen. 12:1). In other words, Abraham began his journey not knowing the destination. He was going, not knowing.

Like Abraham, we don't fully know where God is sending us. If we have it all planned out, it is likely in the flesh.

God gave Abraham a vision for becoming the father of a great nation. Yet in his old age he remained childless. But the Bible says he kept believing God. Eventually, his wife gave birth to a boy, Isaac, who had a son Jacob, who was later renamed Israel, whose offspring did become a great nation.

If God has put a vision to serve Him in your heart, however dim or foggy, keep the faith and never give up. The vision from God rarely comes clearly. He gives us enough to begin but not enough to finish. If He gave us the whole vision at once, then we would depend upon ourselves instead of Him. Also, it might scare the wits out of us!

A friend was going through a terrible time of not knowing. He handed me a page from Oswald Chambers's *My Utmost For His Highest,* which said in part:

> God has to take us into the valley and put us through fires and floods to batter us into shape, until we get to the point where He can trust us with the reality of the vision. . . . Allow the Potter to put you on His wheel and whirl you around as He desires. Then as sure as God is God and you are you, you will turn out as an exact likeness of the vision. But don't lose heart in the process. If you have ever had a vision from God, you may try as you will to be satisfied on a lower level, but God will never allow it.[3]

Hardships

Though we can find enormous personal satisfaction in serving Christ, the ultimate purpose of our service is not for our benefit, but for God's. Because of this, our service is often filled with hardships. We see an example of this in Joseph.

God gave a young, boastful Joseph a vision of ruling over his family. That must have been the last thing on his mind when his brothers sold him as a slave to a passing caravan. That must have been the last thing on his mind when his owner Potiphar's wife accused him of rape and he went to prison. God was working some things into Joseph's life, and some things out of Joseph's life.

Then God sent Joseph. Miraculously, he rose to become second only to Pharaoh in the kingdom of Egypt. When his brothers finally showed up in Egypt looking for food because of a famine in their own land, Joseph could say of their sin against him, "You meant it for harm, but God meant it for good—for the saving of many lives."

When God gives you the vision to serve Him, He will also give you everything you need to fulfill the vision, but it won't come without opposition. Ask Joseph, Elijah, Gideon, David, Paul, Nehemiah, Jeremiah, Ezekiel, Daniel, Moses, Asa, Abraham, Peter . . . In other words, ask anyone who has ever done anything significant for God.

We must go through hardships because the people God calls us to minister to go through hardships. Through hardship, God strengthens our character so we can comfort others with the comfort we ourselves have received.

Twelve Suggestions to Discover Your Calling

Let's make some assumptions. Let's assume you know Christ, and you have a growing burden to serve Him. A man filled to the overflow will want to give it away. Let's assume you are not currently involved in a personal ministry. Let's also assume you are looking, or are ready to look, at your work as a sacred, holy calling. What would be the best way to discern how you can begin to produce more fruit?

1. Employ the means of guidance.

To help us discern His will, God has given these means of guidance: the Bible, prayer, the Holy Spirit, a conscience, our circumstances, counsel, and fasting. Use these with liberality, keeping the question before you, "God, what is Your calling for my life?"

2. Discover your spiritual gifts.

Make the effort to learn your spiritual gifts. This will help you discern your direction as much as any single thing. Your church may offer training in spiritual gifts. Ask your pastor. Also, check your local Christian bookstore for books and other resources. Knowing your gifts will help you in your work as well as personal ministry. For example, a man with the gifts of leadership and faith may be suited to his own business.

3. Identify your motivated interests.

Philippians 2:13 says, "For it is God who works in you to will and to act according to his good purpose." In other words, God puts desires into our hearts to do His work. Pay attention to your desires. Pray over them and see if your motives are pure. Getting in touch with your motivated interests can help you direct career choices as well as choose personal ministry opportunities.

4. Complete your written life-purpose statement.

To understand God's larger purpose for your life is to know why you are here and what your life is about. Develop a written life-purpose statement of one or two sentences. Base it upon a Scripture verse if possible. (For a fuller treatment of this topic, see my book, *The Man in the Mirror,* page 68.)

5. Keep a journal.

Consider keeping a written journal of Scriptures that touch you, impressions you have, your concerns, and new insights you learn about yourself, the character of God, and His calling. Look for patterns of interest or concern.

6. Keep driving toward the vision.

Vision is a mental picture of a desirable future. Eventually, God will give you a picture of what He wants you to do. This may be more or less clear. An old country preacher said, "Clarity of vision means an acceleration toward the goal." When early morning fog reduces our vision we must drive more slowly. But when the fog burns off we can speed up. We all go through periods when we know where we want to go, but the way to get there seems fogged up. The key is to always keep driving toward the vision, even if you must drive slowly because you are in a fog. Act in light of what you *do* know. Don't *not* act in light of what you *don't* know.

7. Pray about what to do when strategy is unclear.

God has given me a vision: "To help bring about a spiritual awakening in America by reaching the men and leaders of our nation with Christ." The picture is a spiritually awakened nation. Yet, for over five years the precise *strategies* for the part I'm to play were unclear. That changed recently, for which I'm grateful, and I've accelerated. For over five years, though, all I could do was to keep praying for the strategy—not the "what" to do, but the "how" to do it.

When *how* God wants us to undertake our vision is unclear, we must pray and wait patiently. These are the times when He is equipping us—preparing us—with all we will need to successfully fulfill the vision. It may be His will to keep things unclear for forty years, as in the case of Moses. Keep moving with what you've seen so far, while praying for what you still need to see.

8. Reorganize work life to allow for personal ministry.

Jim refused a promotion because it would put him on the road four days a week. Linn quit a position because his boss wanted him to work seven days a week. He found a job selling light bulbs with 1,325 established accounts that required a normal forty-hour week. Don't be so bogged down in work that you never have time to serve the Lord in other ministry capacities besides your work.

9. Employ the power of faith.

After winning the U.S. Open and Wimbledon, then number-one-ranked tennis pro Pete Sampras was asked if he thought he could win the Grand Slam (the four major international tennis tournaments) like his hero Rod Laver did in 1968. No one since Laver has won it.

He answered no. That pretty well sealed his fate. The negative power of disbelief will cripple your vision. But the power of belief or faith is enormous. Faith is not mere positive thinking; faith is believing God in the face of unbelievable circumstances. It is trusting that what God puts in your heart as desire is within His power to bring about.

10. Maintain priorities.

Regardless of what specific ministry or occupation God gives us, we all have inescapable priorities that we must not neglect; for example, our wives, children, walk with Christ, personal finances, rest, exercise, and work. We must take responsibility for our own private lives.

11. Expect opposition.

Live your life in light of the vision God has given you. Don't let opposition deter you. God gave Nehemiah a vision to rebuild his city, but he encountered stiff opposition. Nehemiah 4:9 says, "We prayed to our God and posted a guard day and night to meet this threat." In other words, praise the Lord and pass the ammunition! In the end, God fulfilled the vision He put in Nehemiah's heart, a vision that at one point appeared dead.

12. Be willing to take some risks.

After an invigorating discussion on calling, equipping, and sending, a man said with tears in his eyes, "But I'm just not feeling called."

The counsel to this man, who at the time was not serving the Lord at all, was, "Do *something*."

Many men never attempt anything significant because they might fail. They would rather be perfect in *potentiality* than imperfect in *actuality*. Are you involved in personal ministry? If not, what is the Lord saying to you? If you are, have you been faithful to the vision God has given to you?

QUESTIONS AND DECISION

1. "As long as we do it honestly, everyone is free to pursue his own self interests." Do you ☐ agree/ ☐ disagree? Explain your answer.

2. To what extent does the following statement reflect your own beliefs? Explain why or why not:

   God has a plan for your life. It is a calling, not just a career. It includes all of your life, including your vocation, your family, your church, your community, your country, and your ministry.

3. Do you consider your career part of your spiritual calling? Why or why not?

4. How would you answer the following questions?

   • I want to serve the Lord, but what can I do?
   • Wouldn't I have to be a minister to serve the Lord?
   • I have the desire to serve God, but how do I go about it?
   • What kind of personal ministry can I do?
   • Is my work part of my calling?
   • Why is it taking so long to get in gear?
   • What is God's will for my life?
   • What does the Bible say about all this?

5. The Bible makes no distinction between *sacred* and *secular*. For the Christian, all of life is spiritual. As Francis Schaeffer said,

   There are certain things which are given as absolutely sinful in the Scripture, and these things we as Christians should not do. . . . But then everything else is spiritual. The painting of a picture, the work of a good shoemaker, the doctor, the lawyer—all these things are spiritual if they are done within the circle of what is taught in Scripture, looking to the Lord day by day for His help.

Does this differ from what you have thought in the past? If yes, how? How would adopting this understanding affect you at work tomorrow? After work tomorrow?

6. Between the *calling* and the *sending* we often go through a season of *equipping*. A lack of clear direction often accompanies a time of equipping. Are you in such a time now? Does the knowledge that this is to be expected help you? If so, how?

7. What do you think God is calling you to do?

8. If you have a burden to serve God and are not involved in work and ministry as a calling, or if you sense your calling is in the process of changing, which of the following suggestions mentioned in the chapter would most help you discover what to do? What specifically can you decide to do to move your search along?

- Employ the means of guidance.
- Discover your spiritual gifts.
- Identify your motivated interests.
- Complete your written life-purpose statement.
- Keep a journal.
- Keep driving toward the vision.
- Pray about what to do when strategy is unclear.
- Reorganize work life to allow for personal ministry.
- Employ the power of faith.
- Maintain priorities.
- Expect opposition.
- Be willing to take some risks.

PART 6

●

THE SEASON OF

SUFFERING

The Nature of Suffering

Your sufferings are the kisses of Jesus.

—*Mother Teresa*

23 In his younger days Ken, a developer, builder, and pilot, was by his own admission a high flier. He didn't marry until he turned thirty-two.

He prayed and asked God to give him a son. The Lord answered his prayer, but the son born to him was brain-damaged. He accepted the news and began to investigate how to best raise him. Many of his friends said, however, "Don't waste your life on that boy."

"But he's my son. He's of my own flesh." Ken found a specialized school in Orlando and moved his family there from Jacksonville, Florida. Since his business was still in Jacksonville, he commuted back and forth for five years, leaving Orlando each Monday morning and returning Friday evening until he was finally able to move his business.

Under the loving tutelage of devoted teachers, young Tommy learned how to read and write. Eventually, he even graduated from the University of Central Florida. Turns out Tommy is a computer whiz, and today he manages the computer system for a privately owned student dormitory.

I asked Ken, "What would you say to those people today who told you, 'Don't waste your life on that boy'?"

After a long, thoughtful pause, he said, "I wouldn't trade this for anything. I thought I was a real mover and shaker. It is as though the Lord wanted me to see that there is a whole other world out there.

"Tommy has taught us how to love, and he has taught us about miracles. My wife, Susan, put it this way. She said, 'God, I am so glad I didn't miss this!' Tommy truly is a joy to Susan.

"When Tommy was growing up, he couldn't understand why girls didn't like him. He has weak eyes—he has to be driven everywhere—and he's not very tall.

"When he was growing up, he would sit around the house and ask, 'Why doesn't anybody ever call me? Why doesn't anyone ever want to do anything with me?'

"This would break our hearts. When he would talk like this, which was often, Susan and I would both become quiet. Each knew what the other was doing. We would each pray silently for God to give Tommy a friend.

"Many, many times within five minutes the phone would ring for Tommy, and someone would say he wanted to come by or go to a movie or something like that. This is how we learned about miracles."

The Questions Suffering Raises

What is suffering? Is what we call suffering really suffering? There can be no question that what Ken, Susan, and their son, Tommy, have had to live through has brought sorrows. Yet, when measured against the greater good that has resulted, who is to say?

Would Ken and Susan have become as close? Would Ken have become such a spiritual man? Would they have relied so completely upon the Lord? Would their character have developed as deeply? Would they have given praise and glory to God as they now do? Would Tommy have been such a blessing to so many people? Would they have learned love, joy, and miracles?

We have all agonized over the question, "Why do bad things happen to good people?"

Perhaps we have agonized even more over the question, "Why do bad things happen to *me?*"

"Why do people suffer?"

"Exactly what is suffering?"

"Is suffering inevitable?"

"What causes suffering?"

And perhaps the most difficult question is, "Why does there have to be suffering at all?"

Here is the heart of the problem of suffering: If God is good, then why is there suffering? If God is great, then why doesn't He remove all suffering?

Respected Christian philosopher Alvin Plantinga has said that the most impressive argument of the atheist has to do with the problem of evil.[1]

David Hume framed the problem well when he wrote, "Epicurus's old questions are yet unanswered. Is He willing to prevent evil, but not able? Then He is impotent. Is He able, but not willing? Then He is malevolent. Is He both able and willing? Whence then is evil?"[2]

Humanly speaking, the implications about our sufferings are that:

1. God doesn't know (*ignorance*, He is not *all-knowing*).
2. God can't do anything about it (*impotence*, He is not *all-powerful*).
3. God doesn't care (*malevolence*, He is not *all-good*).

Either God is sovereign or not, and either God is good or not. Is God sovereign? All-powerful? In control of all things? The unequivocal claim of Scripture is yes. Is God good? All-benevolent? Committed to our good? The unequivocal claim of Scripture is yes. Can we fully understand how God is in complete control and completely good? No, we cannot. But we can trust Him. He works for our good, as the following story illustrates.

The Character of God

Two days before she was to arrive home from college for the Thanksgiving break, our freshman daughter phoned.

We had missed her deeply, and like all her classmates, she was really getting homesick. When she phoned this particular Sunday night, she was suffering. She wept as she told how she had less than four dollars in cash and didn't know how she was going to get home.

She was also going through some culture shock that had her feeling down. She was used to warm, hugging, joking-around relationships with all the kids, both boys and girls, from the small Christian high school from which she graduated.

To top things off, she had two papers due and a major exam to study for, all of which when added together had her totally stressed out.

Money problems. Social problems. School problems. All in all, it pushed her into overload.

My wife, Patsy, listened on one extension of the phone and I was on another. As our daughter talked and occasionally broke down, my breathing labored, and my heart felt like it was breaking. More than anything else in the whole world, I wanted to reach out, wave a magic wand, and make every problem go away. Yet, I also knew that would be exactly the wrong thing to do.

We encouraged her, mostly by listening, and agreed with her how good it would be to see each other. Her mother explained how to charge gas and food for the ten-hour drive home with the credit card we had given her for emergencies. As Patsy and I hung up the phone, I had to brush tears from the corners of my eyes.

Patsy and I talked the situation over, and we agreed: The worst possible thing we could have done for our beloved daughter would have been to rescue her from her problems. In other words, *truly loving parents have goals for their children that are larger than their immediate sufferings.*

Our main desire for our children (who both already walk with the Lord) is for good character. We know we can't help our daughter develop good character unless we help her take responsibility for her life. She must learn how her choices have consequences—that Mom and Dad won't always be there to bail out bad decisions. She must learn to cope with heartache. In short, we must help her move from dependence upon us to dependence upon Christ and the abilities He gave her.

We know that some short-term pain will result in long-term benefits to her character. She will have deeper courage, higher integrity, and broader confidence in her own abilities. She will also realize that if you spend your monthly allowance too quickly, you will surely suffer at the end of the month!

Now, let me say that as her father, I had to use every ounce of willpower not to wire her one hundred dollars to tide her over. I wanted to rush to the campus to type her term papers for her, even though it's a ten-hour drive. Though these were my strongest impulses, they were not my only impulses.

We love our daughter more than life itself, and would do anything possible to make her life easier unless in the end it would make her life harder. But we know that her present circumstances, as hard as they may now appear, will result in a greater good in the long run.

So, we allow her to suffer so that she may grow, become strong in character, develop discipline, learn responsibility, gain confidence, learn to trust God more, and in the end, be a better person. For her own good we disciplined her, as we thought best, by not rescuing her.

And that's a picture of how God operates with us; that's the character of God.

Our Father in heaven, in ways far more loving and tender, deals with each of us in precisely the same manner. He loves us with an everlasting love. He would never do anything for our harm; He works only for our good. God never allows any suffering, pain, or evil to touch us unless it will bring about a greater good or prevent a greater evil. That's what He is like; it's His character.

For example, our son wanted to go wakeboarding (water skiing on something like a surfboard) with a friend. We said no because he had an ear infection. He was upset, but we knew preventing him from going was necessary to avoid a greater evil, namely, a worse ear infection.

Bump Pain

Pain is often God's warning system. A few days ago I bumped my knee on my desk, and it really hurt. The knee is a sensitive, important part of my body. God invented "bump pain" to warn us that harder blows will create even more pain. Bump pain teaches us to be more careful. Bump pain protects us from greater harm. The pain of an argument with your wife is a warning system to settle things with her so a greater calamity doesn't happen later.

When the props get knocked out, God is often showing us how we have built with "wood, hay, stubble." Or maybe how we have been trying to control things. Or perhaps how little we depend upon Him. This smaller suffering now is good because it prevents a greater suffering later if we were to continue on the same wrong road.

God, as a parent, loves us enough to put the development of our character before the development of our circumstances. When He allows a season of suffering, you can be sure that a personal enlargement lies ahead. God will always add to your suffering the necessary ingredients to turn it into a blessing, even if it must wait for the age to come. The sufferings He allows are never for your harm, but always for your eventual well-being.

Thoughtfully read what the Bible says about the discipline of God:

AND YOU HAVE FORGOTTEN THAT WORD OF ENCOURAGEMENT THAT ADDRESSES YOU AS SONS:
"MY SON, DO NOT MAKE LIGHT OF THE LORD'S DISCIPLINE, AND DO NOT LOSE HEART WHEN HE REBUKES YOU, BECAUSE THE LORD

DISCIPLINES THOSE HE LOVES, AND HE PUNISHES EVERYONE HE
ACCEPTS AS A SON."
ENDURE HARDSHIP AS DISCIPLINE; GOD IS TREATING YOU AS SONS.
FOR WHAT SON IS NOT DISCIPLINED BY HIS FATHER? IF YOU ARE NOT
DISCIPLINED (AND EVERYONE UNDERGOES DISCIPLINE), THEN YOU
ARE ILLEGITIMATE CHILDREN AND NOT TRUE SONS. MOREOVER, WE
HAVE ALL HAD HUMAN FATHERS WHO DISCIPLINED US AND WE
RESPECTED THEM FOR IT. HOW MUCH MORE SHOULD WE SUBMIT TO
THE FATHER OF OUR SPIRITS AND LIVE! OUR FATHERS DISCIPLINED
US FOR A LITTLE WHILE AS THEY THOUGHT BEST; BUT GOD
DISCIPLINES US FOR OUR GOOD, THAT WE MAY SHARE IN HIS
HOLINESS. NO DISCIPLINE SEEMS PLEASANT AT THE TIME, BUT
PAINFUL. LATER ON, HOWEVER, IT PRODUCES A HARVEST OF
RIGHTEOUSNESS AND PEACE FOR THOSE WHO HAVE BEEN TRAINED
BY IT. (Heb. 12:5-11)

The children of overly permissive parents destroy themselves. As God's
children, we need God's discipline.

Is Suffering Good or Bad?

Once upon a time a farmer captured a wild stallion. His neighbor said
to him, "Sure glad to hear your good news."

The farmer replied, "Good news, bad news, who knows?"

A few days later the farmer's son asked if he could break in the horse.
The stallion threw him off, and he broke his leg.

The farmer's neighbor said, "Sorry to hear your bad news."

The farmer replied, "Good news, bad news, who knows?"

A week later war broke out, and all the young men in the city were
drafted to go off to fight.

The neighbor leaned across the fence and said, "Sure turned out to be
good news, the way your boy broke his leg and all."

The farmer replied, "Good news, bad news, who knows?"

We do not see the larger picture of what God is doing in the world.
Things that appear to be suffering and hardship, biblically speaking, form
the ingredients of greater goods and the means to prevent greater evils. In
fact, God actually uses hardship to liberate us from sin and bring about our
salvation:

FOR THE CREATION WAS SUBJECTED TO FRUSTRATION, NOT BY ITS OWN CHOICE, BUT BY THE WILL OF THE ONE [GOD] WHO SUBJECTED IT, IN HOPE THAT THE CREATION ITSELF WILL BE LIBERATED FROM ITS BONDAGE TO DECAY AND BROUGHT INTO THE GLORIOUS FREEDOM OF THE CHILDREN OF GOD. (Rom. 8:20–21)

We should be cautious about thinking of our hardships as hardships. Rather, what we often think of as suffering is really the means of grace to bring us into a closer reliance upon God. God's blows redirect us to the right path. Our sufferings are actually blessings—"the kisses of Jesus."

Certainly, I'm not saying our sufferings don't hurt. I'm not suggesting the pain is not real. Rather, they are peccadilloes compared to the benefits they achieve for us. Why does a bodybuilder endure pain until his muscles groan for rest? He does so because he knows it is the only way he can achieve his goal. In the same way, the Bible says that "our light and momentary troubles are achieving for us an eternal glory that far outweighs them all" (2 Cor. 4:17).

Here's what real suffering is: To be allowed to completely direct our own lives to our eventual destruction. Tragic suffering results when we rebel and abandon the chastening that comes from a loving Father.

We do not know what a day may bring forth, but we do know who brings forth the day. God is a God of purpose. He is working out everything in conformity to the purpose of His will. What men mean for harm, God means for good, for the saving of many lives. God even uses the evil men perpetrate upon us for good.

Three Ways We Suffer

We may suffer for one or more of three reasons:

1. for doing wrong
2. for doing right
3. for no apparent reason

How we respond to our suffering depends on why we are suffering in the first place. It is wise to give some thought to why you are suffering. For example, if God is chastening you for doing a wrong thing, then you know you must submit to the blows of His loving correction. On the other hand, if you are going through a season of suffering because you stood up for right, then you can be glad (Matt. 10–12; Phil. 1:29; 3:10; 1 Peter 4:12–15).

Many times, however, we don't have a clue about why we are going through various trials and temptations. Our sufferings seem to be without reason or logic. It is as though we were standing around minding our own business and all of a sudden, "life" happened. Perhaps the hardest to understand sufferings of all are the seemingly random acts of pain that befall us all from time to time. In such situations we must submit ourselves to the mercy of God and continue to do good.

The Gift of Suffering

An American Christian and a Chinese Christian were speaking to each other. The American said, "I've always wondered, if God loves the Chinese people, why does He let them suffer?"

"That's interesting," replied the Chinese believer. "I've always wondered, if God loves the American people, why doesn't He let them suffer?"

Tim and Joyce formed a partnership with a builder to remodel a house for profit. The builder turned out to be a bad actor, and they got stuck with house payments on two homes.

One day Joyce's father was expressing concern and asked, "How rough is it?"

"Oh, Dad," she said. "This is the greatest challenge to the strength of our marriage we have ever had to face. But, Dad, I wouldn't trade this time for anything. Tim and I have never felt more close to each other. We are reading the Bible together, and we are praying together like we have never done before. We are learning so much."

Why let people suffer? Suffering is a gift of God through which He works out His plan for our lives.

Here is the lesson: Never ask God to shorten the duration of your hard times. Rather, ask God to teach you every lesson He intends for you during your hard time, lest you have to travel that road again.

Suffering will make us bitter or better. The choice is ours.

QUESTIONS AND DECISIONS

1. Are you in a season of suffering right now? If so, do you sense you are handling it well? Are you growing? Has it made you bitter or better?

2. Which of the following questions do you still struggle over?

   • "Why do bad things happen to good people?"
   • "Why do bad things happen to *me?*"
   • "Why do people suffer?"
   • "Exactly what is suffering?"
   • "Is suffering inevitable?"
   • "What causes suffering?"
   • "Why does there have to be suffering at all?"

3. Do you consider suffering to raise a question about the character of God—His greatness and His goodness? If so, what have you learned in this chapter that has helped your thinking?

4. How have your sufferings been like the discipline of a loving father? What greater good has come about or greater evil been prevented?

5. Looking into your past, how have your seasons of suffering been for your good? In what ways have circumstances that looked like bad news turned out for good?

6. When we are suffering, we sometimes think our suffering is going to work for our ultimate harm. According to Romans 8:28, is that really true? In what ways does suffering achieve greater things (2 Cor. 4:17; Rom. 8:20–21)?

7. Do you agree with the following idea or not? Why? What would be the value in adopting this idea as a philosophy of life?

Never ask God to shorten the duration of your hard times. Rather, ask God to teach you every lesson He intends for you during your hard time lest you have to travel that road again.

8. Are you willing to trust God that His Word is true, in spite of your feelings, and that your sufferings are "light and momentary troubles" (2 Cor. 4:17)? If so, pray and ask God to work in and through your sufferings to make you into the kind of man He wants you to be.

Four Consoling Truths
about Suffering

The only problems mankind faces fall into three categories—sin, suffering, and death. The Bible is the only book that speaks adequately to these issues.

—Adrian Rodgers[1]

24 Once during a message I gave near year-end I asked the men in an audience, "How many of you have experienced great *joy* this past year? If so, please raise your hands." Every man in the room raised his hand.

Then I asked, "How many of you have experienced *suffering* this last year? If so, would you please raise your hands." Again, every man in the room raised his hand.

Life simultaneously chugs along two tracks: the track of joy and the track of suffering. When we took our wedding vows, we conceded to the certainty of joy and suffering as we pledged our love "in sickness and in health, in plenty and in want, in joy and in sorrow, as long as we both shall live."

Actually, we frequently find ourselves immersed in joy and sorrow at the same time. We lose a big sale after months of hard work, but come home to the news that our son made the basketball team. Or the boss brags about us in front of the whole company, but on the way home we must drop in on our slowly becoming-senile parents who require daily supervision.

Think for a moment of the great seasons of suffering in your life. I am not talking about opposition. Every day we face opposition—resistance—to leading a successful life. Rather, I'm speaking to those significant periods when circumstances collided and crashed together to overwhelm you for a season.

In my own life I can recall seven major seasons of suffering:

1. the period of *disillusionment* and *lack of meaning* that led me to drop out of high school

2. a prolonged time of *loneliness* and *emptiness* while in the U.S. Army
3. the *despair* early in my marriage, which resulted in surrendering my life to Christ
4. six months of depressed feelings from *unmet* business *expectations* and *financial pressure* early in my business career
5. pain from migraine headaches, which deeply *discouraged* me
6. the tragic *death* of my younger brother
7. five years of *crisis, business troubles,* and *fear of failure* following the Tax Reform Act of 1986

No two- or three-day-long trifles, these seasons of suffering became my consuming focus for months on end—even though I would try to wear a mask that said, "Everything's just great."

What have been your seasons of suffering? You may be in such a season now. Let me suggest that you write them down, perhaps on the margin of this page.

From the Bible we can glean four truths about suffering that I hope will console you:

1. Certainty: In this world you will suffer.
2. Calling: We are called to suffer.
3. Purpose: There is purpose to suffering.
4. Comfort: There is comfort in suffering.

1. The Certainty of Suffering

Faithful Christians suffer.

About two and one half years ago Daryll received a call that his wife had been in an automobile accident. Since that day, she has never had a full night's sleep. The synapses at the base of her skull were damaged, and the nerve endings make her sleep fitfully. It has put a real damper on their lives.

A Christian businessman faces bankruptcy. Another man who misses his daughter deals silently with an empty nest. Another man must cope with a teenager making all the wrong choices.

An attorney faces a dwindling practice against competitors who advertise. A middle-aged man struggles to maintain his lifestyle on the reduced income of a new career. An older man struggles to adjust to the loss of his wife to cancer. A young man faces the daily depression of a pending divorce. Another man's marriage is not making it, and no one knows.

During the Passover meal, Jews symbolically dip parsley in salt water because "life is immersed in tears."

Joseph Parker said, "If you speak to broken hearts, you will always have a congregation. There is one in every pew."

We suffer in many ways: financial pain, relationship pain, emotional pain, physical pain, identity pain, and pain from lack of purpose or direction. Everyone suffers. Faithful Christians suffer. Suffering is certain. In this world you will suffer. Peter said, "Dear friends, do not be surprised at the painful trial you are suffering, as though something strange were happening to you" (1 Peter 4:12). Jesus said, "In this world you will have trouble" (John 16:33).

From Genesis to Revelation, from creation to the present, the Bible describes a great cosmic struggle between the forces of good and the forces of evil culminating in human suffering. The prophets suffered. Jesus suffered. The disciples suffered. We suffer.

As John Guest put it, "We all have one choice to make: Each of us can suffer with Christ or without him."

Expect to suffer, even for doing right. Suffering is certain.

Have you thought of suffering as a certain fate or something you could avoid with enough careful planning?

2. The Calling to Suffer

Chuck Swindoll said, "For God to do an impossible work he must take an impossible man and crush him."

The witty Jamie Buckingham was a bit more direct when he said with tongue in cheek, "He whom God loveth, He beateth the hell out of."

We find in the Bible a call to suffer that chafes against the call to comfort we find glorified in much of today's Christian culture. Please read carefully these verses that accentuate the Christian call to suffer:

- "For it has been granted to you on behalf of Christ not only to believe on him, but also to suffer for him" (Phil. 1:29).
- "To this you were called, because Christ suffered for you, leaving you an example, that you should follow in his steps" (1 Peter 2:21).
- "We must go through many hardships to enter the kingdom of God" (Acts 14:22).

- "Do not be surprised, my brothers, if the world hates you" (1 John 3:13).
- "If the world hates you, keep in mind that it hated me (Jesus) first" (John 15:18).
- "In fact, everyone who wants to live a godly life in Christ Jesus will be persecuted" (2 Tim. 3:12).
- "Consider it pure joy, my brothers, whenever you face trials of many kinds" (James 1:2).
- "If you are insulted because of the name of Christ, you are blessed, for the Spirit of glory and of God rests on you" (1 Peter 4:14).

Compared to all the Bible has to say on the subject, these Scriptures are a mere smattering on the call to suffer for the sake of Christ.

We are presented with two choices. First, we can join in the crusade to shape the world into a utopia by seeking to eliminate all sources of potential pain. Or, second, we can accept that "this world in its present form is passing away" (1 Cor. 7:31) and enter into the Bible's call to suffer.

Have you thought you could remove the pain from your life, or have you accepted that to suffer is a calling?

3. The Purpose of Suffering

People can handle almost any amount of evil and suffering if they believe it is for a purpose.

In a Nazi concentration camp, prisoners were forced to work in a vile, stinking factory to convert human waste and garbage into a fuel additive for the Nazi war machine.

One day an attack by Allied aircraft leveled the factory. The next day the prison guards herded several hundred inmates to one end of the remains. A Nazi officer ordered them to shovel sand into carts and push it to the other end of the plant.

The next day they received orders to move the sand back. And so it went, day after day, hauling the same pile of sand back and forth.

The pressure mounted until, finally, one older man started sobbing uncontrollably. Another screamed, and they beat him into silence. A three-year veteran of the camp broke into a run toward an electrified fence, which killed him.

Dozens of prisoners went mad and ran during the days that followed. The guards shot the ones not electrocuted by the fence.[2]

We can handle almost any kind of suffering as long as we believe it has purpose. Even especially cruel imprisonment and work to help an enemy can be tolerated if they are for a purpose. But remove purpose and suffering is intolerable.

There is purpose to suffering.

Look at what the Scriptures have to say about some purposes for suffering:

- so that we may be delivered from bondage to decay and become children of God (Rom. 8:20–21)
- so that we will rely not upon ourselves but upon God (2 Cor. 1:9)
- so that we may be made more sensitive to others, that we can comfort them with the comfort we ourselves have received (2 Cor. 1:4; Luke 22:31–33)
- so that through our sufferings, the saving grace of God will reach more and more people (2 Cor. 4:15)
- so that God may receive praise (1 Peter 1:6–7)
- so that evil may be punished (Deut. 9:4–5)
- so that we may draw closer to God (2 Cor. 1:4)
- so that we will be corrected by discipline (Heb. 12:5–11)
- so that our character may be developed (Rom. 5:3–5)

There is no *meaningless* suffering. That people suffer for no *apparent* reason does not mean there is no reason.

The familiar passage of Romans 8:28, says, "And we know that in all things God works for the good of those who love him, who have been called according to his purpose." The clear meaning of this verse is that whatever befalls the believer, it works for his good (whether in this life or only eternally we cannot be certain).

Proverbs 12:21 puts it this way: "No harm befalls the righteous,/ but the wicked have their fill of trouble." The word for "harm" is translated "evil" in the King James Version. The Hebrew word for "harm" means "to come to naught or nothingness."[3] Said differently, then, nothing that happens to the righteous will "come to naught"—suffering is not meaningless.

As one man experiencing arrhythmia said, "My crisis was good—it brought me back to reality." It was not meaningless.

As someone has said, "Now the whole answer to the problem of apparently useless suffering is that no suffering is really useless."

God puts things in front of us that are bigger than we are so that we must depend upon Him.

On a Sunday morning in a small Alabama town, a tornado ripped through a Methodist church during the worship service at 11:32 A.M. In the disaster, the pastor's four-year-old child died. In a news conference this pastor expressed a poignant truth, "We don't need faith for the things we understand. We need faith for the things we don't understand."

Actually, it would be more in tune with our experience to suggest there is meaningless or purposeless suffering. However, there are no instances of meaningless suffering in the Bible.

The Bible is our final court of appeal on matters of feeling and experience. We do not interpret our Bible by our experience; we interpret our experience by our Bible. In the end, you and I must live by faith: "We live by faith, not by sight" (2 Cor. 5:7).

The one question we cannot answer is, "Why is there suffering at all?" We simply don't know. It is part of the secret will of God: "The secret things belong to the Lord our God" (Deut. 29:29). But this we do know: God is good.

Though we cannot know why there is suffering at all, we do know from Romans 8:28 that God uses suffering for good. God is always working. If God calls a man to suffer, it is because that is how that man will grow. Pain is for growth. Pain is God's grace for growth.

4. The Comfort in Suffering

Some years ago I had just finished speaking at an evangelistic prayer breakfast in Vero Beach, Florida. As I drove back to Orlando, I passed very near to the site of the last property problem that could put me under.

I eased off the interstate and drove to the buildings. Workmen were busily building out a tenant space, but it was too little too late. I circled the buildings and drove slowly around to the back, parked my car, and got out.

The emotional tension this deal had produced was wrapped around my chest like tight steel bands. After glancing both ways to make sure no one was watching, I lay prostrate on the grass and prayed to God for deliverance and mercy.

Near the beginning of this fresh-in-my-memory season of suffering, I had discovered a wonderful promise from God: "Call upon me in the day of trouble;/ I will deliver you, and you will honor me" (Ps. 50:15). This promise is simple. If we call upon the Lord in our day of trouble, He will deliver us. But notice the promise also includes an obligation. The delivered man is instructed to honor the Lord.

When I first read this verse, I made a pledge to God that if He would deliver me from my suffering, I would praise, honor, and glorify His name for His mercies, which is why I'm telling you this story.

Eventually, we were able to settle up, and God did deliver me. And I followed the psalmist's instructions: "Give thanks to the Lord, call on his name;/ make known among the nations what he has done" (Ps. 105:1).

Although I pray I never have to go through a season of suffering like that again, I wouldn't trade the experience for any amount of fame, fortune, power, or prestige. I truly thank God for the suffering. He reshaped my character and kept me from running headlong into certain disaster.

Because there is purpose *to* suffering, there is comfort *in* suffering.

God knows what He is doing. He is completely dependable and trustworthy. We can count on Him. He will always do what is right. Through our suffering, He corrects our faulty thinking, spares us from greater evils, and brings about greater goods. He leads us to repent of our sins. He produces in us the character of His Son, Jesus. He disciplines us, molds us, and shapes us.

Can we become all that God wants us to be without affliction? The Bible indicates the answer is no. We need the grace of affliction. Yes, trials and tribulations are painful at the time, and we should never seek them out. Yet, when they come, they come as the sweet fragrance of God's grace to help us grow, mature, and stay on the right path. King David understood that affliction is actually a blessing:

IT WAS GOOD FOR ME TO BE AFFLICTED
  SO THAT I MIGHT LEARN YOUR DECREES. . . .
BEFORE I WAS AFFLICTED I WENT ASTRAY,
  BUT NOW I OBEY YOUR WORD. . . .
I KNOW, O LORD, THAT YOUR LAWS ARE RIGHTEOUS,
  AND IN FAITHFULNESS YOU HAVE AFFLICTED ME. . . .
IF YOUR LAW HAD NOT BEEN MY DELIGHT,
  I WOULD HAVE PERISHED IN MY AFFLICTION.
(Ps. 119:71, 67, 75, 92)

The Bible encourages you to "cast all your anxiety on him because he cares for you" (1 Peter 5:7).

Charles's wife died after a lengthy battle with cancer. For many months he grieved deeply over the passing of his best friend. Indeed, she was an encouragement and source of increased faith to all who knew her. One day while riding in his car, Charles started yelling *at* God in anguish. When he had completely vented himself, the only thing left to do was to yell *to* God, "Now what?"

"Now what" for you? Where are you today? Perhaps you have made your peace with suffering. Or maybe you are struggling to accept suffering as part of life. Perhaps you can't seem to see any purpose to it. Possibly you long for your joy to return. You may need to be comforted. Comfort is available. Come to Jesus. Throw yourself upon His mercy and goodness. Be patient and wait for Him to act. God will rescue you in due season.

QUESTIONS AND DECISIONS

1. Are you in a season of suffering? Where are you hurting and why?

2. *Certainty:* Have you thought of suffering as a certain fate or something you could avoid with enough careful planning?

3. *Calling:* Have you thought you could remove the pain from your life, or have you accepted that to suffer is a calling?

4. What should be our attitude toward suffering based upon each of the following verses? Have you ever considered suffering as a Christian calling? How do these verses affect your thinking?

   • John 16:33 _____
   • Philippians 1:29 _____
   • 1 Peter 4:12–14 _____
   • James 1:2 _____
   • Acts 14:22 _____

5. *Purpose:* From your experience, do you have the sense that suffering has purpose to it, or does it seem meaningless? Explain your answer.

6. What does the Bible say about the purpose of suffering?

   • Romans 5:3–5 _____
   • 2 Corinthians 1:4, 9 _____
   • Romans 8:20–21 _____
   • James 1:2–4 _____
   • 1 Peter 1:6–7 _____

7. *Comfort:* How do the three previous biblical truths we have discussed provide us with comfort in suffering?

   • Certainty: In this world you will suffer.
   • Calling: We are called to suffer.
   • Purpose: There is purpose to suffering.

8. "The Bible is our final court of appeal on matters of feeling and experience. We do not interpret our Bible by our experience; we interpret our experience by our Bible." Do you ☐ agree/ ☐ disagree? Explain your answer. Why should we base our understanding of suffering on the Bible rather than on our experience?

PART 7

•

THE SEASON OF

SUCCESS

The Four "Attitudes" of Successful Men

Many of life's failures are men who did not realize how close they were to success when they gave up.

—*Unknown*

It is a great deal better to do all things you should do, than to spend the rest of your life wishing you had.

—*Unknown*

25 A ruddy young man bends down, reaches into a trickling seasonal stream, selects five stones polished smooth by time, faces off against a nine-foot-tall giant who talks too much, hurls a single stone that sinks deep into his forehead, cuts off his head, and saves his people from annihilation. It was quite a day.

The people cheered their new hero, David. As a reward for his bravery he rose to a high rank in the king's army, pleasing everyone. The Bible says, "In everything he did he had great success, because the Lord was with him" (1 Sam. 18:14). It was a season of success. This was his beginning.

No man who ever lived has been more successful than David. The Bible records that "he died at a good old age, having enjoyed long life, wealth, and honor" (1 Chron. 29:28). This was his end.

What kind of man was David? The Bible tells us that God declared, "I have found David son of Jesse a man after my own heart; he will do everything I want him to do" (Acts 13:22). His heart was fully devoted to the Lord (1 Kings 11:4). God said he "kept my commands and followed me with all his heart, doing only what was right in my eyes" (1 Kings 14:8).

No man in the Bible ever received more approval from God than David. No man represents a better model for how we should live our lives. What more could you or I ever hope for than to be called a man after God's own heart?

God had a purpose for David's life. David "served God's purpose in his own generation" (Acts 13:36). God has a purpose for your life too.

David knew that his success was not for himself only, but also for the sake of others. The Bible says, "David knew that the Lord had established him as king over Israel and had exalted his kingdom for the sake of his people Israel" (2 Sam. 5:12). Whatever success you and I enjoy, part of the purpose God gives success is for the benefit of others.

The "Character of David" Test

As you read this page, David is with God in heaven. He learned the secrets of success. He became a man worthy of receiving God's favor. Are you such a man? Are you, like David, a man after God's own heart? Answer these questions honestly, and if need be, make some decisions about where you go from here.

- Are you a man after God's own heart?
- Will you do everything the Lord wants you to do?
- Is your heart fully devoted to the Lord?
- Do you keep His commandments?
- Do you follow Him with all your heart?
- Do you do only what is right in God's eyes?
- Are you serving God's purpose in your generation?

David stands at the head of a long line of Bible heroes after whom we can pattern our lives. God gave Nehemiah the vision to rebuild the city of his fathers. God anointed Daniel to preserve the kingdom of God while his nation was exiled to Babylon. God used Asa to reform Judah from its wicked ways. God sent Joseph to Egypt ahead of his family to save their lives. God called Noah to build an ark to preserve the human race. God raised up Moses to lead his people out of slavery.

If David and this gallery of heroes could speak to us from the grave, what advice would they give us about how to lead a successful life? What would they lay down as the attitudes of success?

Attitude #1: Take Some Risks

First, our gallery of heroes would say, "Have the courage to take some risks others are not willing to take." No one else would go out to fight against Goliath, but David risked almost certain death and went. When everyone else's courage melted, David did not lose heart. So that you don't think He was some naive, inexperienced teenage boy, remember that this boy had a track record. He had killed both lion and bear with his bare hands. It was not an uncalculated risk.

Like David, we should take more risks, but not without some calculation and preparation. Success is that point at which preparation meets opportunity. For example, it would be foolish to risk your life savings on a small business if you have no business experience at all. On the other hand, if God calls you to start your own business after serving as an administrator to another businessman for fifteen years, perhaps you should take a calculated, considered risk.

Take divinely inspired risks. Many people never attempt anything significant because they might fail. Not Abraham. Not Joshua. Not Noah. Not Gideon. Not Daniel. Not Paul. They heard God's calling on their lives and took calculated risks because they believed God was able to complete what He put in their hearts to do.

Hudson Taylor said, "Many Christians estimate difficulties in light of their own resources, and thus attempt little and often fail in the little they do attempt. All God's giants have been weak men who did great things for God because they reckoned on His power and presence being with them."

Courage is not the absence of fear but a willingness to trust God anyway in the presence of fear. Right now I'm investigating a drive-time radio show for men. Frankly, my strongest impulse is not to do it. Why? Well, fear. What if it fails? What if people don't like me? What if I can't fund it? What if I am criticized? Or worse still, ridiculed?

Fifty people over the age of ninety-five were asked on an open-ended basis, "If you could live your life over again, what would you do differently?" As you can imagine, the answers covered a wide range. However, one answer that kept showing up over and over was this: "If I had it to do over again, I would risk more."[1] Are you afraid to stick your neck out on something God is leading you to do?

Attitude #2: Depend on God

Second, David and his friends would tell us, "Do everything you do in the name of the Lord." David was scrupulous to follow the Lord's leading. The few times he acted in the flesh he suffered deeply. For example, many people died when he took a forbidden census, and when he committed adultery with Bathsheba, the baby born to them died. He was human. So are we. But David learned to repent and to give God glory in all things, and God gave David victory and success in return.

King Asa was a brilliant, relentless reformer of ancient Judah. He cleaned up the nation and made laws that required people to seek the Lord and obey His commands (Asa was his own Congress). He created an economic boom and prospered, but what did he get for his labors? An army of one million troops marched against him.

Asa responded, "Lord, there is no one like you to help the powerless against the mighty. Help us, O Lord our God, for we rely on you, and in your name we have come against this vast army. O Lord, you are our God; do not let man prevail against you" (2 Chron. 14:11).

I picture Asa running around telling everyone, "Hey! Don't worry about these suckers. We rely on God! There's no one like God. We'll go out against this army in the name of the Lord! They can't whip us until they finish whipping God!"

Notice what Asa did. Asa put God's reputation on the line. He so closely identified everything he did with the reputation of God that before men could prevail against him, they first had to prevail against God.

Today, too many men think they are saved by faith, but somehow the rest is up to them. They have a *saving* faith, but not a *living* faith. God wants us to live all of our lives with His name on our lips.

Once I was negotiating for a piece of property. As often happens, at the critical moment the seller brought up the proverbial straw man—that "other" buyer waiting in the wings—to knock me off balance.

He harassed me with this antic several times, but I simply ignored him. Finally, he played his trump card, and I told him, "Look, if it is God's sovereign plan for us to buy this property, there is nothing I can do *not* to get it. On the other hand, if it is God's sovereign plan for us not to get it, nothing I can do will make it happen. So you go ahead and do what you have to do." (This statement must have rattled him because after that the sale went through like a breeze.)

One of our greatest temptations is to depend upon our own strengths that we make into feeble little gods upon which we falsely depend:

- a good plan
- experience
- natural ability
- resources available
- strength of will and character
- other men
- our integrity

To depend on any of these rather than on God is to make an idol. Granted, these are the *means* through which God will work, but let us always remember it is God who does the working.

Once you believe you have the vision of God, depend utterly on Him. So closely identify everything you do with God that before men can prevail against you, they must first prevail against God.

Are you giving God the glory in everything you do? Are you depending on God to bring about your seasons of success?

Attitude #3: Take Responsibility

Third, our hall of heroes would want us to know, "You must take personal responsibility for your life."

Muhammad Ali was describing a religious experience to a reporter. The reporter said, "It must be a great comfort to know that God is with you there in the corner of the ring." Ali replied, "Yes, it is a great comfort, but make no mistake about it. When the bell rings, that guy on the other side of the ring comes over and hits *me!*"

David depended completely on God, but it wasn't God who hurled the stone and cut off Goliath's head—David did. We must take responsibility for the outcome of our lives.

The license plate on a friend's car reads: UP 2 YOU. "I'm tired of Christians blaming others and using that as an excuse for not making a contribution," he says. "We must go on from here. You have to take personal responsibility for who you are and what you will become."

At first these two ideas—depend on God and take responsibility—look as if they contradict each other. On further examination, though, we see they are complementary, not contradictory.

We could put it this way (notice the nuancing):

- Success is the result of God's blessing, not man's effort.
- Success does not depend on man's effort, but rarely comes without hard work.

Work hard. You can't expect God to work if you don't work. Aggressively follow up whatever God reveals to do. Be thankful for whatever God decides to do.

The apostle Paul put it this way: "I worked harder than all of them—yet not I, but the grace of God that was with me" (1 Cor. 15:10). Even though he worked very hard, he attributed his efforts to the grace of God at work within him. In essence, he was saying, "I worked hard, but I always knew it depended on God, not me."

Dwight L. Moody put it this way: "We pray like it is all up to God. We work like it is all up to us." This makes good theology.

Working hard will not guarantee success, but not working hard will guarantee failure. Unfortunately, success does not always come in direct proportion to the amount of effort we put forth, but failure always comes in direct proportion to our laziness.

While writing this manuscript, I ran into a brief cash-flow problem. I could have said, "I can't worry about that. I'm too busy right now." But instead I stopped writing for a while to straighten out the problem. That's life.

Someone has said, "One hundred percent + 100 percent = 100 percent," meaning that our 100 percent plus God's 100 percent ends up producing 100 percent of God's will. What is our 100 percent? We are responsible to be faithful. *God is not calling men to be successful; He is calling men to be faithful.* What is God's 100 percent? God is responsible to do whatever He wants, because He is God.

If we are faithful, we will be successful in the way God wants us to be—and that should be enough. If it's not, we've got a problem. Christian men living in a world that has become a festering sore of violence, crime, drugs, poverty, racism, and despair can no longer afford to view success the way the world views success—through the narrow lens of "What's in it for me?"

To what extent have you been seeking success based on your own effort apart from God? On the other hand, are you being diligent, or are you guilty of spiritualizing lazy habits? Take responsibility for your life.

Attitude #4: Expect Opposition

Fourth, David and company would want to say to us, "You must expect opposition, even when you are doing God's will."

When Nehemiah heard that the captives who returned to Jerusalem from the Babylonian captivity had not been able to rebuild their city, even after eleven years, God put a vision in his heart to help them rebuild the city and the wall around it. What is the vision God has put in your heart?

God provided Nehemiah with all the resources he needed to rebuild the city where he grew up. But when Nehemiah began to rebuild, he encountered stiff opposition. Opposition came from enemies who taunted them, rubble that discouraged them, famine that debilitated them, taxes that sapped them, and slavery that dehumanized them. They suffered through external threats, natural disasters, government interference, and economic hardships.

The problem with life is that there is opposition. A young man who had played especially well during basketball training camp did awful in his first game. The coach pulled him aside and asked, "What's going on?"

The young man said, "Coach, I would be doing great, but there are all these tall guys running around waving their hands in my face!"

In a fallen world we must expect opposition. When Paul was writing to tell the Corinthians he wanted to visit them, he said, "But I will stay on at Ephesus until Pentecost, because a great door for effective work has opened to me, and there are many who oppose me" (1 Cor. 16:8–9). Notice how a great opportunity was accompanied by a great opposition. Paul produced fruit, but not without resistance. This we must learn to expect. Consider the following verses:

WE HAD PREVIOUSLY SUFFERED AND BEEN INSULTED IN PHILIPPI, AS YOU KNOW, BUT WITH THE HELP OF OUR GOD WE DARED TO TELL YOU HIS GOSPEL IN SPITE OF STRONG OPPOSITION. (1 Thess. 2:2)

ENDURE HARDSHIP WITH US LIKE A GOOD SOLDIER OF CHRIST JESUS. (2 Tim. 2:3)

THEREFORE, SINCE WE ARE SURROUNDED BY SUCH A GREAT CLOUD OF WITNESSES, LET US THROW OFF EVERYTHING THAT HINDERS AND THE SIN THAT SO EASILY ENTANGLES, AND LET US RUN WITH PERSEVERANCE THE RACE MARKED OUT FOR US. LET US FIX OUR EYES ON JESUS, THE AUTHOR AND PERFECTER OF OUR FAITH, WHO FOR THE JOY SET BEFORE HIM ENDURED THE CROSS, SCORNING ITS SHAME, AND SAT DOWN AT THE RIGHT HAND OF THE THRONE OF GOD. CONSIDER HIM WHO ENDURED SUCH OPPOSITION FROM SINFUL MEN, SO THAT YOU WILL NOT GROW WEARY AND LOSE HEART. (Heb. 12:1–3)

Nehemiah handled his opposition this way: "Therefore I stationed some of the people behind the lowest points of the wall . . . with their swords, spears and bows. . . . From that day on, half of my men did the work, while the other half were equipped with spears, shields, bows and armor" (Neh. 4:13, 16). Nehemiah depended on the Lord but also took responsibility for the call God put on his life. And because he expected opposition, he was prepared and not overwhelmed.

Where are you getting opposition? Are you surprised? Is it from a quarter you least expected? Are you prepared so that you will not be overwhelmed?

These four attitudes of success form a vital foundation for building success that won't collapse when the storm comes. Keeping these four attitudes on our screen will help us manage our success so that it will last.

QUESTIONS AND DECISIONS

1. Read Matthew 7:24–27 and 1 Corinthians 3:11–13. What is the only sure foundation of success?

2. We looked at four attitudes of successful men in this chapter. The first attitude of success is to *have the courage to take some risks*. Where have you been less than courageous in your life? What changes would you like to make? Who can you talk to for counsel and advice?

3. The second attitude of success is to *depend on God and not your own abilities*. Do you do everything in the name of the Lord? What happens when you depend on yourself?

4. The third attitude of success is to *take personal responsibility for your life*. To what extent have you over-spiritualized your life and not taken responsibility? To what extent have you under-spiritualized and taken too much control over your circumstances? What is the right balance?

5. The fourth attitude of success is to *expect opposition*. In what ways have you been overwhelmed with opposition? In what ways have you underestimated the influence of this fallen world on your life? In what ways have you given the devil too much credit and overemphasized his power?

6. If you have not already done so, take the "Character of David" Test by answering these questions:

   - Are you a man after God's own heart?
   - Will you do everything the Lord wants you to do?
   - Is your heart fully devoted to the Lord?
   - Do you keep His commandments?
   - Do you follow Him with all your heart?
   - Do you do only what is right in God's eyes?
   - Are you serving God's purpose in your generation?

Have you been a man after God's own heart? Willing to do what He wants? Keeping His commands? Following Him with all your heart? Doing what is right in His eyes? If so, thank God in prayer for giving you the desire to follow and serve Him wholeheartedly. If not, what remains between you and a full, complete, no-regrets surrender to the Lord? If now, near the end of this book, you are ready to surrender all to Christ, tell Him in prayer right now using your own words.

True Success

Our tendency is to overestimate what we can accomplish in one year and underestimate what we can accomplish in ten years.

—*Richard Foster*[1]

26 When I opened the morning paper, I was stung by the headline. One of our city's most prominent businessmen was dead. For several days shock waves rippled through our business community. Everyone was stunned as details became available about the tragic airplane crash that took the life of such a big player.

That was about ten years ago. I must tell you that today no one misses the man. In fact, since his funeral, I have heard his name mentioned only one time. You see, his death was shocking but not tragic. His prominence created a shock, but because he had invested only in things rather than in people, hardly anyone was saddened by his death. In other words, he was commercially successful but relationally poor. He was a man who lived only for his own self-interests. He did not invest in other people. Everything he did, he did for himself.

The True Meaning of Success

Any man who says he doesn't want to be successful is a liar or a fool or both. The only issue is, "What is *true* success?"

In one sense, this entire book has been about success. From page one we have been leading up to this chapter. Let's begin by making sure we are on the same page about what success really is.

What is *true* success? First, can any man be considered truly successful who does not have an assurance that when he dies he will go to heaven? I think not. The Bible asks, "What can be compared with the value of eternal life?" (Matt. 16:26 TLB). No matter how many good deeds you perform, accolades you receive, poor people you feed, or how much money you give to the church, unless you have asked Jesus to forgive your sins and trusted Him to be your Savior and Lord, you are no success.

Conversely, can any man be considered a failure if he knows Christ? Actually, yes. Even though you succeed *spiritually* (you have the assurance of eternal life), you can still fail *morally* (living without integrity), *relationally* (failure to love others as Christ commands), or *financially* (failure to provide for your family). You may go to heaven, but ignominiously: "He himself will be saved, but only as one escaping through the flames" (1 Cor. 3:15). To not live a life of love, faith, obedience, and service in your marriage, family, work, church, and community is to build with "wood, hay, stubble" (1 Cor. 3:12).

My brother-in-law was offered a lucrative job with a major software company. During the interview, it became clear that the position required a great deal of travel.

"How many days a month would I be on the road traveling?" he asked.

The recruiter laughed and said, "You've asked the wrong question, Hal. The question is, 'How many days would you be home?'"

"Okay, how many days would I be home?"

"Three or four days a month, and that includes weekends."

He turned down the offer. Sure, he wanted to advance his career and make more money. Who doesn't? But he didn't let his personal ambition detour him from his calling. He understood a few key principles we have already discussed that deserve a brief review. As has already been said, the problem for many men is not so much that they are failing. Rather, the problem is that they are achieving their goals, but they are the wrong goals. Failure means to succeed in a way that doesn't really matter.

There are many ways to measure success beyond career success. No amount of success at work will compensate for failure at home. To succeed in your career but fail at home is to fail completely.

True success is to satisfy your *calling*, not your *ambition*.

How Are You Doing?

How we decide we are doing depends on where we have placed value. In other words, "What's important to me?"

The problem is that unless we remain vigilant to "take captive every thought to make it obedient to Christ" (2 Cor. 10:5), we become products, even prisoners, of our own culture. Then, once culture-bound to a man-centered world, we tend to evaluate (read: e-"value"-ate) how we are doing on the basis of the world's default values:

- performance
- production
- prestige
- possessions
- perception
- status
- strokes
- acceptance
- appearances
- physical attractiveness
- athleticism
- happiness
- finances
- IQ

[handwritten: GOALS VS RESULTS]

Our culture offers value only to people who possess the above attributes. Our culture grants human worth to you in proportion to how good you look, how smart you are, how much money you have, and/or how athletic you are.

To be considered successful in the eyes of the world, you are required to display one or more of the four killer "bees": *beauty, brains, bucks,* and *brawn.* If you don't have one of these attributes, forget it. The emphasis is always on externals—what you have and do—rather than on who you are.

When we accept the default values of our age, we become culture bound. We allow "how we are doing" to be determined by the standards of the world rather than the Word of God.

The Word of God says that as Samuel looked over Jesse's boys to anoint one of them king, God said, "Do not consider his appearance or his height. . . . The Lord does not look at the things man looks at. Man looks at the outward appearance, but the Lord looks at the heart" (1 Sam. 16:7).

How do you decide how you are doing? Review the list above. Be honest. How many of these points are axial forces in your life? An axis is the center line around which a body or object rotates. Around what center lines does your life rotate?

How *should* we decide how we are doing? The Bible helps us refocus on those priorities in life that really count. Consider these centering questions:

- Am I putting God first in my life (Matt. 6:33)?
- Am I maintaining my first love, Jesus Christ (Rev. 2:4)?
- Am I in the center of God's will (Phil. 2:13)?
- Am I constantly seeking after the will of God (Rom. 12:2)?
- Am I the husband, father, and provider I should be (1 Tim. 5:8)?
- Am I a faithful, diligent, honest employee or employer (Col. 3:23–25)?
- Am I seeking to be financially responsible (Luke 16:10–12)?

When men sincerely ask these questions of themselves on a regular basis, they will find a true success that really matters.

Don't get caught up in the world. Wear the world loosely like the old, frumpy, tattered suit that it is. Already threadbare, soon it will be gone.

The "Ten Measures of True Success" Quiz

Success that really matters means a full-orbed, well-balanced, priority-based, thought-through success. I do not think a man will feel and sense that his life has been successful unless he can honestly answer yes to all of the following ten questions.

1. Am I performing fulfilling work?
2. Am I a good provider?
3. Am I doing everything possible to help my children become responsible adults?
4. Am I building a strong, loving marriage?
5. Am I doing everything possible to introduce my family to faith in Christ?
6. Am I investing in other people's lives as a friend, counselor, accountability partner, and mentor?
7. Am I living a life of good deeds?
8. Am I living a life of integrity?
9. Am I walking closely with the Lord Jesus every day?
10. Will I go to heaven when I die?

This is success. If failure means to succeed in a way that doesn't really matter, then these are the ways that really matter.

Time for a pop quiz. To which of these ten questions can you answer yes? To which must you answer no?

No matter how poorly you may have rated yourself, the good news with Christ is that He is the God of redemption. He is a healer, the Great Physician. It's never too late with God. No matter how much of your life you have allowed to slip by without paying attention to success that really matters, He will help you redeem the time. It's never too late to become a real man.

What Makes a Real Man?

1. *A real man is a man of courage.*

He is not afraid to do what a real man ought to do. He is not afraid to love his Lord, to cherish his wife, to nurture his children, to be excellent in his work, to be faithful in his service, and to be vulnerable with his friends. And he does all this before a watching world, unashamed.

2. *A real man is a man of wisdom.*

He doesn't take himself too seriously. As he gets older, he laughs more. He learns to let little offenses go. In fact, bigger and bigger offenses seem smaller and smaller in his mind. He realizes people are weak, and he himself is far weaker than he once thought. He seeks more advice, and he doesn't always accept the first solution to his problems as the best solution.

3. *A real man is a man of commitments.*

He has consciously decided to set aside his personal, selfish goals and ask how he can live for Christ. He has decided to make the four commitments of a kingdom builder. A kingdom builder commits to *build the kingdom* (the Great Commission [Matt. 28:18–20]). A kingdom builder commits to *tend the culture* (the Cultural Commission [Genesis 1:28]). A kingdom builder commits to *love other people* (the New Commandment [John 13:34–35]). A kingdom builder commits to *love the King* (the Great Commandment [Matt. 22:37–38]).

4. *A real man is a man of balance.*

He loves God without neglecting to serve Him. He cherishes and nurtures his family without neglecting to work hard to provide for them. He enjoys each day as a gift from God without neglecting to provide for retirement and the risk of early death. He gives his employer a full day's work without neglecting to save enough energy for the ones who will sit on the front row at his funeral.

Have you been pursuing true success, a success that really matters? How are you doing? How should you be doing? If you died in a plane crash today, would anyone really care? What changes do you need to make to find real success?

Carefully consider the words of this prayer:

Prayer by an Unknown Confederate Soldier

I asked God for strength, that I might achieve.
I was made weak, that I might learn humbly to obey.

I asked for health, that I might do greater things.
I was given infirmity, that I might do better things.

I asked for riches, that I might be happy.
I was given poverty, that I might be wise.

I asked for power, that I might have the praise of men.
I was given weakness, that I might feel the need of God.

I asked for all things, that I might enjoy life.
I was given life, that I might enjoy all things.

I got nothing that I asked for—but everything I had hoped for.
Almost despite myself, my unspoken prayers were answered.

I am among all men, most richly blessed.

We can learn much from this unknown soldier. Like us, he prayed for what he thought he wanted. What do we think we want? Strength, health, riches, power—all things. And why do we want it? So that we might achieve, do greater things, be happy, receive the praise of men, and enjoy life.

In His kindness God answers the misguided prayer, not with what we want but what we need. Sometimes He gives infirmity, poverty, weakness— but always life. And why? So that we might learn to obey, do better things, be wise, feel the need of God, and enjoy all things.

When we get nothing we ask for, let us be mindful that our great God will give us everything we need and all that we hope for—almost despite ourselves.

I would like to share a poignant truth with you: *The great secret of contentment is not getting what you want, but wanting what you get.*

Success in the Public Square

I would like to conclude by discussing a great problem that Christian men must take the leadership to solve. There can be no meaningful personal success without addressing this issue.

We live in an era in which the leavening influence of Christian faith on American society and culture has eroded like a washed-out road. In one generation we have witnessed a catastrophic decline in education, law, government, the arts, entertainment, and every other arena. Simultaneously, we have witnessed a meteoric rise in Christian divorce, sexual perversion, violence, abortion, drug abuse, youth gangs, inner-city despair, and much more. Could anyone deny that, by and large, the church is losing the battle for the culture? Why is this? And where is the compelling draw of a gospel that changes men's lives?

If 60 million people claim to be born again—and they do—then how could this decline of culture possibly take place? Good question. The reason is the problem of Cultural Christianity versus Biblical Christianity.

Are not 60 million Christians enough yeast to make the "bread of life" rise in our society? Unfortunately, a Gallup Poll showed that only 10 percent of these 60 million people are deeply committed (or Biblical) Christians. Because most of these 60 million people are Cultural Christians, they have a faith that is, as Os Guiness says, "privately engaging but publicly irrelevant."

The unhappy result of Cultural Christianity is an impotent, self-centered faith that doesn't change things. In short, Cultural Christians live mostly for themselves. They don't make an investment in the kingdom.

Here is a great problem in the world today: Men have overemphasized their private faith to the detriment of their public duties.

To be a truly successful man requires that you take responsibility for your private life—your relationships with your wife and children, your finances, health, and walk with God—and that you also take responsibility for building the kingdom and tending the culture.

The irony is that we are there—Christians are everywhere, only silent. Except for a few voices, ours has been a generation uninvolved in the debates taking place on the public square. I'm not suggesting Christian men should try to usher in Christian government, media, or marketplace.

But we should be vitally involved in working for government that governs Christianly, media that report fairly, and a marketplace that competes with integrity.

What can we do? We can say, "I want my life to count. I want my life to have mattered." We can take on some public duties. We can become involved in discipling other men to become spiritual leaders. We can recommend Biblical Christianity. We can help men convert from cultural Christianity. We can show men a picture of what a Biblical Christian would look like by our lives. We can challenge men to build the kingdom.

Personally, I sense the most strategic use of my time is to intentionally invest my life in men who will invest their lives in other men (2 Tim. 2:2). I'm implementing this strategy principally by meeting with a few FAT men (faithful, available, and teachable), and by doing more writing and speaking. What do you sense are your public duties?

If men across this nation who *know* Christ in *private* will also *live* for Christ in *public*, we can experience a return to sanity. Children will grow up in godly homes, wives will be happy, businesses will deal honestly, government will be just, the education system will teach values, the media will report fairly, the judicial system will be equal for all, the arts will uplift, entertainment will refresh, professional sports will set an example, the church will be pure, the poor will be fed, the naked will be clothed, the sick and imprisoned will be visited, and God will be glorified. God has made an investment in you. Have you invested in the kingdom?

And so here is my conclusion: We don't need any more Christians to win our nation back to God. All we need is for the Christians we already have to *be* Christian, wherever they are.

Leave the World Better Than You Found It

Recently, someone shared this. Someone had passed it along to him, and I pass it along to you.

- The world is a better place because Michaelangelo didn't say, "I don't do ceilings."
- The world is a better place because Martin Luther didn't say, "I don't do doors."
- The world is a better place because Noah didn't say, "I don't do arks."

- The world is a better place because David didn't say, "I don't do giants."
- The world is a better place because Jeremiah didn't say, "I don't do weeping."
- The world is a better place because Peter didn't say, "I don't do Gentiles."
- The world is a better place because Paul didn't say, "I don't do letters."
- The world is a better place because Mary didn't say, "I don't do virgin births."
- The world is a better place because Jesus didn't say, "I don't do crosses."

Will the world be a better place because you didn't say, "I don't do _____"? Will you leave the world a better place than you found it? What will you put in the blank space? What will be your legacy? Will you discover and answer God's calling, both private and public?

Dwight L. Moody, the Billy Graham of the 19th century, one day heard these challenging words which marked the beginning of a new era in his life: "The world has yet to see what God will do, with, and for, and through, and in, and by, the man who is fully and wholly consecrated to Him."

"He said 'a man,'" thought Moody. *"He did not say a great man, nor a learned man, nor a rich man, nor a wise man, nor an eloquent man, nor a 'smart' man, but simply 'a man.' I am a man, and it lies with the man himself whether he will, or will not, make that entire and full consecration. I will try my utmost to be that man."*[2]

Will you try your utmost to be that man? What will you do with your "dash"?

Conclusion

During our lifetimes, we will each feel the gentle breeze of success and the harsh wind of suffering many times. We can no more control our seasons than we can control winter, spring, summer, and fall. At the height of financial success, tragedy may strike. In the depth of despair, light breaks through.

Although we can't control our seasons, we can control ourselves. We can live worthy of God's calling. Each of us can seek to be the kind of man that God will want to bless. In this book we have sought to show

men how to build with "silver, gold, and costly stones" on the only foundation that will survive, the foundation of Jesus Christ and His Word (Matt.
7:24–27; 1 Cor. 3:11–13).

As you go from this book back into the seasons of your life, remember
that God has a purpose for your life, a calling. God has put you in whatever
life situation you occupy for a reason. God wants you to go into your arena—
whether business, the trades, government, education, medicine, law, the
arts, entertainment, sports, the military, science, or religion—and be a
witness for Him among the idols of the world, to build the kingdom and
tend the culture. Go into your arena and be faithful there, whether or not
you achieve worldly success. Use your skill, cling to your integrity, and do
not be ashamed of your piety.

As you turn now to that unique set of problems and opportunities that
only you face, know that you are not alone, for God makes the seasons.

QUESTIONS AND DECISIONS

1. How do you define true success?

2. In this chapter, four ways were mentioned in which a man can fail:

   • spiritually
   • morally
   • relationally
   • financially

   Which of these areas are strengths for you? Which are weaknesses?

3. Which of the following default values of the world most influence the way you measure "how you are doing"? Pick the top four and number them in order.

   • performance
   • production
   • prestige
   • possessions
   • perception
   • status
   • strokes
   • acceptance
   • appearances
   • physical attractiveness
   • athleticism
   • happiness
   • finances
   • IQ

4. What percentage of your values would you say comes from the world and Cultural Christianity, and what percentage comes from Biblical Christianity (for example, 25/75)?

5. To have value in the world you must have beauty, brains, bucks, or brawn. According to 1 Samuel 16:7, how does God evaluate you?

6. Here are the ways we should decide how we are doing. Answer the following questions. How are you doing on this basis?

- Am I putting God first in my life (Matt. 6:33)?
- Am I maintaining my first love, Jesus Christ (Rev. 2:4)?
- Am I in the center of God's will (Phil. 2:13)?
- Am I constantly seeking after the will of God (Rom. 12:2)?
- Am I the husband, father, and provider I should be (1 Tim. 5:8)?
- Am I a faithful, diligent, honest employee or employer (Col. 3:23–25)?
- Am I seeking to be financially responsible (Luke 16:10–12)?

7. In this chapter, ten elements of a well-balanced, priority-based success that really matters were posed as questions. If you did not complete those questions as you were reading, do them now.

☐ 1. Am I performing fulfilling work?
☐ 2. Am I a good provider?
☐ 3. Am I doing everything possible to help my children become responsible adults?
☐ 4. Am I building a strong, loving marriage?
☐ 5. Am I doing everything possible to introduce my family to faith in Christ?
☐ 6. Am I investing in other people's lives as a friend, counselor, accountability partner, and mentor?
☐ 7. Am I living a life of good deeds?
☐ 8. Am I living a life of integrity?
☐ 9. Am I walking closely with the Lord Jesus every day?
☐ 10. Will I go to heaven when I die?

How did you do? What changes do you need to make based on your answers?

8. If you died in a plane crash today, would anyone really care? What changes do you need to make to find real success?

9. Will the world be a better place because you didn't say, "I don't do _____"? Will you leave the world a better place than you found it? What will be your legacy? Will you discover and answer God's calling, both private and public? What will you do with your "dash"?

Discussion Leader's Guide

Any man interested in starting a group to discuss *The Seven Seasons of a Man's Life* can successfully do so and lead a lively discussion by following these guidelines:

1. Decide how many weeks your group will meet and pick the chapters to read and discuss each week. Groups may be existing Bible studies, fellowship groups, prayer groups, or Sunday school classes (women can be included). Or, you may want to start a group from scratch.

2. How to Start a New Group: Photocopy the Table of Contents and the questions at the end of a couple of chapters, and give a copy to the men you want to meet with. Ask them if they would like to be in a discussion group that would read the book and answer the discussion questions at the end of each chapter. This can be a group from work, church, your neighborhood, or a combination. The optimum-sized group would be eight to twelve men (assuming some men will have to miss a week occasionally). Decide to meet for a set number of weeks. If the group gels, you may want to suggest the group continue to meet after you are finished studying *The Seven Seasons of a Man's Life.*

3. First Week: Distribute a copy of the book to each member together with a typed schedule. Assign the first chapter as next week's reading assignment and ask them to be prepared to answer the questions at the end of the chapter. Then go around the room and ask each man to share with the group where he is on his spiritual pilgrimage. This is a great ice-breaker, and the men will be encouraged and enjoy learning about where other men are on their pilgrimage. Be sure to point out that there are no wrong answers to this question. Some may just be starting on their pilgrimage; others may be well down the road. Close with a prayer. Always adjourn exactly when you said you would.

4. Typical Week: Begin with an ice-breaker question. As an alternative, you may ask a different man each week to give a maximum five-minute personal testimony of how he became a Christian. During a one-hour meeting, a good schedule to follow would be:

• Ice-breaker question	5 minutes
• Discussion questions	45 minutes
• Group prayer	10 minutes

5. Alternative Typical Week: Prepare a twenty-minute lecture based on the chapter. After your presentation, spend thirty minutes discussing the questions and ten minutes in prayer. Use your creativity to think of other ways to help men deal with the material.

6. Have coffee and soft drinks available. If you meet over lunch or breakfast, allow an extra fifteen minutes for eating, if possible.

7. Leading a Discussion: The key to a successful discussion group will be your ability to ensure that each member gets "air time." Your role is to encourage each man to render his thoughts and ideas on the subject of the day. If off-the-subject questions are asked, simply suggest that you discuss them at a separate time. If someone rambles too much, privately ask him to help you draw out the more shy members of the group. Take each question in succession, and make sure everyone has the opportunity to comment. If you have a shy member, take the initiative and ask, "_____, how would you answer question number 3?"

8. You don't have to be an experienced Bible teacher to lead a discussion about *The Seven Seasons of a Man's Life*. If someone asks you a question beyond your scope, simply say so and move on.

9. The pleasure and added understanding you will experience from a group discussion will prove to be well worth the effort on your part.

Notes

Chapter 2

1. William Safire, comp., *Lend Me Your Ears: Great Speeches in History* (New York: W. W. Norton, 1992), 445.

Chapter 3

1. "Bill(ionaire) Gates to Give Away Fortune in His 50s," *Orlando Sentinel,* 3 June 1993.
2. Todd Balf and David Zinczenko, "Get Past Tense," *Men's Health,* May 1994, 62ff.
3. Cathryn Conroy, "Pushing the Envelope Away," *CompuServe Magazine,* December 1994, 35.

Chapter 4

1. Douglas Coupland, *Life After God* (New York: Pocket Books, 1994), 309, 359.
2. John T. McNeill, ed., *Calvin: Institutes of the Christian Religion* (Philadelphia: Westminster Press, 1960), 35–37.
3. Ibid, 36.

Chapter 5

1. C. S. Lewis, *Mere Christianity* (New York: MacMillan, 1952), 56.
2. J. Gresham Machen, *Christianity and Liberalism* (Grand Rapids: Eerdmans, 1923), 80ff.

Chapter 6

1. H. Norman Schwarzkopf, *It Doesn't Take a Hero* (New York: Linda Grey Bantam Books, 1992), 212–13.

Chapter 7

1. Weldon M. Hardenbrook, *Missing from Action* (Nashville: Thomas Nelson, 1987), 87–88.
2. James Strong, *Strong's Exhaustive Concordance of the Bible* (Nashville: Abingdon Press, 1980).
3. Ibid.

4. Patrick Morley, *Two Part Harmony* (Nashville: Thomas Nelson, 1994).
5. Donna Wilkinson, "The Modern Family Man," *Orlando Sentinel*, 10 March 1994.

Chapter 8
1. Morley, *Two Part Harmony*.
2. "Students: We Want Parents to Push Us," *Orlando Sentinel*, 13 May 1992.
3. Ronald H. Nash, *Faith and Reason* (Grand Rapids: Academie Books, 1988), 21ff.
4. James Davison Hunter, *Culture Wars* (New York: Basic Books, Harper-Collins, 1991), 204–05.

Chapter 9
1. Ron Blue, *Master Your Money* (Nashville: Thomas Nelson, 1986).

Chapter 11
1. "Stress," *Men's Health*, November 1993, 60ff.
2. Ibid.
3. Cynthia K. Walker, "Stressed to Kill," *Business and Health*, September 1991, 42ff.
4. Jim Conway, *Men in Mid-Life Crisis* (Elgin, IL: David C. Cook, 1978), 26–27.

Chapter 12
1. St. John of the Cross, *The Ascent of Mount Carmel* (New York: Triumph Books), 19.
2. Ibid, 30.
3. Ibid.
4. "Spiritual America, In God We Trust," *U.S. News and World Report*, 4 April 1994, 50, 53–54.
5. Linell Smith, "Are People Responsible for Their Bad Acts?," *Orlando Sentinel*, 17 August 1994, E-1.
6. Bill Hybels, "Reading Your Gauges" in Bill Bright, ed., *The Greatest Lesson I've Ever Learned* (San Bernardino: Here's Life Publishers, 1991), 110.

Chapter 14
1. Francis A. Schaeffer, *Escape from Reason* (Downers Grove: InterVarsity Press, 1968), 9.

Chapter 16
1. Anthony Robbins, *Awaken the Giant Within* (New York: Simon & Schuster, 1991), 490.
2. Harry S. Dent, *Cover Up* (San Bernardino: Here's Life Publishers, 1986), 33–34.
3. H. Richard Neibuhr, *Christ and Culture* (New York: Harper Torchbooks, 1951), 236.

Chapter 17
1. Deitrich Bonhoeffer, *The Cost of Discipleship* (New York: Collier Books, 1959), 175–79.
2. Andrew Murray, *Humility* (Springdale: Whitaker House, 1982), 46–47.

Chapter 20
1. Oswald Chambers, *My Utmost for His Highest* (Westwood: Barbour and Company, Inc., 1963), August 23, 173.
2. Dallas Willard, *The Spirit of the Disciplines* (San Francisco: HarperCollins, 1988), 153.
3. Jim Wilson, *Principles of War* (Random Press, 1983), 67–70.

Chapter 21
1. Richard Foster, *Celebration of Discipline*, rev. ed. (San Francisco: Harper and Row, 1978, 1988), 1.
2. Robert N. Bellah, et. al., *Habits of the Heart* (New York: Harper and Row, 1985), 228.

Chapter 22
1. Brother Lawrence of the Resurrection, *The Practice of the Presence of God*, trans. John J. Delaney (New York: Doubleday, 1977), 108.
2. Francis A. Schaeffer, *Letters of Francis A. Schaeffer* (Westchester: Crossway Books, 1985), 144, 168.
3. Oswald Chambers, *My Utmost for His Highest* (Grand Rapids: Discovery House, 1992).

Chapter 23

1. Alvin Plantinga, *God and Other Minds* (Ithaca: Cornell University Press, 1966), 115.
2. David Hume, *God and the Problem of Evil* (from *Dialogues Concerning Natural Religion*), in William L. Rowe and William J. Wainwright, eds., *Philosophy of Religion: Selected Readings* (New York: Harcourt Brace Jovanowich, 1973), 187.

Chapter 24

1. *Brightside*, Vol. 27, no. 10, 4.
2. Charles Colson, *Kingdoms in Conflict* (William Morrow and Zondervan, 1987), 67–68.
3. *Strong's Exhaustive Concordance*.

Chapter 25

1. Tony Campolo, *Who Switched the Price Tags?* (Dallas: Word, 1986), 28–29.

Chapter 26

1. Foster, *Celebration of Discipline*, 107.
2. W. P. Moody, *The Life of Dwight L. Moody* (Westwood: Barbour and Company, Inc., 1985), 122.

Index

About the Author

Business leader, author, and speaker Patrick Morley has been used throughout the world to help men and leaders think more deeply about their lives and to equip them to have a larger impact on the world. He has been the president or managing partner of fifty-nine companies and partnerships. He founded Morley Properties, which during the 1980s was one of Florida's one hundred largest privately-held companies.

Mr. Morley has also served as president or chairman of numerous civic and professional organizations. He serves on the board of directors of Campus Crusade for Christ and the editorial board of *New Man* magazine.

Mr. Morley graduated with honors from the University of Central Florida, which selected him to receive its Distinguished Alumnus Award in 1984. He is a graduate of the Harvard Graduate School of Business Owner/President Management Program and Reformed Theological Seminary.

Mr. Morley is the bestselling author of several books, including the award-winning *The Man in the Mirror* as well as *Walking with Christ in the Details of Life, The Rest of Your Life, Getting to Know the Man in the Mirror,* and *Two Part Harmony: A Devotional for Couples.* He teaches a weekly Bible study to 125 businessmen and leaders. He resides with his family in Orlando, Florida.